Discourses
ON Cosmic Law

Discourses
ON Cosmic Law

— Volume 1 —

Mark L. Prophet

SUMMIT UNIVERSITY ❧ PRESS®

Gardiner, Montana

Discourses on Cosmic Law • Volume 1
by Mark L. Prophet
Copyright © 2020 The Summit Lighthouse, Inc. All rights reserved.

For information, contact
The Summit Lighthouse, 63 Summit Way, Gardiner, MT 59030 USA
Tel: 1-800-245-5445 or +1 (406) 848-9500
TSLinfo@TSL.org
www.SummitLighthouse.org

Library of Congress Control Number: 2020949271
ISBN: 978-1-60988-352-2 (softbound)
ISBN: 978-1-60988-353-9 (eBook)

SUMMIT UNIVERSITY 🦢 PRESS®

23 22 21 20   1 2 3 4

Contents

Foreword

The messenger Mark L. Prophet, anointed by God to bring forth his teachings for the Aquarian age, walked before us as a friend on the Path. "Seized with a passion that is the love of God," Mark illustrated truth as a day-to-day experience of God that could come to all. For him the path of Truth led to cosmic consciousness.

He won because he never stopped loving people—all kinds of people. And he never lost patience with seeing through to the end the needs of his friends. He was equally enduring with strangers and even the self-styled enemies that everyone who truly loves encounters on life's way.

While showing a rare tenderness and deep sensitivity to his students' innermost needs, he was well known for his instant intolerance toward the assailants of the soul's upward striving—those assassins of one's own highest virtues that from time to time rise up from the mists of the subconscious.

Master psychologist—for he read the soul and heart of a man as no other could—fearless defender of the integrity of the individual, lover of Christ and feeder of his sheep, this giant of a man was never so tall as to not bend to the lowliest among us and lift up that one as a babe in arms to the point of self-recognition in God.

"Because Thou art, I AM!" was his mantra of be-ness, and he affirmed it for all until they, no longer content to walk in his shadow, would follow the pathway of personal God-realization to the Sun.

Yes, he endured his own imperfections as Paul did before him, who was never without his "thorn in the flesh," as he put it. But God in him was greater than all of that. In him we saw the timeless ritual of the Lord's sweeping down upon his anointed, raising him up for a holy purpose, and, in the very process, the Son of God transcending the son of man.

Then one day the Prophet spoke to us no more, and his voice became the echo of conscience in our souls. But for you, dear friend, he left footprints—big and well-outlined—of his path of practical "Christ-I AM-ity," as he loved to call the Way of his Saviour.

Simple yet profound, serious to the nth and suddenly laughable by sheer buffoonery as in self-mockery, he would teach us the cardinal rule of life—"Don't take yourself too seriously. Don't be seized by your own self-importance."

Disarming as in the role of pure fool, he would, with rapier thrust worthy of Launcelot, thrust home to our souls the piercing wisdom that laid bare the phantom of personal pride. And suddenly we would be free as he, uninhibited, little-boy-and-girlish—embarrassed by our supercilious egos and so glad he had dismissed the specters of our yesterdays before anyone saw just how nonsensical those ancient idols were.

And so by relentless holiness this divine comédien—who would first disarm the carnal mind and then summarily bind the beasts that preyed upon our innocence—this twentieth-century adept let us know that it's okay to be human as long as you remember you're divine. But if you think you're all divine, you're probably too divine to be human. And after all, it's in our very humanness that we can afford to love and win!

ELIZABETH CLARE PROPHET

CHAPTER 1

The Avatar

The question before us this morning concerns the arhat or the avatar or the individual who has not only given complete dedication of their life unto the highest purpose but also, in addition to having given their all to the highest purpose, has accepted the highest purpose within themselves as the lodestone that they will use in directing the course of their life.

We observe a river from above as a bird flying over the water and we see the meandering of the stream. But sometimes we do not realize the simple mathematical formula that the shortest distance between two points is a straight line. And so what do we do? We are meandering through the land from the source, the beginning, to the end, or the ocean of being.

You see, this happens to us, yet the mathematical law remains that the shortest distance between two points is a straight line. "Strait is the gate, and narrow is the way... and few there be that find it," the Master Jesus said.[1] Isn't it true?

Yet although we have all this direction before us, we sometimes forget it and we take this winding, sinuous, stream-like road through the land, and then we lament and bemoan the fact that our progress is not swifter. Who is to blame for our progress, God or ourselves?

Yet we say that we are God. And so the transfer of the torch of divine authority comes to us, and it comes to us with great clearness.

There is a duality manifest in man. There is an id, an identity, a selfhood which we can either utilize for the glories of the ephemeral, of the temporal, or we can put it into the framework of the eternal. The avatar has done this. The avatar always will do this.

And so those of you who are here dedicated to the purposes of the Eternal should understand that the happenings in your life that occur are somewhat in your own control. For example, in a recent *Pearl*, the great Ascended Master Hilarion revealed in the almost perfect manner of Saint Paul his thinking about the darkness in ourselves.[2] In other words, the darkness does not always come from the level of the demon.

Although it may have been at one time demon-inspired, satanic, the darkness in people comes from the namby-pamby, willy-nilly attitudes that we sometimes show toward ourselves, our failures to reject what we ought to reject and our failures to accept what we ought to accept and our failures to understand this law of the shortest distance between two points being a straight line. It is ourselves. It is the darkness we allow or permit to permeate our being.

It is not permanent. It will not remain permanent, because the chastisement of life—"whom the Lord loveth he chasteneth"—will occur and every son that he receiveth will be scourged[3] because the scourging is for the sake of the purification of the man or the woman.

When you chastise your child, why do you do it? You chastise your child for love's sake. You have and you feel love for the child. Can you believe that God would do otherwise? For one minute could you imagine that God would not chastise? God is all things here. He is not only the God of complete love in the highest octave. He is also the God of justice, justice being one of his qualities. And as a part of divine justice, it is not just that God wants to exact his Shylock pound of flesh and say, "You did it. You'll have to clean it up."

That's not the idea. What God is concerned with is not punitive.

The chastisement of heaven is to make us aware. It is like the spur that the rider wears with which he chastens the horse. God goads us into action. He shows us clearly that this straight line is before us, and he shows us that we have taken the winding and devious course. Do you see?

So there is no chastisement from heaven. Perhaps in one sense of the word the God aspect of *ourselves* is what really acts to chasten us. God has said, "Mine eyes are too pure to behold iniquity."[4] So God doesn't dwell upon the darkness—the temporal, ephemeral darkness of our world.

I think that all of you expect to see a gradual improvement, do you not, in this place? Don't you expect an improvement to occur? Don't you expect an improvement to occur in us? Of course you do, and I do too. We all expect that our attitudes toward the world will become more like the masters'. And so this is exactly what is going to take place within us. It does take place. It is taking place. Step by step we are being led to greater evolutions.

But of course, these things are not charted. You cannot chart this journey on paper as you would if you were to make a safari to the Sahara Desert. These things are charted by the eyes of the soul. And the eyes of the soul are not open in many.

And so we look, we gaze upon what is happening in the world, what is happening to ourselves, what is happening to our fellow men, and we do not see all the progress that occurs—nor do we often see the retrogression that occurs in some people. These things are subtle, and all should understand the meaning of "subtle" because that is what subtle is. It is almost hidden. In fact, it may be hidden, and it is the uncovering of the depth of our progress that is very momentous.

This is a great gift from heaven to all of us. It is a magnificent gift, just think, that we are making progress.

I think it's wrong for people to have an arrogant progress that looks down on their fellow men. I see this in religious work all the time. People have an elite society, and when the neophyte comes into this society, the neophyte is made to feel that he is now talking to the great initiate.

And the great initiate deigns to bow down his head a little bit, and he says, "One day you'll know, but now you don't." Yet the same thing could be said by the master. Do you see what I mean? This is subtlety. If the Master said it, "One day you'll know," it would be true. And so we see that subtlety deals with truth and also deals with truth mounted on the staff of error.

People whose lives are not really complete and still remain relatively imperfect, who have just started on the Path, certainly have no right to be arrogant toward other people who are just beginning on the Path—in practically the same position they are. Why do they do this? What is the reason, the motivation behind it? It is ignorance.

We want none of the people in this activity to feel any false sense of security, any false sense of ignorance that will act in their worlds so that they can be patronizing to the man or woman that comes in here. Be like a child. Be like a lamb of God. Be like the Lamb of God that taketh away the sins of the world. You don't have to do anything more than be cuddly and wooly, because that is what it means. You are that, you see.

You don't have to look down on them from the mountaintop and say, "You vile creature, you sinner down there. I was once there, of course, but I've forgotten it now because I'm a part of all the loftiness of heaven."

No! Be the servant of all, as the Master taught. Wash their feet. Wash their consciousness. Let them tell you how wise they are. Listen, and don't always talk. And then when you do talk, try to let it be some sweet and simple words of love and advice that they can appreciate, but not given in the patronizing manner.

That is the problem in the world today, the world of religion. People have made of religion a commodity to be marketed in the bazaars. They stretch their great bazaars out before the people and then they say, "We have a greater commodity," when there is only one God and we all share and drink in the life that he gives to us.

Man tends to be very sonorous and to sound off and tell everyone how great the teachings that *he* has are, because there is the prerogative of simply gazing at something and saying, "This is mine. This is my church, my pastor, my religion, my God, me, mine"—but often not "ours." So we say today, "Our Lord," and we say it not of The Summit Lighthouse but of the world—and also of The Summit Lighthouse, because then it truly is ours.

The world is in great darkness today and great dangers of darkness, and the chastening hand of heaven will rest upon the world. Fear not. Let us not hasten that day, but rather hasten the day of mercy, because he "is a jealous God, showing mercy unto thousands of them that love him and keep his commandments."[5] This is true. And I believe that "his mercy endureth forever"[6] and I believe that his mercy is functional even in the domain of the chastening.

We come here, then, both to be chastened and to be healed, because the Master who has said, "Let that which is lame and that which is halt and that which is blind be healed. Let it be turned back on the pathway of the divine."

That's the whole of it, don't you see? It's not to remain as a little ball that is rolled into a slot, a rut. The only difference between a rut and a grave is one of depth. Remember that. So let's not roll into these slots and say, "This is a niche that I can't get out of."

I was watching this morning as our tiny little one tried very desperately to turn over. This for her was a colossal task, one which she cannot yet do, although almost. And I say to myself now, How prone we are to take for granted the potentials we have of movement and of life and the qualities of life within ourselves, and how little appreciation we sometimes feel for even the ability to manipulate and to move our physical body and to move the great ship of the mind out into the ocean of the mind, to be able to raise the sails and watch as they billow out and as movement occurs.

For we journey into the infinite—but an infinite that is not understood is not a journey. Do you see? Going somewhere when we know not the way is of very little value, and being someone is the key that will take us where we want to go, because it will show us the way and reveal not only the scenery on the path but our identification with it.

The identification of each one of us with God is the most key and important factor of our lives. This great mystery, this enigma, this obscurity now becomes the light. It *is* the light.

The meaning of "the white stone that no man knoweth saving he that receiveth it"[7] is seen in this concept. The white stone upon the path is clear. It is a stone that is as long as the path and as short as the journey. For the journey may be short or long, it matters not. And the stone, the rock of the ages, will be secure beneath our feet. Only the debris we place upon the rock can become the mud and slime upon which we slip. It's the debris that we place there, that we allow to be placed in our pathway, the impediments that we permit to be placed in the pathway of others.

I have thought and I have pondered in the name of heaven upon the situations involving this world. And I have seen the clashes in the name of religion all the way from the Crusades unto the present time, those circumstances in the name of Christ which are calculated to bring death and every quality into the world that is not the quality of the Prince of Peace. And I ask myself, as I'm sure you have asked yourself, "How long, O Lord? And why?"

But yet many of us have been caught in the net of this both in this life as well as in previous lives. We have been caught in these nets, the innuendos that are thrust upon all in the world that are the tactics that delay the God-realization of the avatar, of the Son of God.

It seemed very far from us, perhaps, when first we heard or read the words, "Truly this man was the Son of God."[8] This was spoken by the cross. What a delight it should be to our souls today to realize that this is also spoken of us, that the immaculate example given by

Jesus and by other avatars, as brothers and sons of God also upon the spiritual path in the great diorama of history, are all examples to us so that we may then be examples to an age to come.

It is folly for us to seek a memorial of stone and wood and brass. Rather let us make a memorial of our lives so that God may inhabit our lives. Then it does not matter what the world may say of us, because even now it matters only what he says of us and what he thinks of us.

And he thinks within you. This is one of the strangest things you have ever heard. But the guilt in man, the guilt that man feels sometimes for his own errors and mistakes, is a chastening to heaven itself—because God has to think within the molds and matrices *you* create. Some portion of himself, be it ever so tiny, must encase itself in the neurons of the brain, in the memory cells, and retain those impressions of guilt and condemnation that you have.

And what did the Master say? "I am come that ye might have life and that more abundantly."[9] Why, watch as the drama unfolds and see the eggshell of life just crack under this blinding, blazing metamorphosis, this great change that comes. And then all at once we look and we say, "Why, everything is just the same, but I feel different about it." You see, it's all here.

A man may have a feeling of guilt and condemnation and say, "I am not worthy, O Lord, to inhabit your heaven. I'm here on earth and I deserve, I'm sure, to go wherever the children go that have failed to keep thy commandments and to love thee properly."

Inwardly we consent to this. We allow the perfect matrix of our brain to hold the imperfect thought of ourselves, and in the holding of this thought for ourselves, to hold the permanent chastening of others. I'm not referring to the ability of man to be able to judge right and wrong acts. I'm talking about permanent chastening because we never allow ourselves to enter the newness of life. Instead we become confined within the old prison houses of our darkness and our imaginations, and our "foolish heart," as Saint Paul said, "was darkened."[10] Our heart is darkened because we will not allow ourselves to see on the horizon of our own life the time when we become the avatar.

Do you think in God's name, in the name of the God of love, in the name of the living Christ, that any in this world who are the avatars, who are the sons of God, those who are "called according to his purpose,"[11] those who were chosen—whether they dwell in India or whether they dwell in America or South America, down in the Amazon or up at the North Pole or the South Pole in an igloo, wherever they are, they who are avatars, the sons of God, the flowers breathing forth the fragrances of heaven into space—that these want to hold you back?

They only want to kindle in you a flame and a fire as to what you will be. They want you to get the *vision* of yourself as this, but for goodness' sake, don't be stuck-up by it, because this will cast you down and all your progress will be turned into retrogression. We have enough of these people in the world today.

In The Summit Lighthouse activity, the spiritual hierarchy want *you* to manifest the power of the avatar. It's time that some of you begin to manifest precipitation. It's time that some of you begin to manifest dominion over demons.

Oh, yes, Sweathog* is here in Denver. That of course is a manifestation of a demon. Those people today, the fallen Atlanteans and those who have fitted themselves into the matrices of Atlantis, who are now delivering the specific rock and roll tactics to the world, whose vibrations are turning our young people into pathways of darkness, these are manipulated by demons as a puppeteer plays with his little puppets.

The demons move through their consciousness. They control them. It gives them a field day in the world. They are no longer confined to the Hades of darkness, but they are now given entrée into the world, into our world, to our young people, to those that

---

*An American rock band.

God and Saint Germain and Jesus and all the great masters would nurture and guide.

It doesn't matter that you have made a mistake or that I have made a mistake. The point is, we are going to come to the area where we will not make mistakes, because we are dealing with the principles of heaven. We are dealing with the principles of immortality. Unless he be born in thee, his birth in Bethlehem remains in vain for thee.

And so what is an incarnation? If a man would be an incarnation such as Lord Krishna or if one would be an incarnation such as Lord Shankaracharya, what difference would it make?

These examples are set before you by the living God in obscure places on the earth so that you may understand that there is a phenomenal manifestation here and there on the planet, that there has been such a phenomenal manifestation upon the planet in the past, that holy men and saints do come from somewhere and go somewhere, that you came from somewhere and you will go somewhere and you are in the process of going, that movement and function is taking place in your lives, whether it be retrogressive or whether it be progressive.

Heaven is now, according to the cries of man, reaching to the position where heaven demands from the lives of those who are dedicated to Saint Germain, to Jesus and to every one of the great masters a new form of life, a new lifestyle on your part in the mood and fashion of the angels. It is not enough to carry the crutch, the cane, the appliance of man's inability to locomote. No, none of that is enough.

We need now to realize that all infirmities must be put aside. When we read Morya's words, "Even the best zurnas lacked some strings,"[12] we are reminded that out of infirmity, sometimes, the greatest strength is born. We can if we will coddle ourselves. Any of us can do this.

But we are not here to condemn one another but to give one

another this firmness that lays hold on life and grasps it and says, "This tender hand I hold is a hand of flesh" and knows that "this hand I hold is the living God." What is meant by "a new heart of flesh" is the contrasting of the stony heart of man's feelings that reject man made in the image of God constantly and sit in critical judgment upon their fellow men, those whom they even know not.

Ours must be a message of infinite love and we must demonstrate that love to the world. We must show that we have greater capacities, greater storehouses in reserve than have ever before been thought possible by us.

I urge you today to increase your own belief in the potential of God inside of you. I urge you to stop placing the lines of limitation upon yourself. I do not mean that the just limitations imposed upon us by God should be revoked. For the world is governed somewhat by all of this, and it would be a sad thing indeed if people were to reach the form of magic as in the book *The Morning of the Magicians* and if our consciousness would become absorbed with how much magic or phenomena we could do. This is not the pathway toward light.

In the greater light of heaven all share equally in the government of heaven. But when you deal with a child that is maturing, you wait until he has come of years to give him his inheritance. For to give it prematurely unto man's hand would surely establish rivalry. For he would not yet understand the great capacities that are given to a Christ, which we hold within the chaliced cup of the Last Supper within ourselves—the Last Supper signifying the finality of our own individual Communion with God, when we will take from his hand the torch that heaven has already passed, and holding it into our grasp and consciousness, see clearly that we have a reasonable power to prevail upon heaven and demand, at this Last Supper, the vestments, the garments of the Christ, to walk the earth as an ascended being.

We have the right "to ask and it shall be given unto us, to seek and we shall find, to knock and it shall be opened unto us."[13] There has been too much limitation in the world and too much criticism, too much self-imposed criticism. And yet indulgence lingers, self-indulgence as well, where we find ourselves face to face with varying potentialities, manifold potentialities, in fact. And we stand for a moment in confusion, our minds literally reeling. Which way shall I go, Lord?

"I am the way, the truth, and the life. No man cometh unto the Father but by me. If any man climb up any other way, he is both a thief and a robber."[14]

We understand, then, that it is not just to seize control of the power strings of heaven that we live, but to master ourselves and say, as a little child would say, even when we already know that we are a man, "O God, I am thine. I came into this world to minister unto thine. I pray only that they may receive thee as I have received thee. For thou art the dawn of purpose, the zenith of purpose and the setting sun of purpose fulfilled. The long day of life is a day that has no end, in reality, for when purpose is fulfilled, we behold again the dawn and thy cycles proceed in orderly fashion from thy hand and there is no ceasing of the flow of thy energy and thy plan. And thy plan for me is as clear as the crystal sea, and I wait upon thee, O God."

And then, you see, all at once we're going to feel a little different toward everyone. We don't stand and look at the halt and the lame and the blind. We don't stand and look at those who are in error's way as if we would mimic them or criticize them, nor even criticize the haltingness of self when we ourselves falter on the way.

But we keep our eyes unflinchingly upon the goal of our God Presence and we see in *that Presence* the restoration of our domain and the restoration of the destiny of man. And we perceive that all purpose, both that which is in east and west and north and south, is indeed the flaming power that is held by the wind to carry the seeds, the divine seeds over the whole earth and to kindle a fire upon earth that shall never be extinguished or burn out, because that which is on earth here below will only be a memorial to that which is already established above—perfection and life and paradise and the Eden of purpose.

This is destiny. We are destiny. But be not afraid to cast our weight upon the magic carpet of the wind of the moment, for it, too, will carry us where we ought to go as our mind directs it in its course. And our mind is best when harnessed by God's mind. And to invoke his purpose is to secure his assistance.

And so as we ponder, then, this day the matter of the avatar, let us see this individual as an example only and see ourselves as the avatar, as the Son of God, as the master of purpose. For only then will all of heaven be satisfied with us.

They expect, as we also ought to expect, no fragmentation of purpose but a unification of the whole. And when the unification is achieved, and when the divine sense is completed within ourselves, then all will be fulfilled. We must perceive the mastery of cycles that climbs the steps to the landing and then onward to the next step and the next landing and does not falter because of the austerity or longevity of the stairways that are there to climb. But rather, let us receive these stairs with joy and place our feet upon them and see that in the climb is the great challenge of life.

And who cannot say that a greater elevator of the wind will not also come and bear us away beyond those stairs at some point in our development where the Godhead suddenly says to his lofty sons and daughters, "You have struggled now many a year and cycle to complete thy destiny. Thy feet have wandered far, and you have not perceived the beauty in my star, and now I claim you. I claim your vow. I lift you. I bring you now unto my heart. This great magnet of fiery destiny is fulfilled within you. This is the purpose of life. For lo, in you I AM."

Do you see how simple it really is and how beautiful it is—not a struggle of little people trying to fulfill some greater purpose and yet manifesting the shades of ugliness, but instead all people, both great and small, fulfilling their purposes together and coinciding, in the only way that man can, with perfect unity.

For who amongst us can in one year meet all of the people that are upon this planet? Or can we play upon the whole great organ of heaven with our fingers? Can the fingers of our mind span the octaves of universal being, see the great chords that are there or hear them? Our ears are not able.

And so through the process of union with God, we are able to be truly united in the only way man ever can be, and that is with the highest Self of all. Let us be up and doing.

As Jesus said long ago, "Cannot ye watch with me one hour?"[15] Our whole life and all that remains of it now, all that is in the hourglass is just one hour. Do you understand? One hour remains and all shall be fulfilled. This whole life span is that hour, but there is a day also and a year and a cycle and a cosmos and eternity.

Let the smile, *the smile* of cosmic purpose rest upon our hearts' chalices today, and let us determine through no outer-world drama but through the hidden drama of the heart that we will fulfill our destiny, that we will make this order one of infinite dedication. And so the world shall be blessed by that dedication and each of us in return shall receive the mantle of our united reward.

God bless you.

April 16, 1972
Colorado Springs, Colorado

CHAPTER 2

Antahkarana, the Web of Life

The idea or the concept that man is consciousness is correct, because only in the ocean of consciousness can we find the answer to problems of time and space, to the continuity of life. Consciousness, however, ocean that it is of infinity, is like the most massive computer that was ever built. It has the power to receive the ripples and impressions from untold numbers of people.

Cosmic beings, angelic beings, human beings, dwarfs, gnomes, sylphs of the air, elementals of the fire and beings of the sea, the undines, in fact every creature that exists in the universe is able to make its imprint upon this great universal brain or manifestation or the fluid of life or the great cosmic ocean, the universal consciousness field. Everything flows into it and everything flows out of it.

This giant computer, which in one sense of the word I would like to call the web of life, fills all known space and embraces comprehensively the total stream of time from any conceivable beginning to any conceivable end, in other words, in a vast, continuous circle. It receives every impression and it gives out every impression and it separates the planes of consciousness within its own great and blessed being. In fact, everything from the lowest astral levels and the levels of decomposition physically to the highest levels of

God-realization and manifestation, the very height of God himself, is recorded in this universal ocean that spans space, exceeds space and fills the whole stream of time with all of its far-reaching little niches and alcoves and tortuous windings.

Beautiful, isn't it? It's a beautiful concept. In this great concept of this massive, circular ocean, the whole law of cycles is included. Nothing, then, is excluded from this massive computer system. Nothing that is, at all, can be excluded from it, you see. It has to be there.

Unfortunately, the dispersion of consciousness has not been understood by men, and they have thought of consciousness as occupying the relative space of the physical brain or the body. They do not quite understand yet, either scientifically or spiritually, the omnipresence of God. Nor do they seem to understand the statute of divine limitations.

To illustrate this, Jesus was a friend to Lazarus, who was the brother to Mary and Martha. Jesus loved Lazarus with a very deep love, the deepest possible love for the Master to have. And when Lazarus died, far away in space from where Jesus was, and they didn't have Western Union or any message system, the Master possessed the capacity, you must understand, and the capability of having the knowledge that Lazarus was dead.

The fact that he had not appropriated that knowledge from the universal ocean of life was shown in the fact that when it was revealed to him for the first time, he wept. And the shortest verse in the Bible is the statement, a little verse, "Jesus wept."[1] I know because the ladies in the Methodist church where I grew up loved to quote that when they were called upon to give a Bible verse. "Jesus wept," they could remember it, so easy. One after another they would get up, "Jesus wept."

However, the important thing that we derive from that knowledge is that while the Master possessed the perfect capability of dipping into the stream and ocean of God's mind, this vast computer that fills time and space and exceeds it all, he did not do it. This in no way was an expression of Jesus' limitation. It did not indicate that Jesus was a limited being at all. He simply was not appropriating the power, the reserve that he already had. He was not appropriating and using it because he was involved in so many divine schemes, so much assistance to mankind, that in his own embodied state he was unable to cope with all of it at once, you see.

Rather than say, then, that we have limited the Master, I will say that we have shown the laws of limitations governing embodiments and the fact that when you are in embodiment and engrossed in many things, it is possible that you do not make an attunement or do not receive the impressions sent to you from the Universal. Now, this does not mean that you're bad, that you're limited, that there's anything necessarily wrong with you. It simply shows that the vastness of the whole cosmic scheme can scarcely be realized by flesh and blood and by the limitations thereof. Yet the Master demonstrated tremendous proficiency.

Rather than feel that this limits him, I feel that it comforts us to know that with all of his greatness he did not always appropriate all of the knowledge the Universal held. And this shouldn't make us feel too bad when we consider that the Master Jesus said, with his great love ray, "The things that I do ye shall do also, and greater things shall ye do because I go unto my Father."[2] In other words, "Because I have lived, because I have loved, because I have given myself to God and developed new systems of communication with the Father, you are going to be able to do greater things because the Universal Mind will now hold the patterns that I have brought forth in my mission."

This is the highest transcendentalism that can be revealed or that up to that time had ever been revealed by any Master or any man or any avatar. Since then men have fulfilled his prediction. They have done greater things than he did. And they, too, have proceeded back to God, and they are now one with God. And we have their momentum of generated service to add to the power of the Godhead and the power of the Christ and the power of possibility to embodied men.

Therefore, in one sense of the word, the pathway to God is easier today because these men lived. The question, then, before us is, "Will the pathway be easier tomorrow because *you* have lived?"

When I hear people constantly moaning and complaining about how awful their life is or how everything is going the wrong way for them or how "Nobody loves me anymore" and "I can't seem to do the right thing" and "I'm afflicted and overcome with adversity," I cannot help but feel that these blessed people had better understand that if they are having these experiences, it either means that they are doing something wrong, therefore reaping the karma of the wrong that they're doing, they're cleaning up the karma they made in past embodiments, or they're being attacked because of the tremendous service they're rendering to life right now. There are three reasons.

So nobody really knows what the reason is, do they? And it's kind of difficult for people to say when someone suffers adversity, "Well, you're one of these people that is reaping karma from the past" or "You did something yesterday that brought this on you today." But they don't usually do anything else but say that. Very few people will say, "Oh well, it must be because you've taken a stand for the Light."

Well, if you're moaning about this and groaning about this, I don't believe you've taken a stand for the light. The people who are taking a stand for the light will *never* moan and groan at adversity. That's the key that you can use to determine whether or not you are reaping your karma or whether or not it is the karma of the past or the karma of the present. That's the criterion. Are you hollering about it? Are you screaming about it? Are you complaining about it? Are you dumping a burden upon everyone else and feeling so sorry for yourself that you could almost weep?

Jesus contributed immensely to the betterment of all humanity upon every system of worlds. And when we are to understand antahkarana, the web of life, it means that what happens within the limited circle is also macrocosmically projected into the larger circle. And if we go to Ezekiel's wheels within wheels,[3] which restates and rephrases and convinces us of the law of cycles, we are able to perceive in that idea that all of these spheres of influence exist in perfect order from the highest circles of cosmos to the lowest little circle of the nucleus of being, our own individual life.

Now the blessed Master Jesus one time made a statement that riled up his enemies quite a bit. He said, "You are whited sepulchers full of dead men's bones. You don't enter into the kingdom of heaven yourself and you hinder those who are entering in from entering in."[4] Hard words, but true. "You are whited sepulchers full of dead men's bones."

I used to wonder at that expression until it was revealed to me just what it really is. A sepulcher is a place of burial. A whited sepulcher is a place of burial whitewashed by human consciousness to look like it's something else. The dead men's bones within are the failures of consciousness and the engravings of hopelessness and the negative ambitions and despairs of life. These literally record themselves upon our bones. Our forms are distorted by ignorance, our minds are warped by error and our consciousness spurns regenerate identity.

You need to think about that for a moment in order to understand antahkarana, for antahkarana is basic to the law of cycles and the law of waves and radiation, or radiant energy. Whenever you tremble a spider's web anywhere on the web, the whole web trembles. Therefore, when you're having your little crying spell in Podunk, Kentucky, and you're down there with Moses in the bulrushes or something, and you feel terribly sorry for yourself, just realize that you are adding to the weight of sorrow of your family, of your state and city, of your nation, and of this world. And carrying it a bit farther, through antahkarana, the web of life, you are trembling the universe with your vibrations of negativity. If you stop and consider the real truth of this, do you see what an impetus you have for a better life?

A lot of people don't mind if they do wrong as long as the wrong is done to themselves. They seem to feel that it is justifiable that they can wrong themselves with impunity, but they must not wrong others. This is an error. You are an emanation from the Master's molding wheel of life, from the hand of the Master Potter. God made you. And when he made you, he made you in his image. And your responsibility is to manifest his image everywhere.

We all have erred, and the lives of all men are full of many shames. We know this is true, but that past is prologue. And if we are to emerge as victorious human beings and add to the credit side of the ledger, we must recognize the effect we have upon all life by manifesting negative states and creating indignities in life.

We are not our own, as Saint Paul said; "Ye are bought with a price."⁵ The price of Godhood was paid by the Universal Christ Mind, because when God, the perfection of the perfect cube, descended into form and the triad of spiritual precipitation stood over it in the divine geometry, when God did this, he assumed, from the standpoint of the mystery of the law of assumption, the identity of the created. And until you understand that, you do not understand antahkarana. And you should.

God assumed your identity. And the only way a transfer could be made of consciousness to you was by God giving you a part of himself. And that took that part of himself out of the Universal and put it in the coat of skins of you, in the consciousness, in the identity, in the personality and every part of you. And in a very real sense God is crucified in matter.

And what is the true meaning of *matter*? Matter means "mater."* And here we find that the physical world is the Mother of God because God himself impregnates mater with Spirit-spark identity. Then the womb of mater, of material substance, becomes the generative point for the manifestation of the Christ-intelligence of regeneration.

---

*Latin for "mother."

We are giving you a branch of the lesser Christian mysteries that has not been expounded upon too much in this world. But it is important because every decree uttered through your lips, every prayer breathed through your being, every benign act, every attempt to control your human appetites, every time you move toward some degree of mastery, you are actively engaged in a service of chiseling out the divine image in physical manifestation, where it will be caught up into the heavens and changed in the twinkling of an eye by the Spirit of God into that Christ, God, universal reality that it already is.

The veil of Isis is the dual veil of is-is. It means that that which seems to be and is not. This is the beast referred to in Revelations as that beast which was, the beast which is and the beast which is to come.[6] The beast which was, of course, is scarcely understood by human beings, but it is the historical man. The beast which is, is man in the state of becoming. And the beast that is to come is man prior to his assumption into his divine identity. Because one moment from the identity of the Godhood you still embrace a little of the beast, until it is finally shed.

Somehow or other I think one of the ways that the dark forces have gained so much control over the mind of men is because they can promulgate the idea that no one is perfect. The moment we begin to say, "Well, no one is perfect," we immediately excuse ourselves and we say, "Well, charity covers a multitude of sins."[7] No one is perfect. And that excuses everything, doesn't it? We can tremble the web of life. We can agitate our neighbors. We can produce vibrations and put them into that cosmic bank, that recorder within their own plane.

And the LORD God placed eastward in Eden a flaming sword to keep the way of the tree of life.[8] This beautiful computer, this universal antahkarana, this web of life has the beautiful capacity of separating the planes. And thus, the earth plane maintains its own identity. The astral maintains its own identity.

Do you know what it means to cancel out a sum upon an adding machine? To punch the figures and they're wrong, they're erroneous, and then clear the whole board with one sweep of the hand, you know what it means? It's easier electronically than mechanically, but you can do it both ways. All of these little figures fall back to zero. Well, that's how easy it would be for God to roll up the scroll of all of his creation. He could just clear the board. And every act and every word and every thought and every deed would pass away. What does it say, what did Jesus say? "Heaven and earth shall pass away, but my word shall never pass away."[9]

Someday, then, somewhere, all of these sums, the trembling of the web of life, the depositing of negativity into the body of antah-karana, must cease and a clearance of the board occur when the heaven and earth of human thoughts and ideas passes away. "But my word shall never pass away." The secret of immortality, then, is identification with the Word, with the Christ image. This is the only way human beings can actually achieve immortality.

The brothers of the shadow are quite crafty. They have intelligence. It is the intelligence of the serpent mind—sinuous, tortuous, twisting, warped, and deceiving. It says, "You shall not surely die."[10] And many other lies does this carnal mind tell us, but these lies have no power to deceive the soul of God. They cannot deceive the spirit of God that is within us. They only trick the mind, and the mind is the turning point. The mind is the delicately balanced jewel where people can pivot either on error or on truth, as the case may be. And it is the mind that is attacked, that ultimately allows the emotions to run away with the prize.

The rationale of the mind that authorizes us to accept that which we cannot or should not accept causes us, then, to cut loose in our emotions and we say, "Well, I'm going to do it anyway. Whatever it is, we're going to do it anyway. It doesn't matter what the consequences are."

I have received letters from those I sought to help, utterly condemning me. Persons who came to me for help, asked my help, implored it and were given it, turned around and said, "You told me thus and thus and thus, and what you told me was tyranny." But all I told them was the truth of God's law.

The masters do likewise; they continually release truth. And do you know what happens to us individually if we spurn the truth that they offer us? Well, I'm going to tell you. The biggest, the worst punishment that happens is not given by them; it's given by cosmic law. And it means, "I will cut them off from thy fount of wisdom."

After the Universal has given us so many precepts of knowledge and then we have spurned that knowledge again and again and again, after a while the cosmic law steps in and says, "All right, you have had the knowledge for your freedom and you have rejected it. Now we are going to cut you off and we are not going to give you any more instruction. You're going to have to find out the hard way, beat your head against the wall, let the world be your guru. Find out through the hardness of the Law and the return of your own karma just what you are producing by your acts and conduct."

People looking at this say, "My, the Law is hard." Not so. The Law is extremely gentle. For I think that if the Law were to continue always in gentility, ultimately people would go the broad way that leads to destruction[11] and say, "Well, we will carry on as we have because we enjoy it and it won't make any difference to us. We've got lots of time. Don't you know that God is eternity? Why do you have to go ahead and bother about getting perfected now? That's a hard job, to get perfected. You might have to give up something. You might have to change something. You might have to change an idea. Maybe it'll be a bit uncomfortable to change. After all, you might be thought funny by someone."

And you know, those threescore and ten, of which most of us live out twenty years before we even know we're alive, is gone by so quickly. The first thing you know, you're twenty, and then you're forty, and then you start moving the other way because by the time you get to eighty, you know, well, it's twenty-three skiddoo, for most people, unless they're real good students of the masters. And then we have several of them that seem to survive to ninety and up to a hundred. They still haven't equaled Methuselah, have they?

We're coming back now to the truth of life. We have to take a stand someplace, somewhere for the honesty of the Law, and as long as the enemy can trick us and say, "Well, you're not perfect," he can keep excusing anything you do. We have people in this town that have come up here and heard the masters' dictations. They know that something wonderful is taking place, and they've told us so. But where are they on Saturday night or Sunday night? Many times these same people are in a restaurant somewhere, maybe down at Canyon City or somewhere, having lunch or they're watching a television program. They're not here decreeing and they don't realize that in any sudden moment they may be catapulted out of the body into the astral realm.

We have classes here, and if we have enough interest we would have more classes. Now we are growing and we are getting more interest and we're going to have more classes. But our classes do give training in what to expect at the change called death and how to prepare for your ascension and cheat death if you can. Some people will definitely be able to cheat death in this embodiment if they continue on their present course. Others will not. They will have another embodiment and some will have more than one.

But whatever the case, the knowledge of how to act and behave in the spiritual world, the knowledge of what to do with your spiritual body when you have vacated this body, the knowledge of how to bring yourself to waking consciousness, how to start the balancing process from inner levels that will help you to work out a little of your karma between embodiments, all this is vital to your existence.

These things take time. I have seen people who were in an accident where their body is laying there dead, and they suddenly stand beside their body and look down on it. This is a situation unparalleled in their life. It's like the story of the Jewish man's horse, where he comes to the door and says, "My horse just died. He never did that before."

Well, you never died before. So here you are dead and you're looking at your body. You still are conscious. You know your name. You know where your family is. You see the car. You see everything, but you can't move. You just stand and look at it.

It's like the incident told by Norman Vincent Peale in one of his *Guideposts* magazines, where a man crashed an airplane and his spirit went way up in the air about two hundred feet. He is looking down at his body, he sees the plane, he watches as they cut the fence and they come across the field. His wife is way out at the highway coming in her car, and she's running over toward the plane. And one woman over there says, "I bet he was drunk."

Pretty soon he starts going down toward his body and he gets close to it and he gets in his body, and then he feels like he's whirling around as when you're on the operating table before you go out with ether. The next thing you know, he blinks his eyes, he's looking up, and he sees that woman in the crowd who said he was drunk. He looks up at her and he says, "I was not drunk." And she gets scared because she knows that she was way over in the field, two hundred yards away. And so she runs away and the man lives.

But you see, the circumstances involved here are real. And I think that the fact that we survive the body, that we survive death should be a vital factor to people. I think it would be a lot more interesting, as far as atheism goes, if people didn't survive. They could say, "Well, good. When the end comes, it comes. So let us eat and drink and be merry, for tomorrow we die."[12] It doesn't make any difference if you're not going to live again. If you're just going to snuff it all out, well, it doesn't matter, ethics do not matter, how you treat your neighbor doesn't matter. "Let's get all the good we can get according to the human idea of materialism because we only live once and when we're dead, we're dead and that's all."

That's real good, isn't it? But it isn't so. People do reembody, and they do have a period and span between embodiments, and they do pass through astral terrors. The statement of Jesus, "Thou wilt not leave my soul in hell nor permit thine Holy One to see corruption,"[13] referenced the fact that God would not allow his soul or his spirit to actually abide and dwell in the realm of the astral hordes, the realm of hell. And the purgatory spoken of by the Catholic Church and the hell spoken of by the Christian Bible are basically the astral realm, especially the lower astral realm.

And if you want to get an idea what some of the creatures look like that dwell there, go over to France and look at the gargoyles on the cathedrals. That will give you some idea of what you will see in the astral hell. And this is what men see when they get delirium tremens, when they get the DTs and get good and drunk. They see that astral realm and the veil is thinned and that's what they dwell in and they go mad. They run absolutely berserk. They climb the walls. They put them in straitjackets. They're almost insane and they are, in fact, insane.

Now this is the realm that we are trying to show you how to get out of and stay out of. Because someday, you know very well according to statistics, you're either going to go up or you're going to go down. And the up and down here that we're referencing is either you're going to ascend or you're going to just be buried. And if you're buried, your spirit is still there and your being and consciousness can very well be awake as it is in some cases. Some people die and go to sleep and don't know anything for weeks and months or maybe years. Others die and they are wide awake. And you have to learn how to guide yourself so that you can be a master of antahkarana.

This is better than karate. In karate you can fight off the denizens of the crime world, you see, unless they have a gun, which is supposed to be a great equalizer. But in the world of antahkarana, the world of the spirit, in order to master that realm you have to have some knowledge of that realm. Jesus had knowledge.

That's what the mystery schools were supposed to teach. But you see, the dark forces don't want that. They just love the innocent little neophyte who comes out of the body and stands there and says, "Gee, I don't know where I am or who I am." And they say, "Well, we'll tell you who you are, come and follow us." And there they are, waiting to try to vampirize that person and take them over and lead them down the spiral negative pathway.

I'm sorry that these are the facts of life. I'm very, very sorry. But the only way that God could give man Godhood was to put him in a freewill situation. And it is our misuse of the free will that has put us into this situation, and nothing else.

Some people argue and say, "Well, God has all power. Why doesn't he just go ahead and pass a law that all of our sins would be wiped out immediately and that we would be perfect? And why do we have to go through all of this in order to experience this?" Well, dear hearts, remember that God is going through it with you. He is crucified in matter. Remember that.

This should give you a tremendous comfort because the only way that your soul could ever be immortalized is to have the divine companion right, right, right within you. That divine companion is the mold of the Christ. That's the divine image. The divine image is there, and by conformity to it you become one with the Universal Christ and you attain your true spiritual identity.

But in the meantime, what is really happening in the world is this: All over the world the tyrants like the Hitlers and the Mussolinis and all these people are doing these control factors and they're trembling the web of life and demanding their pound of flesh, like Shylock of old in *The Merchant of Venice*.

Oh, they all want to control something. "Knowledge is power," they say. Well, it is. And the wrong kind of knowledge is the wrong kind of power, and the right kind of knowledge is the right kind of power.

So antahkarana is basically a most magnificent concept because it shows that all of the myriad planes of identity function within, their own ideational levels. And when you climb the ladder of life, you climb from plane to plane to plane to plane till you reach the highest. And these masters have the knowledge they have because they've gone through all these planes, and they just keep right on going up. And there wouldn't be much incentive for them to keep climbing if there was nowhere to climb to, if they could go up and just sit down on the right hand of God and have dinner.

Well, this would be a very easy and simple thing, but the nature of God is transcendent, and God himself transcends himself each day that exists. The God of today is actually in one sense not the God of yesterday, because God himself is evolving through the creation. Now, I know that may sound blasphemous to some people who have the idea that God is already created. Well, they also had the idea that the world was already created in seven days and that God is now resting somewhere. That is erroneous, too, because the perfect creation is never finished.

"Finish, then, thy new creation / Pure and sinless let us be,"[14] do you see? Finish, then, thy perfect creation—this means that the perfect creation of God was made in the mind of God in the seven days of creation, the seventh day being the day of rest and completion or finality. But that is in the dual nature of God. That is, in one sense, the night side of God to us because it is the invisible realm that holds the pattern. And when we bring it forth in the figure eight, in the configuration of the eight, into the physical manifestation, then it returns back to Spirit ultimately. But it first has to come forth and the divine matrix has to encompass it round about.

Oh, these things are deep, I know. But you can understand the spider's web, can't you? You've seen a spider's web. You can understand that the web of the universe is vast, that it covers all the known and unknown cosmos everywhere. You can understand that what trembles one part of life trembles another. You can understand that all those who teach Christ, who preach Christ, who glorify Christ, who lift up God, who exhibit faith—you understand? Faith—they enhance creation, don't they, for all of us. And every part of life is blessed by that.

And everyone who curses life by saying, "I want to end it all. I don't want any part of it. I'm going to commit suicide. I'm not getting anything out of it," well, you're not putting anything into it, either. And that's basic truth. People who are busy putting something into life don't have time to even die. They're too busy.

I've heard quite a few of them say, "I'm just staying around to cheat the undertaker." I've never heard any of them say that they were staying around to cheat the uptaker, though. I think they're staying around to please the uptaker. And the uptaker is our own divine God Presence, who takes us up and changes us from glory to glory even by his own spirit.

So in conclusion, can you not see that all of the mysteries of God are in this beautiful computer, this infinite ocean? Can you not see that all good and all evil is deposited in there, in its plane? Can you not see that the sword of truth that God put between Eden, which is the higher planes, and the lower planes where identity is being worked out[15] remains there to separate the error of man from the perfection of God so that there is no contamination above?

Can you not see, then, that this pure state above is the goal of us all? That this state below is the school of us all? That the two-edged sword remains to separate it? And that in that which is below the two-edged sword, the law of cause and effect functions primarily? That there the web of life is trembling in its negative way as well as its positive way? But above, all good is added to the Church daily, even as the souls of men are added to the Church Universal and Triumphant daily.

All good goes above and accrues. But all evil becomes mere record, cause, effect, record and memory here below—below the realm of the sword. But the sword is eastward in Eden, eastward meaning within, and within here referencing not just simply the inside of your body but the inside of consciousness. Jesus said, "You cleanse the outside of the platter, you cleanse the outside of the form, but the inside is full of dead men's bones." Do you see? And this is what we call psychic episode.

The Divine Director told me one time, "You know, Mark, every single program on television, every book that is written, every novel is psychic episode." I think he put that in one of his *Pearls*, too, if I remember right. But he told me this. He said it's psychic episode. It's somebody's life pattern in an imperfect state. It's not a perfect state in most cases. They're writing about people and their mistakes and their heartaches and their triumphs, too, sometimes, but always human.

You know how they have that Horatio Alger series where the boy wins his fortune in the big city? Well, all of these books, everything that's written, is all psychic episode. And it all brings us in to a point of interest about human beings.

But what's going to happen if we just fill ourselves with that garbage? Ultimately, we're going to be more and more human and less and less divine. And we're interested in getting out of it. So I don't say that there are not interesting stories on television and in movies and in radio that cannot act as a diversion. I have heard, although I don't know if it is true or not, that the late Paramahansa Yogananda used to love to read Wild West stories as a diversion.

I have heard that one of the great masters who is now ascended (and I'd rather not name him because he was here on earth not too long ago) used to enjoy going to the movies once in a while because it was a relief for him. But I really think that if he were here today and saw the type of diet that he'd get in the movies, he would have a hard time finding one. On board ship, I walked out of *Thoroughly Modern Millie*. I had enough almost as soon as I got in. I just thought I'd see what it was like to see a theater on board a ship and to rock along the waves while you're looking at the movies.

But I think that by this understanding of antahkarana, by our understanding of how we as individuals can hurt life by what we think or help life by what we think, we can see an enormous potential for good. Can you imagine the thought power of a million people concentrating on the betterment of their community if they lived in a city? Tremendous, wouldn't it be? Can you imagine the thought power of healing that a little group can engage in?

You probably may remember the time they projected the heart attack at me, and the doctor said I had one notch out of five that was hanging. All the rest of my heart was destroyed. I had one muscle left. Well, I got up here and delivered a dictation the next night. Did you know that? It was unheard of. People just don't do that. And they took a reading afterward, and he says, "Well, I can't understand it. Your heart seems very good." Well, they can project anything at you—anything.

So you see, by this understanding of antahkarana, that right where you are is the center of the universe. As far as you are concerned, your heart is the center of the universe and you tremble the whole universe from that point in space where you are. And every other person has their own center that connects. And actually, in one sense, it's like the teacher with the eyes in the back of her head. The light rays that go out from your heart and connect you with the whole universe flow periphically, terrifically. They flow out around the whole globe. They don't just go out like these rays here on a flat plane. They go out in all directions, do you understand, like the rays from a light bulb. No matter which angle you're looking down or up at it, they are always emitting energy.

When you light a candle up on top of Pike's Peak over here, if you were millions of light-years away from the earth, if you had a powerful enough telescope, you should be able to see that, because once the light rays begin to travel from that candle, small as it is, they never stop traveling. They just keep going out in the universe. Actually, they curve in, if you really want to know, and they come back to the source. They are circular. But they travel an awful long way before the curve is made. I'm telling tales out of school, the curvilinear universe.

But at the same time this demonstrates the law of cause and effect, it brings back to you almost on a roller coaster every thought and everything that you think. And this is why the field of consciousness is the field of identity. And the field of consciousness is able to have what we call the night and day side.

The night side of consciousness can reach out as far as God reaches, every way, and then come back. We call it the night side because we can't perceive the light that's in it. But the day side of consciousness may be no bigger than a walnut for some people. It's very small. They haven't gone out very far in their imagination. The action of being has not expanded in the antahkarana of cosmic magnificence.

And this is a very important point that illustrates why one star differs from another star in glory.[16] It's because although all men have in the antahkaranic dual pattern the complete manifestation of the seven days of creation, they have probably not got to the first hour of the first day of creation in their outer manifestation. And you will find in measuring people that they range all the way from the first hour of the wailing, lusty cosmic infant to the old, mature man with a long white beard in the seventh cycle of life, just about ready to go upstairs and join Saint Germain and Jesus.

Where you are, I don't know. It's like that old saying, "Round she goes and where she stops nobody knows." I don't pretend to know exactly where everyone is. I have a good idea if I take a spectrum of the aura and analyze it. I don't have time to do it. I'm not curious about each one of you. I don't care in the sense that I want to be curious. I care in the sense that I want to help everyone, but certainly not just to peek into your world and say, "Peek-a-boo! Here I am. I know what *you're* thinking."

When you once taste of human vanity in yourself, you've had enough. You don't have to look in somebody else's mind to be able to realize what human beings think. And if you get to that stage, then you say, "God help me that I can be able to get acquainted with the masters and begin to think some of the masters' thoughts."

Must have been wonderful to have been in the mind of Jesus when he was raising Jairus' daughter. Wouldn't you like to have had the experience? Well, you know you can through assumption. You can assume the identity of any ascended master. Did you know that? But be very careful when you do this. Don't go around and tell people that you're Napoleon or somebody. They have a habit of locking these people up. And people that run around and say, "I'm Jesus," well, they'll lock those people up, too, or the men in little white coats cart them away.

But it doesn't hurt to be able to conceive of the Christ-identity as your own. You can claim the identity of Saint Germain. You can claim it in its essence and let it be a guiding star to your life to expand your consciousness into the master's consciousness. This is the trembling of antahkarana according to the initiatic process. You gain the master's consciousness by assuming his identity.

The only thing is, don't try to tell somebody else that you are the master. Just appreciate the fact that you can assume the identity, and as you do it, you will get some of the master's assistance into your world because you tune in with his vibration by doing it.

Now I've given you a secret. Good night.

October 12, 1968
Colorado Springs, Colorado

CHAPTER 3

The Artisan in the Temple

The artisan in the temple is always each individual. All of us are consecrated to being workmen to build the temple of God. Somewhere along the line in the snarl of the human personality, we become involved in the concept of saying, "Someone else but not I."

We do this through several methods. We eliminate ourselves from becoming artisans by saying we are not worthy of being artisans. We eliminate ourselves from becoming artisans by saying other people do not think we are worthy to be. Therefore, the first concept that is utterly important to us is the concept of recognizing not what man thinks but what God thinks and what God has thought.

The primal purpose of the Creator, to make of man an artisan in the temple, then, is an activity of the wise Masterbuilders of the race, the ascended masters. Many times we are prone also to fail in the recognition of their role in our development. This is done through many methods. Again, "I am not worthy," or, "Someone does not think me worthy." And this is always based on past performance and the assessment of either the individual or the other person of our value in life.

And our value in life is, in reality, on a sliding scale. Which way do you want to slide? That's what it boils down to. Personally,

I don't think that we should slide either way. I think we should move forward and be propelled forward by the great motor of life, which is joy.

Saint Germain has referred to joy as the motor of life. I think that joy in being an artisan in the temple is probably the most important function that a human being can actually engage in.

We have many functions from the cradle to the grave, but our destiny lies not there. We eat, we sleep, we procreate, we marry, we are given in marriage, we enjoy nature, we work. We may amass money or we may have no money. We may develop a little or we may not develop at all. It's all a matter of what takes place in our individual worlds. For here man is very much the individual. And the artisan in the temple is first of all an individual.

It is true, of course, that we're all a part of God. We can apply this to the whole world. We can say that Adolf Hitler was a part of God as well as we can say that Mother Cabrini was a part of God. We can apply this term, this epithet to the most sublime individual or the most ridiculous individual, the Austrian paperhanger who ruled an empire.

It doesn't matter, some people say; I say that is does matter. And the masters say that it does matter. And our Presence tells us that it matters. It matters very much what we do and what we think. "As a man thinketh in his heart, so is he"[1] is not only a truism, it is a statement and restatement of the old law.

Therefore, the artisan in the temple must be aware of his thoughts about himself—because our thoughts about ourselves are indeed effective. They're effective, and they're affective. They affect us for good or ill and they affect others for good or ill, *our* thoughts.

And so, I want to discuss with you, in connection with this sermon this morning on the artisan in the temple, the question of spiritual facility, in other words, the opening up of spiritual vision, the powers of spiritual perception. This seems to be a goal in the lives of many people—the desire to be able to do the same things that

Jesus did, that the great masters do. And they will apply it to seership as well and say, "I would like to possess the power to be able to see into the invisible, to be able to hear at a distance, to be able to project the consciousness out of the body."

Recently I visited with a man who was assisting Tom Miller in making our movie. And on his desk I found, where the nameplate usually goes, a plate that said Chairman of the Bored, b-o-r-e-d. And I realized full well, even in that whimsical statement, that many people today are bored because they are not artisans in the temple consciously.

If we are integrated into a master plan or integrated into *the* master plan in our consciousness, we have an entirely different sense of doing. Everything we do takes on a different phase of meaning. The little boring task becomes a movement in the mainstream that is leading us to a final goal, which final goal we recognize is only final in a cyclic sense, because once it is achieved, a greater goal is beyond it; and the ultimate purpose is thereby served.

But now we return to the thought, the very key thought, about the artisan in the temple, the thought of opening the centers, the thought of having spiritual perception. They say that knowledge is power. And whereas physical and material knowledge has always been considered to be power (thus we have secular education), spiritual knowledge, or seership, the ability to be able to see at a distance, to possess psychic faculties, seems to be a premium in the consciousness of people today, who feel that once they have this power, they have achieved the ultimate.

I would point out today in the name of El Morya and at his request the grave dangers attendant upon the opening of the centers prematurely and the great good fortune that comes to people who do not open the centers prematurely.

Long ago, in a lecture I gave, I referenced the concept of "Thank God you cannot hear the footsteps of a fly." And this is very important, because if we had a magnification per se in our hearing, making it so keen and acute that we could hear the moth consuming our garments in the closet and everything were to manifest in a similar scale, we would often find that life is deafening to us, even physically, and we would not live in a world of peace or quiet, even in our sleep. We would be constantly disturbed by this super-hearing. So, you see, dramatically we can reveal to you the blessedness of tempering the wind to the shorn lamb.

Now, then, let us deal with the problem of the opening of the centers prematurely from the masters' vision and from what is right and what is real and what should be, rather than what is. What should be is the ennoblement of the character. This means taking on *the vestments of the Master*, investing one's consciousness in the Master's sense about everything, leaving alone the human sense.

When we take on the Master's character and ideals, we become a different person; we are changed. This alteration, then, is a prerequisite to the opening of the centers. But those who put the cart before the horse, and many are doing it, will often find themselves a helpless victim of a macrocosmic world where they are a microcosmic entity.

A moving picture was shown on television recently, a rerun of an old movie, called *The Incredible Shrinking Man*. It dramatically illustrated this whole concept. The man began to shrink until eventually he had to live in a doll house. Then from the doll house he went down to the point when he could crawl into a mouse hole and he had to run from the house cat.

At the end of the movie, after having had a battle with a spider wherein he used a pin as a harpoon and finally impaled the spider on this pin, he escaped into the grass (which was a forest of giant trees) through an opening in the screen (which was larger than a window). And he continued to shrink.

And as he looked out there in the grass at the whole universe and at the stars, he said, "In reality, all is a matter of relativity." So he felt he was going into an infinity within as well as if he had become one who continually enlarged, the enlarging man, because, after all, he found that he had all the faculties of consciousness when he shrunk, you see.

Now, what I am trying to do this morning is to illustrate for you, for all time, I hope, the principle that the horse must be *before* the cart—the horse of development, of character ideals, of spiritual rapport with God and the masters that enables us to think in their terms and in their frame of reference before we open those ghastly centers which can become the means, yes, of our reaching into the macrocosm and finding God but, when opened prematurely, can cause us no end of grief because we find ourselves helpless, naked before this whirlwind of psychic forces which will be able to move us as easily as a straw that is cast into the wind.

So above all things, then, understand that the artisan must first of all develop the consciousness of the temple of God. He must recognize that his body is the temple of God, but he must carry it a step further and say that his *mind* is the temple of God.

People don't understand Saint Paul—they don't understand the scriptures that refer to the fact that the body of man is the temple of God.[2] And they don't understand that the body is always fourfold. When the phrase is used in the scriptures, "the body is the temple of God," it means the body, the consciousness, the mind, the feeling world, the allness of man, of individuality, is the temple of God.

But we seem to think in terms of the body, and we wash the outside of the platter scrupulously clean. We clean our ears, we clean our noses, we clean our face, we clean all over physically. But we are dirty in our minds and dirty in our consciousness and dirty in our feeling world without ever realizing it, because we attach "scrupularity," the state of being scrupulous, to the physical self and often overlook the real human being, the total consciousness of our being.

And this is why I say that it is very clear to me now that the artisan must always *first* develop his spirituality, his spiritual nature. He must develop his feelings of love and obedience to the Christ, his feelings of respect for human beings that are here on earth besides him.

Right beside us people are living and they have rights. We see it on the nation's highways. We saw it again dramatically illustrated, that almost every single time that we went forward to pass, even if we were only ten feet behind another car, the other car, if it was a Volkswagen or a huge van, would pull out directly in front of us, having no regard whatsoever for their own life or limb or for ours.

And the speed didn't seem to matter. We could be coming at them at eighty miles an hour or coming at them at twenty miles an hour—they would still dart out, you see, showing that the problem that the world has today is a problem of recognizing one's brother and showing, evidencing concern for his life, not just our own.

We find that in organizations such as the Communist Party and the Center for the Study of Democratic Institutions,[3] in Santa Barbara, that these social aspects are stressed, and they are considered as human problems, soluble in the chemistry of humanity.

But the centuries have not demonstrated that man by intellectualism is able to effect emotional control. On the contrary, those who are at all versed in skillful diplomacy soon come to realize that there is no question about it: you have to win the *feelings* of people before you can even direct or guide their minds. So we again learn about others and we learn about ourselves in those interpersonal relationships that we engage in through what we term friendship and through this business of living.

So the artisan in the temple must be exceedingly aware of himself. And the artisan in the temple must be aware of the need to first develop the Christ aspect of the person and then to understand that once the Christ aspect is developed, that it itself possesses the natural quality of triggering the stream of natural unfoldment whereby the spiritual, the psychic senses, the seeing at a distance, the penetrating vision will unfold with it.

And I can cite—although I do it humbly in God's eyes—to a very limited degree my own experience. I never did stress developing along the path of reading people's auras, looking into their past, finding out who I was in some past life. I never stressed being able to project my consciousness at a distance to control the forces of nature, to bring the elements under obedience. No. Instead of that I stressed proximity to the Deity, both as the Deity and as the ideals of the Deity.

We must recognize, then, dear hearts (and I hope you're not too tired to listen to me, because this is a very important concept), that the Deity as a person is one aspect, but the Deity as his own law is another vital aspect. And you cannot, I repeat, *you cannot* validly separate the laws of the Deity from the Deity. To make a friend out of God and to flaunt his laws will always bring about an attendant manifestation of human jangle and discord in your world that will bring you down and will not raise you up, which should be your aim.

So I want to stress that friendship with God means friendship with his laws also—of reasonability, of decency, toward our fellowmen and to organizational purposes. But now, for a moment, we stop our process on the artisan in the temple, and we begin to examine the artisan in the temple from the standpoint of the guild. We are going to look at group activity in the temple for a moment.

We talk about individuality and individuality of expression. But we ask ourselves, in the business of the workaday world and the business of living, what can we do as a group that we cannot do as an individual? And we find that we have multiplied the power of the individual enormously in the world scene when we harness the individual's talents and abilities in group action.

And so here we have the developing of what we will term a spiritual guild. And the forming of the spiritual guild is in essence the activity of the Great White Brotherhood.* You might apply it to The Summit Lighthouse as an organization and say that we are members of the guild, that this is our guild hall, that we are artisans in the guild or workmen in the Lord's temple, that we are a part of

---

*The term "white" refers not to race but to the aura of white light that surrounds these immortals, who have risen from every race and walk of life.

the building of the temple in this age.

This epoch is ours, our energies are ours. What we do with those energies is the question—what we do with our lives, how much we contribute of meaningful activity to the aspect of the guild and hence to the manifestation of the total culture which, I will bring out, is the Great White Brotherhood. In other words, the Great White Brotherhood represents the culture, the guild is the Summit, and the artisan is the individual Summiteer, the member of The Summit Lighthouse.

We must have some developed sense of this and a realization that we cannot put the cart before the horse and try to develop some super-seership which seeks to evade responsibility by making us possessed with a capacity which we do not really have, thus fooling ourselves. We have to cast this aside. Instead of this, we must face up to reality.

I suspect that this last statement may not have been fully grasped by all of you, so I would like to point out that there is a tendency toward spiritual sloth on the part of practically everyone.

Thus, we must equate the scriptures that Jesus brought out with the subject matter at hand and remember that his words must in this case be taken literally, as in many cases they should, where he says, "My Father worketh hitherto, and I work."[4]

I think that if you could take people out on the lawn and then have them weave garlands of flowers and dance around and play little games, that they would expend enormous quantities of energy most happily and give that energy happily, but when that has to be employed in the aspect of work, then we find sometimes that the artisan balks at the fact that *he must work*. And therefore we come around to the subject of the Father working hitherto and I work.

In my discussions with the masters, I have learned that their service after the ascension is enormous, that after they pass through the change into the higher octaves, they just *begin* to work. And at that level they have a distinct realization that would not come to us ordinarily of the terrific problems encountered in the structures that human beings have created in consciousness, in the electronic belt, and in the four lower bodies.

In other words, we have a tremendous structuring of distortion which has occurred in most people. The artisans at the Summit here are no exception. Just because we join the guild does not immediately transform us electrically, electronically, so that we can fit the highest schema of the masters. On the contrary, all it does is open the door or afford us an opportunity for the expansion of our identity.

We are cells in the body of God. But unless we are working cells, with a capacity for expression of the Deific idea that is actually the concept of God for the guild, the concept of God for the culture, then, you see, we are working against nature, not flowing in the mainstream thereof.

Now, this particular talk that I'm giving to you was prepared by Master El Morya and placed in my consciousness in order to acquaint you with the fact that there is a meaningful structure existing here but that the power to enhance the structure lies within the hands of the artisan. It cannot lie entirely in the hands of the group or the guild, because the guild is no greater in its expression than the sum total of the greatness of the individuals put together.

At this point, we introduce that which is not new to us but still has to fall in the category of the eternally new: the idea of an ever-new presence of order. I find that the greatest problem in the universe is really chaos, because chaos is any form of disorder. It doesn't matter how minute it may express.

You wear glasses. You have misplaced them. You reach for the glasses. You cannot see without them. You cannot read a word of print. You immediately are faced with a dilemma of "Where are my glasses?" You use money in order to pay for goods or services. You are in a restaurant or a doctor's office, and it says, "Cash on the spot, Johnny," and you reach in your pocket and your wallet is missing. Someone stole it or you left it at home. You immediately face a dilemma. What are you going to do about it? The man wants his money.

So we live in a very, very practical world where chaos introduced into that world shows the need for order. And therefore the Master has stressed to me that the time has come for what he calls the guild-hall consciousness, to enter into the artisan's sense, and for the artisan to now begin the development of his sense as a workman in the house of God.

I suspect that sloth is probably the devil's greatest tool—one of the greatest—that and discouragement. And I think nothing discourages us more than sloth. I am not implying, nor is the Master implying, that we have sloth here. He is merely pointing out that there is a tendency toward sloth as there is a tendency toward gravity. And gravity and sloth are almost hand in hand.

A state of consciousness that wants to work in the Master's temple as an artisan, to be a part of the guild, to assist and contribute to his greatness, to the guild-hall greatness, must recognize that his natural tendency, from the human level, not the divine level, is to have the gravity of sloth tending toward chaos in his world.

It takes an effort to think and have a place to keep your glasses, to have a place to keep your wallet, to have a place for everything with everything in place. It takes an enormous amount of thought and planning to actually furnish a house or to buy groceries for a given period of time. Tasks that seem very simple are actually colossal when they're multiplied numerically. And therefore the problems, the logistics, of the whole world complex are today staggering to the imagination.

Is it any wonder, then, that the benefit of computers was given to our society? And actually, if you will only think of it that way, when you order your life, you are utilizing a giant computer, you are using the whole facility of being, of self, to produce a wanted situation of order in your life.

Now, I regret very much that I have to take your time for this discussion, if I bore any of you, but I assure you that the Master has said that this is a very important message. Just because it may have the earmarks of the obvious about it does not mean it is not important.

The Master says the word *artisan*, the word *guild*, the word *culture* judged from the spiritual aspect are very vital because they are keys to a functional manifestation of hierarchy upon the planet. Hierarchy is not going to manifest just through the intellect. Hierarchy will manifest through the fourfold nature of man. When we do not need this body anymore, we can shed it. As long as we need it, we should have it in good health and have it in joy.

I think, then, that if we will recognize the forming of good habits and feeding them into our computer, it is going to make automatic a great many of our normal functions. And as it makes these functions automatic, it will take more and more of the strain off of the developing embryo from a spiritual standpoint.

We are embryonic gods. As long as we are involved in the temple magic of just working on the physical body to see that it produces a feeling of élan, of well-being, as long as what we're doing is just that, we are neglecting the developing of our immortal soul. So, therefore, shall we then dispense with the physical body? How ridiculous can we be? Of course not!

The physical body is an important function or we would not have it. *But, don't make it any more important than twenty-five percent of the business of living.* Take the mind and make it a separate thing, if you will, but always realize the four functions of the four lower bodies must be integrated into the square. And eventually the square, when the physical form is no longer needed, becomes a triad, a triadic manifestation.

But it is always three that agree in one.[5] For in reality, what is most important to us is our state of consciousness. Consciousness is capable of absolutely manifesting a state of bliss, and bliss is the natural divine state when that divine state is free from the *sense* of bliss and enters into bliss in a natural manner. So long as a person is seeking bliss for the sake of enjoyment without the actual honoring of the Creator by understanding that they are expected to manifest his nature, they are falling short of the mark.

Some people say, "I just *love* to give decrees." Others say, "I don't give a fig for decrees, but I do it." The point is, we should neither be doing things because we enjoy them or because we do them from a sense of duty, but we should do whatever we do as artisans to God as a part of the whole noble process.

You take, for example, Leonardo da Vinci and his sculpturing. We understand that he first drew in charcoal the anatomy of the perfection he sought to express. The charcoal image was lacking in the glamour of the finished product. The things that we have to do in order to prepare the groundwork for our finished product, our divine self, to manifest, may sometimes seem laborious, even lugubrious, heavy.

But when we forget the self, when we enter into the state of the order and natural perfection of the universe and see that as we manifest that order and perfection through our consciousness—the social consciousness, the religious consciousness, the sense of self all put together—we are making great possibilities of change in our realm of purpose, the realm of the individual's purposes. And we are allying or aligning these changes with the perfection of God.

Now, if we do not do this, the whole process may be incomprehensible to us. For it is in the doing that we are actually seeing. And this is what was meant by the statement, "For we shall see him as he is, for we shall be like him."[6] It is a matter of the artisan becoming the image of the Master Artisan. And oh, what tremendous joy the artisan can develop as he becomes imbued with the natural joy of the Master Artisan.

The guild, then, becomes the brotherhood of man; the culture becomes the cosmos. It is a constant expansion, and it reminds me of that "Little drops of water / Little grains of sand / Make the mighty ocean / And the pleasant land."[7]

We are often caught in the jaws of the trap that says, "You're not making any progress. What's happening to you? You're just doing this and you're doing that and you're not getting anywhere." This is a case of our failures to see. And I think that we sometimes feel that if we ourselves only had enough spiritual vision, we could penetrate the opacities that surround us, we could somehow or other trace the realities of self and bring them into view.

And this is the greatest fallacy there is, because we first must bring forth the character from the unseen. Blessed are those that believe and have seen. But *more* blessed are those that believe and have not seen.[8]

You see, we must have the faith. Faith is the substance of things hoped for, the evidence of things not seen as yet.[9] We must function from the level of faith by realizing that God is the rewarder of them that diligently seek him,[10] by realizing that his laws are just, that whatever good things we do we will receive, as evil will be received or returned to us for recompense.

We must recognize, then, that the greater order we can produce in our individual life—whether it be the rearrangement of the cards in our wallet or the rearrangement of our pocketbook for greater ease in serving our needs or a kitchen cupboard or a desk drawer or a work position or a garden for better harvesting and planting—whatever we do to produce order in our world is a part of the macrocosmic scheme, even though it is involved in the most intricate microcosmic miasma.

Order your life, then, and you bring about heaven's first law as the artisan of God in the temple of being. Order your life, then, and you take the first step to produce the building of the pyramid. Order your life, then, and you join issue with the problems that confront us as a nation, as a world, as a people.

Because order is the key to it all. And this is not something that we do once and then it is always done forever. We are ordering and we are reordering. And our reordering is often more important than our original ordering, because hopefully we have established in the field of mind, in the field of the feeling world, a greater sense of what we are doing.

And this is why I say to you today, as we stand upon the threshold of a great springboard that is going to catapult us into prominence in the world, that unless we are ready for that, unless we are ready for Saint Germain's plan, unless we are ready with our visual aids, unless we have the facilities to train the people and the program developed here in our pilot activities, we are going to be caught in the middle of the stream and we're not going to have anything that we can travel on. We're going to drown, then, or be inundated in the new age, and we ourselves will not be ready for it.

Now, the young people all over America today are clamoring in the excitement of life, for reality. And all that the world is giving them is a constant repetitious boring cycle of sex and more sex from a face that is a little more vivacious or a little more interesting than the other face. And youth is constantly supplying these new goddesses of the screen, the sirens that lure men to their doom. And what they can't do with sex, they're doing now with glamour and they're doing it also with greed.

They're showing them, "If you had this money, you could have a bigger car. You could travel all over the world. You could have more women than you have now, and higher-up women, women that are better. You've been playing around with trash, now, fellow. If you just had a little more money, you could get into the big circuit."

If we're going to move in that mainstream, where are we? We're nowhere. And the Church today is totally confused about the nature of being. What we need, then, is the artisan in the temple who will understand the direction in which he is moving. He will understand the direction of the flow of the mainstream of spiritual life. He will understand how to guide his four lower bodies.

Krishnamurti, when he was under the direction of Lord Maitreya, said your body is "the horse upon which you ride."[11] Many of the Theosophical tenets were imbued with more knowledge of the Christ than anything that has ever come down to us since, until the masters in this time through the Summit and other avenues finally opened up the consciousness of man to the I AM Presence and Holy Christ Self. And that, of course, has opened up new vistas.

Now, today we are bringing forth materials in preparation for supplying the needs of millions of young men and women, disillusioned by drugs, disillusioned by sex, disillusioned by money, disillusioned with their world. They will reach up and say, "Where can I touch the reality of the face of the Christ?"

And we must be ready! We must be ready with the visual aids and everything that is needed in films, in music, in decrees, in prose, in instruction books, in classroom techniques, in scientific instruments, in the university and in universities, in instructors, in ministers, in musicians and in workmen of all sorts who will form by their craft the total guild-hall production of victory for this planet.

This is the movement of the new age. This is the plan of the Master that stood behind the purpose of Santa Barbara. And when I recently stood in Santa Barbara and I saw the arch that was not the arch of triumph, because against it leaned the broken-over and bent, old gas pump from probably 1925, as I gazed at that arch, cracked by earthquakes, and I realized that we had to mend the arch, I saw not only the mending of that arch by the work of our hands and the devotion of our hearts, but I also saw the preparing of the necessary classrooms for the first teachers to be turned out by the Summit. Because there at Santa Barbara is going to be the esoteric school of the Fraternity of the Keepers of the Flame.

Here will arise, if the plan be followed—and I always put an *if* in, because you people are the if and so am I. We are the ifs. On our backs rides the power of the future. What we do will be determined not by Stringfellow Barr of the Center for the Study of Democratic Institutions or by Robert Maynard Hutchins or by those people who feel that they are intellectually the elite of the planet and thus the architects of the new age. It will be, and I say ought to be, determined by the ascended masters, by those who understand how to hold in their hands a culture and *pass* that culture to us. That is what is needed.

And therefore we are preparing to counteract the vicious socialistic forces that seek the regimentation of man and the binding of man to the wheel of the ancient law of the ox cart, just treading the treadmill of existence in a social dream fostered by the illusions of some intellectual. In its place the greatest mind of the ages that will span the beginnings and the endings of vast cycles beyond comprehension, the mind of God, comes to us, the vital intelling of the realities of not only the microcosmic man but of the macrocosmic world.

The whole of it all in all of its interesting panorama of variety is all manifest on the screen of consciousness. And it is not a harbinger of doom, but a manifestation of vitalized hope, because it sings to us a song, the song that could almost be called a lullaby of the Mother of the World, that the Mother of the World seeks to rock in her arms the infant humanity that today are gazing upon human illusion and divine reality and cannot tell the difference.

Our role is to *expound* upon the realities of God and *expunge* from society the darkness, the confusion, and the pain that have brought so much blight into manifestation temporally! We will replace it in the name of Almighty God, by his grace and his reality. Do you have a part in it? If you do, then nothing else is *as* important.

Thank you.

August 3, 1969
Colorado Springs, Colorado

CHAPTER 4

Exhalation and Inhalation
of the Breath of God

We would like to think this morning of the exhalation of the breath of God and the inhalation of the breath of God, because in early Genesis we were told that the LORD God breathed into the nostrils of man the breath of life, and man became a living soul.[1]

As we stop, then, all of us, and ponder upon that subject, the breath of life, we realize that it has great import. If our breath is cut off, we no longer have life, do we? So the breath of life is extremely important. Some people, of course, are of the opinion that the breath of life is only conforming to the physical body and is merely a part of the pneumatic system whereby the lungs, as a bellows, open and draw in the fresh oxygen, which is through the systems of the alveoli of the lungs put into the bloodstream.

I want to point out that actually there is a spiritual breath of life, because it states that "man became a living soul." Now a soul is not a body. A soul is a soul. We always talk about the soul leaving the body at the passing. We hear people say this, that the soul leaves the body. But you see, the breath of life, then, is not only a physical thing but it has a divine counterpart in the soul. And man is renewed in his soul, or solar, energy patterns just as well as he is renewed in his physical body. So we see that the soul could not live either without the breath of life.

And then we are brought face to face with the breath of God— the exhaling of the divine breath and the inhaling. Now, we understand from the ancient Hindu scriptures, the sacred Vedas, that Brahma exhaled and that all of the creation is the exhalation of God, that there is a period like the diastole and systole of the heartbeat, the ebb and flow of the tides, that there is a period of sustainment where the breath of God is going out. It reaches a certain zenith, like a noonday, and then it sustains itself and holds, coming, of course, to the point where the breath is not actually moving at all. This precedes the time when God begins to inhale.

God, of course, is referenced here not as a human figure but as a cosmic configuration. You don't think of God as being a man sitting up on a pink cloud somewhere and blowing out his breath. You're thinking now of the release of the Spirit into form, and this release is the energy of the Word that creates the form. And when the form of one cycle of the divine breath goes out, which may take millions and millions of years, then that is drawn back, and that is the inhalation.

It has been considered as proper, according to the ancient scriptures, that God will exhale as creative process, that the exhalation of the breath of God is the creative process manifesting in the womb of matter and creating the suns and the moons and the stars, the planets, and the crystals, and the hearts of men in physical bodies, the wind, the tides, everything. But after a certain point of time, he calls all this back to himself, and the calling of it back to himself is the end of its cycle. And it is actually brought into the cosmic center of universal creation, to the very heart of God, if you will. There it rests for a certain prescribed period of time, as we see in the Hindu dance of creation where the dance comes to an end and the dancer falls to the floor and folds his arms forward and bows his head down and is absolutely still.

This period of stillness is comparable to the gestation period of a child, which is nine months (actually it's twelve months*). I think that this gestation period is the night of Brahma, when all of this is drawn back into the Godhead and there is a rest period.

During the rest period, the patterns are being gathered within. It's like a seed. We find that God is functioning now as a seed, and during this period of rest, the lacy patterns of the creation—when I say lacy patterns I'm referring to the whole divine DNA chain, if you will, the patterns that God makes by which stars will be born and spiral nebulae and whole systems, and galaxies—these patterns are created there. And inside the galactic patterns are created the solar patterns; inside the solar patterns there are created the planetary patterns or the luminous orbs, and inside the luminous orbs are created the moon patterns or satellite patterns. And then inside of the luminous orb patterns of an earth, we find that it will begin to create all of the systems that are going to be involved in the earth, the growing things, the trees, and the water and everything.

It's all programmed. It can be compared to a giant computer. And we have to recognize that during this period of rest, there is an actual manifestation of divine intelligence—the stirring, the shaking of divine intelligence in the sea—and that this shaking is the drawing by the fingers of God of the various graphs and patterns and hieroglyphs that are going to manifest in the various systems of worlds.

When the whole is complete—which is supposed to be during the night of Brahma, during the period of rest—then once again comes the dawn of creation and the exhalation of the breath of God. And the whole system is repeated over again.

---

*Elizabeth Clare Prophet has placed the nine months of the gestation of a child on the cosmic clock starting at the three o'clock line, corresponding to three months each for the development of the mental, emotional and physical bodies. Mark may be extending this cycle back three months before conception to the twelve o'clock line, which is where all cycles begin.

Supposedly, according to what knowledge we can have, and there are few of us that remember these processes, the whole process is transcendent. Each issuing forth, supposedly, has within itself various opportunities for growth and expansion and transmutation and exaltation above and beyond any one part. In other words, Sirius, for example, could evolve more than Andromeda. That is, there could be within the universe, according to the response of the various parts, a greater advancement of one part compared to another, as one star differing from another star in glory.[2] You find this in the universe, and you find it in people. Some people avail themselves more of the divine opportunity. Some systems seem to evolve more than others.

But the whole, taken as a whole now, not as a part, is supposed to be transcending itself each sosophoric round. Every time there is the issuing forth of the breath of God, it is supposed to jump over a higher hurdle of accomplishment. And the process itself is the witness of eternal life. In other words, this is the game of God, the great Creator; this is his business. You and I may be artisans. We may be writers. We may be musicians, sculptors, housewives, tillers of the soil, architects. Whatever we are, God is the master of the creative game.

Now, somehow or other in his consciousness, and while this is not recorded in the scriptures in so many words, it is to be found in the scriptures, nevertheless, if you read between the lines, and Saint Paul himself brings it out in many places, where he says, "Eye has not seen, nor ear heard, neither has entered into the heart of man the things which God has prepared for them that love him,"[3] "to them who are the called according to his purpose."[4]

And so we see that this purpose of God is not—as some of us had imagined, basing this imagination on the scriptures—a matter of a sea of glass and a golden throne and all of the companies of people that have become immortal standing before this throne, plunking on harps and for ever and ever and ever singing, "Holy, holy, holy, Lord God Almighty,"[5] as a great admiration society.

While this is recorded in the scriptures and is absolutely true in its correct meaning, it is not a case of the Father, this great all-wise, all-loving, all-generous father of life, having created all things in order that they might praise him. It's not the case. Actually, what is involved here is the ritual of becoming. And in order for man to become one with God, it is necessary that he praise the highest good.

So we are always dealing with eternal things. We are dealing with eternal things in this very image of the saints all standing there before the throne saying, "Holy, holy, holy, thou alone art holy." Actually, not only would this be boring to men if it were to go on forever in that human thought, if we were to humanize that idea, but it would be boring to the Creator, who I think would become downright embarrassed, seeing that his intention is to convey to the creation the markings of himself.

We find Marie Corelli in her book *A Romance of Two Worlds* brings out the idea that at one point in the initiatic process of men, individuals were given the power to create their own universe, that when they were given this power, in space they said, "Let there be light," just as God did. And they saw the universes springing up beneath their feet. They could see all the star systems and planets, and they went down into the planet to redeem as Christ did.

Then at a certain point they saw that the prayers were all cut off, the people were not praying anymore; they were all involved in doing their own thing. They were no longer concerned about God in any way, and all the light rays of prayers that were coming up were then cut off and there was almost total darkness. And at that point the higher voice, the higher command came and said, "Destroy."

At that point the initiate was very confused. The initiate said, "Oh, but I can't destroy. Don't ask me to destroy these little worlds. Don't ask me to destroy these beautiful little worlds with all these lovely little people on them." And the voice said, "Destroy." And he kept fighting, as Saint Peter did when God told him, "Rise, Peter, kill and eat."[6] He was fighting, struggling with the deity.

And finally the deity said to him, "If thou, O mere mortal, in thy state, in this imaginary world that you have created, feel remorse and an unwillingness to destroy, how do you think, then, that I, who am truly living love, feel about destroying? You are reluctant to destroy this little figment world that we have permitted you to create in space, yet you suppose that I would destroy you." And thus the lesson of divine love and the lesson of compassion were conveyed.

And somehow or other we are brought face to face with the idea that it is the evil, the energy veil of selfishness and greed and narrowness of concept that must be destroyed, not the people—but if the people themselves do not repudiate their own wickedness and turn to God, that they will become destroyers of themselves under cosmic law, that it will not be God at all who is doing the destruction. And of course, this is true, because man has a counterpart known as his angel which is at court.

Most people don't realize this. Jesus said, "And I say unto you that these little ones of mine, their angels do ever behold the face of my Father which is in heaven,"[7] which meant that although these little ones may be urchins in the street covered with mud and covered with dirt and dust, ignorant and struggling to find themselves, that right while this is happening, right while they're down here with dirty faces and hungry looks and in their struggles for recognition, these children have an angel presence and that that presence is beholding God's face right while they're down here simultaneously.

This, then, shows us that there is a concern in the universe for men. This is something that people have forgotten, they forget from time to time. They seem to feel that in their bare struggle for existence, when they are raw and stripped bare, that somehow or other all of the mistakes that they have made render them unfit for the kingdom of God. Then they have to face the concern of God, who never planned for their destruction, who never planned for them to be inadequate to fulfill their purposes, but who planned, on the contrary, for the victory of every lifestream upon the planet.

We ask ourselves, Why? Why, in God's name, should God—the Almighty, the cosmic creator of the universe, the issuer forth of the breath of Brahma and the one who calls it back, who gives the breath of life—have in his own being the slightest thought of failure on behalf of anyone?

You immediately realize this isn't true. God doesn't have it. Then, where does it come from? In heaven's name, where does it come from? It arises out of the uneducated awe with which men behold the universe. They have an uneducated awe, and they see all of this vastness and they stand facing it, the naked reality of the universe, and they feel themselves like a tree that's standing there without bark. You see what I mean.

They feel that the cosmic winds, and there are cosmic winds, they feel the cosmic winds are blowing through the branches of their frail reality and they say to themselves, "Why, I don't amount to a pinhead." And then they start belittling themselves. And like David's sling, they are building up energy with every belittlement, and this energy goes and retreats deep into the subconscious. It goes way down into the subconscious, and the deeper it goes, the more stern and horrible will be the reaction when it suddenly comes forth, this awful retreat of man into nothingness.

That's the source of the superiority complex, because the inferiority complex is the retreat of man back into his consciousness where he is self-belittling and permits and accepts the belittlements of others. But the reaction comes and the further back you draw the sling of energy, the further the rock will go. That is what happens, and it is reaction—reaction that causes people, then, when they felt so badly and felt so small in themselves, to finally decide how very important they really are.

So they begin to feel the need to assert and take their dominion not over themselves but over other people, because in this taking of the dominion over other people they somehow or other have a warped sense of worth. And this is what creates the human struggle, because it is a denial of the reality which comes from the equipoised center where one simply accepts the light ray from God of Being and declares, I AM.

Recently we have heard once again that old and familiar tune from the outer world that denies the power of the I AM, that denies the power of Be-ness, that denies the power of Be-ing. Being and Be-ness, all of this—the realities of God—are. They do not have to be affirmed or sought. They are already a part of each one of us.

The greatest destruction that can be wrought against the I AM is the retreat subconsciously into this feeling world where we begin to be self-belittling or permit other people to belittle us. That's one half of it. The other half of this negative shell is to go the other way and decide how very important you are and then walk around the world with your shoulders thrown back, your head high, and say, "I really am important."

This is a case of where you are bucking up with your energy against the children of God. Why, just think what it would amount to if you have a thousand sons of God and these thousand sons of God have all gone backward and now they all feel the need to assert themselves against each other to prove their worth. Why, these people, a thousand of them, they're all fighting each other instead of actually allowing the kingdom of God to express through them. And here you see a denial of the natural manifestation of the breath of life, of the energy of God, of the simple, sweet, childlike power of Being.

None of us have to struggle to obtain our own reality. We simply have to recognize it. Once we recognize it—here's where the subtle razor's edge manifests—we have recognized the power of the great God Self within, but we have to be extremely careful to realize that we must understand and know that this God is a God of action, not a passive God, in the world of form.

You in your own life can have those same periods of retreat that God has, the diastole and systole of the heart, the ebb and flow of the tides. Your own days and nights are many. We go into a night, a period of rest, but during that time we should recognize that it is the time when we ask God to draw forth our life plan. For we have a personal life plan.

Mazzini said every life is a mission.[8] Well, I think that whether he said it or Christ said it, God said it first. He made every life a mission. But a mission does not mean a mission on behalf of self. It's like the woman said who was out with her tambourine collecting, "I'm taking up a collection for my favorite charity." And in the tavern she was in, the people begin throwing the money in. Someone asks her, "What is your favorite charity?" She says, "Myself."

And so, of course, this is the basic idea. People are often doing things for themselves when God is eager to do things for them. And when he does things for them, this includes the service of the washing of the feet of others by God. What does that mean? It means that any one of you, any one of us, anyone on earth, can get down and wash the feet of another person, and that God inside of us will be washing the feet of the other person. It means that God is not ashamed to cleanse the smallest grain of dust of his whole system. The God of the universe, he's not ashamed, but people are ashamed. We're ashamed for this and we're ashamed for that and we're ashamed for ourselves.

And this is the tool of the dark forces that want to keep this systemic universe in bondage. They have learned the plans governing science, of life, governing the warp and woof of creation. They understand the ergs of energy and how to bottle them up and how to release them. They understand these physical laws of the universe and the spiritual laws of the universe in part.

But they are not congruent with the life plan of the Deity, with the holy triad of being. They do not conform to God's ideas about life. They conform to the idea of "me first" and everybody else afterward. And this is basically what is wrong with society today. But in the midst of all that's wrong with society, we will not correct our own life by condemnation proceedings against this imperfect society. That's why Jesus said, the Son of man came not into the world to condemn the world but that through him they might find eternal life.[9]

We, then, as a part of the Godhead, have in our destiny, locked within it, a significant contribution to the universe once we know this. We must permit ourselves to identify with God in action. We have to recognize that however many people there may be, however many souls there may be in creation, that we have a unique capacity, that this unique capacity of the self, in its minute mathematical part, can actually far exceed what you would think would be the voting rights of that mathematical part in a democracy. In other words, in a cosmic realm, a man is not limited by his portion; he is limited only by the degree and amount of universal love of the divine nature that he can draw forth through the eye of the needle of the self.

If you can think of yourself as an hourglass, and instead of sand falling through, the gold of the divine character falling through into your hands right below the nexus, if you can feel that heaven is bestowing on you its limitless life, then you must accept it as limitless.

In the outer world today we are used to mathematical portions. We say, "What is my inheritance?" Well, you inherited five thousand pounds from your grandfather in English money. Well, when you come to God, if your portion was ten thousand pounds, you're not limited to just accept that, because you're dealing with divine love and divine character. And you have the right to demand of God the allness of God, because that is a part of everyone's inheritance.

In a system where you just cut it up as the Communists do and say, "Well, let's give everybody their share," you could probably conceivably say, "Well, we're going to have very little of God to enjoy because there's so many of us." But God is not that way.

The nature of God is to expand in the domain, and the divine sea out of which the universes were framed—and herein is the mystery of Christ—is transferred to the Logos. And once it reaches the realm of the Logos, the statement of power that is made, which is the fiat of initiation, is, "*All power* in heaven and earth is given unto me."[10]

That is a fiat. Transfer it to the Christ and then accept it from the Christ as your own, and that macrocosmic seed, come now into the realm of the microcosm of the person, can actually expand proportionately within the frame of the person until it is exactly equal—as water seeks its level—in all of its parts in the microcosm as it is equal above in the macrocosm.

And that is a very significant statement when you grasp it, because it provides you not only with the responsibility of responding to the fiats of God but also of exercising your privilege of being a contributor to the magnificence of the greater universe as well. And no one suffers any loss—the loss being suffered when we deny ourselves the gifts and graces of God and the loss being suffered when we refuse to accept that we really are what God has promised us.

We are sons of God. If we're sons of God, then we are, according to the scriptures, "joint heirs with Christ."[11] And if we're joint heirs, then we also can say, "I will sit down on my Father's right hand."[12] And the "right hand" is the right way of living, just as the "left hand" is the wrong way of living—and there are many who have taken the lefthanded path, some ignorantly and some knowingly, I'm sorry to say.

But our responsibility is to understand that this drama is going on permanently. It is not going to stop. Some people have the idea that at one point we will all be perfected and then sort of go into a nirvanic state where we will just sort of titillate in bliss, if you grasp my concept at all. We just sit there in some kind of a blissful state with little ripples of joy running over us and we sit there and do nothing.

This is a perfectly ridiculous thing, because the universe is based on principles of beauty and art. The universe is based on dramatic episodes. The universe is based on a sense of infinite wonder brought down into a crystal, or a child's heart. The universe is based on the grandiose schemes that should not stop.

There is no reason why the creative process should ever stop, because the creative process, in its continuation, as long as it's moving into perfection, is the most wonderful, glorious experience that could ever be had, and those who have attained it from inner levels have told us this again and again: "Eye has not seen nor ear heard, neither have entered into the heart, the things which God has prepared for them that love him."[13]

This doesn't mean that God is going to set us down somewhere on a little slab of crystal light and let our body float there and our mind float in space, and he's going to just make us happy, like some woman sitting there tickling her husband's foot with a feather. It doesn't mean that God is going to do something like this. It means that the challenges of eternity will be before us to create, yes, and even to destroy when we have created wrongly, to destroy any clay that we have formed into an imperfect figure, because it would be like creating crippled children—God does not create crippled children; these are karmic situations—and certainly it would be better to break the forms of these clay imperfect images that we have made and crush them together and put them back on the potter's wheel and issue them forth as more perfect creatures than it would be to leave the imperfect image to live and to produce.

This was the story behind the Flood. This was the mercy of God that brought the Flood forth to destroy the wickedness that men had created here through their own misuse of cosmic energy and its laws.

When we understand all these things, then we see why we must build a more perfect kingdom according to the universal blueprint, according to God's mind, according to God's thoughts and God's concepts. This is why this work is so important.

The outer world in its search for reality could continue to build more perfect socialist republics in which every man supposedly would have a vote but in which today every man does not have equal opportunity but is often subject to the same emotional binges that we have here in America in our union system—if someone doesn't like you for any reason, you're just an outcast from the system.

But you cannot build a perfect Soviet or imperial society based on socialistic principles. And I used the word "imperial" purposely, because they have as much imperialism in their intellectual pride in socialism as the Most High God does in creating more perfect images according to the capacity of God compared to the capacity of man. You understand how I mean that. God is so far above them, but in their own self they take as much pride in creating it almost as God does.

But what they're creating is not reality. It's just someone's imagination of how they think they can make everything fair and square. And you just can't do it, because you're dealing with karma. You've got millions of people on earth, they've created karma in the past, and your government is not going to be able to answer your religious needs to communicate with God. It never will be. You will never find the time in our worldly society where the kingdoms of this world will be able to tell you that they are going to take care of your spiritual needs.

Your spiritual needs are taken care of through the hierarchy and taken care of through your heart—the hierarchy of your heart as it attunes with the heart of God. It's a very individual and unique process in discovering your Real Self. And somehow or other there is a great comfort in realizing that you are not facing a world where there are groups of individuals in a star cluster, and all these little star-cluster groups, made up of eight or ten people, are opposing you as an individual little spark over here. They're all in the same category as you are.

People are not clustered together. Even though they are gregarious in nature and the herd instinct is strong and people unite and form societies and church organizations and racing clubs and enthusiasts in this and that, they're still all one person. Each person is only one, and no one else can be more than you can be, and that's part of God's plan. And you can be just as much in the eyes of God as he is if you have the will to serve and the faith in his plan and the acceptance of that plan, not going backward and saying, "Oh, I'm nothing and I've made so many mistakes."

Sure, your human has made mistakes, but God never made any mistakes. He never made *any* mistakes, because if he had made mistakes, this universe could not have remained as it is today. The very structuring of it would have collapsed upon itself. The way everything is so beautifully organized, the way our flesh form is organized, the way our bloodstream flows through the veins and arteries, the way the thoughts flow across our brain, the whole system of human creation—all of this is too magnificent for any human being or group of scientists themselves to have created it. It had to be cosmic science that created it, and so it was.

And what a wonderful thing it is. The universe expands and blows up like a great soap bubble or a great balloon. And that way, you see, you have the stars pulling apart from each other all the time. They're getting farther and farther apart. Science couldn't figure out why this was happening, but it is because the breath of Brahma is expanding. At a certain point, of course, it will contract and begin to fall all into the center again.

The theory behind it all is that by that time the worlds and orbs should be perfected so that when God takes it back, he takes it back into a perfect state worthy to go back because, you see, once it goes back, anything that isn't perfect is destroyed in the process of inhaling it again. When God inhales, it takes it back to the heart center. If it isn't born of flame, if it hasn't mastered its identity, if it is not welded to Spirit, why, it's just going to melt with a fervent heat and thereby be destroyed in the process.

Therefore there is a certain mercy in the continual expansion of the universe. It does keep expanding. And sometimes it expands and expands and expands, and when it starts to contract it may come back very rapidly to its center and then remain for a prolonged period of time. It could remain for millions of years in the dormant

state as the God intelligence is drawing out the blueprints and dia-
gramming the next release of the breath of Brahma.

Well, of course, the ascended masters and cosmic beings are all
involved in this, and that is why the statement was made, "Let us
go down now and make man in our image,"[14] "down" referring to
going down in vibration, not down in the sense that we're up here
on cloud nine and we're going down to earth. It's not a case of the
masters' being up in space somewhere and going down. It's going
down wherever they are, and they're everywhere, going down in
consciousness, in vibration to the realm of the physical where we're
going to create man in our image and after our likeness.

But now we find that this likeness of man certainly is not the
likeness of God nor do we believe that the flesh form was the created
likeness. We think that it was the soul. The patterns of the great
masters were given to man, to the Adamic and pre-Adamic creation,
but that creation did take on the "coats of skins" after it realized it
was naked in the sense that I was talking about before, "I'm naked
and I'm afraid."[15]

Man became in awe of the universe because he now had the
knowledge of good and evil. He was aware of his potential to do
either good or to do evil. Prior to that he could only do good, because
he only knew good. And therefore the idea of saying, "If you can
only probe this science and understand the science of your being,
you'll be as wise as God is," this is where the serpent was able to
trick man and thus deceive him.[16]

None of the theologians today in the world have really mastered
or understood this process, because they reject some of the ancient
truths of the Vedas. They reject the idea of reembodiment. They
have stultified themselves in dogma and they're stewing in their own
dogmatic juice, and that is exactly why they don't understand it. And
that is why we have to become like little children to pass through
the door. Once we get in, we can grow up. And that's exactly what
we all have to do, to understand our native reality. And when we do

this, we find that we are natives of the cosmos and not just citizens of some nation here.

But while we're here, we have to recognize and respect the lesser dream as we respect the greater dream. And we must respect not only the lesser dream of social life upon this planet, we must also accept the dream of ourselves in our present role.

It's a great mistake for us to reject these opportunities, because God works in strange and very mysterious ways, his wonders to perform,[17] and he does. He works in the humblest little crystal or in the greatest galactic system or in the whole cosmos or in the realm beyond space, in just the realm of pure being.

God works everywhere. And we must see to it that we identify with him and with his plan—not with our own negatives, not with the defense of our own ego, not with the exaltation of ourselves or a sense of struggle, not by the idea that we're going to do it, but by the idea that we are going to accept that magnificent plan, exercise our divine prerogative, use our cosmic vote and serve the cause of our life mission and run our course, as Saint Paul said, with joy,[18] until we finish it and fight the good fight of faith and emerge victoriously. This is every man's mission, and it is yours and mine.

Thank you.

November 10, 1968
Colorado Springs, Colorado

CHAPTER 5

Creation

We are here. There was a day when we held awareness for the first time that we were here on this planet. We do not even remember when that was, but we do know that it seems as though the bond of consciousness had always existed.

Somehow or other, deep down inside of us, either in heart or in mind, somewhere in being—anatomically it does not matter, really—we are persuaded of the truth of being of ourselves. But unfortunately in one way and fortunately in another, every person does not have the same understanding of the elements of consciousness.

Consciousness to some is relegated to the realm of instinctive reaction. We have, then, acting in our world instinctive life, the life of instinct, and we have within our world the life of the intellect. The glory of the instinct is one and the glory of the intellect is another. But these glories are not equal to the Christ mind or the power of the Christ or the power of the masters. For these are spheres of limitation, instinct itself being held in the bondage and jaws of limitation, and intelligence itself being also limited.

For comparative purposes, then, we will first make clear the aspects of instinct as the instinct of the young child who sucks upon the paps of his mother. The child needs no intelligence to do this,

this instinctive reaction being locked within him from the time of the conception, perhaps, certainly being found omnipresent in the child from almost the hour of birth as an active and vital crying out for life. He must draw nourishment and he instinctively knows how.

We can, if we wish, bore you tonight by listing a weighty list of all of the various instinctive reactions which mankind has, but I don't think it's necessary so I won't do it. But I have defined it for you.

Now we will step forward into the realm of intellect. And when we are dealing with intellect, we are referring now to the intelling force that enables the plasticity of the mind to receive impressions and then correct them as a helmsman of a ship is able to make a compass heading and correct his course.

For example, one who is first learning to ride a bicycle or learning to walk does not actually know the principles of balance which are so very automated in us later in life. Later on in life we walk without effort. We ride bicycles. We drive cars. We perform many phenomenal skills without effort. These are automated and they seem almost as instinctive reactions, but actually they were learned. And this is based upon the intelling of the intellect, of the intelligence that is inherent within us that enables us to gather from the sensory world various impressions and then to put these to work in the service of developing the force of the human personality.

But now that we have covered these two subjects and we are dealing with the instinct and the intelligence, let me point out to you that they are the distinguishing characteristics of man. They distinguish man in a way from the animal who is primarily all instinctive.

Man has intelligence and he uses it. Yet he acts very much like the animal, even today, in the world of form. For with all the codification of law, with all the development of society from the time of Hammurabi down to the present day—the age of the Magna Carta, the Declaration of Independence from George III, all of the various episodes that have brought forth instruments of freedom—these have still not been enough to keep the world in a state of peace.

And therefore we see that the warlike instrumentation that is locked into humanity is a result of man's employment of instinctive power and intellectual power. For intellectual power does not in any way assure us that we will have emotional control. It does not assure us that we will develop spirituality.

Spirituality and the spiritual mind with its spiritual secrets and spiritual power are themselves above the ordinary minds of most of the people upon this planet. In fact, many of the people upon this planet would not be able, they do not possess the capacity to understand the higher law and they will first have to forge the vehicles of understanding before they can even be tutored in higher law.

Therefore this in itself may seem a very strange proclamation. But it is not a proclamation that I have issued. It is one that the Brotherhood has declared in its higher understanding of the humanities, and it is an explanation of why we have the strange society that we have today.

We have all of the vital intelligence that creates a society based either upon principles of freedom or communal principles of bondage. We are able to function either in a democratic way, or we're able to function in a communistic way. We are able to function socialistically. We are able to function in a universal sense. But this in itself has not given man his freedom—and I'm talking about philosophical tenets and I'm talking about the characteristics of the present order of humanity upon the earth.

These qualities that we have developed, which enable us to populate our highways with vehicles that give the moving force to life, have not given to mankind the understanding of governing the forces that are now under his control. Yet he continues to cry out for more power. He wants to have power over himself, but more than that he wants to have power over others. And no man has a right to have power over others if he cannot first control and dominate the vital life-forces within himself.

So we see that in the first place the premise is entirely wrong in our society today—to seek power for the sake of power itself or to seek wisdom as an effective means of control or a means of securing greater economic development of our own personal lives. In other words, if I get a diploma, if I secure the knowledge of the world in certain ways, I will be able to command a greater salary. This has nothing to do with the development of the higher powers in man. It is a world in itself.

So we must recognize and understand that there are many minds at work in one body complex, that the citadel of individual man is not a standpat citadel where we have a body with a soul in it. It is a very complex unit. It has a body and it has a soul and it has a spirit that energizes the soul. But it also has a series of minds that, whereas they are linked together, have effective controls of their own particular forte of experience. And by this I reference now the instinctive reactions, the intellectual reactions, and even social reactions that we build up, and the actions of the ego.

The egoistic mind itself is not actually instinctive. If we deal by sheer instinct alone, we will not be able to control ourselves. For the instinct is primarily a matter of survival. The intelligence carries us beyond that. The intelligence carries it into the realm of understanding. We begin to understand the flora and fauna of life. We begin to understand the chemistry of life. We begin to understand the psychology of life. But all this is limited, because it presupposes that man is basically a Darwinian animal, and it does not take into account the evolution of man as he actually was predestined by the Divine Presence that created him.

And so tonight we are going to attempt to convey to you a higher understanding of the creative process, not only involving the Macrocosm but also involving the microcosm, the world of you, right where you are. And out of this understanding, we can hope for the evolvement of an understanding of spiritual evolution in its relationship to the seven days of creation.

And therefore we will be able to explain to you why that

phenomenon which has appeared on the horizon of the world history and is known as Christendom has not been able to complete the process of bringing the world into the divine sheepfold and producing the miracle of the Christ kingdom upon earth—for Christ himself rejected the temporal kingdom and chose instead the eternal kingdom. We are going to prove and show to you tonight what has actually taken place.

As a part of our unfolding drama, then, we must go back to the time of the Emperor Constantine[1] and also back into the early period of the Catholic Church, which at one time was the only Christian church upon this earth. We go back to the era of the Empress Theodora,[2] and we find that Theodora herself could not embrace the doctrine of reembodiment. This was taught in the Catholic Church then, even as it was later proclaimed by Saint Francis of Assisi in the public square, but she could not accept it.

And the reason she could not accept it is because she had been a prostitute and she had now attained to the position of being the empress of the entire country. She felt, then, that the empress was a divine person, and she was afraid that if she accepted reembodiment, that when she returned, she might come back as a scullery maid or something less than that. And she wanted instead to be able to preserve her place in history as an empress, which she felt was a great attainment which she had now won.

She proceeded, then, to have the pope himself killed. She created an alteration which was involved in the Council of Nicea. And that particular alteration has altered the mainstream of the course of Christian history. It has created an entirely different understanding of the creative process than was ever taught by the Master Jesus in all of the great understanding which he had as he came forth out of Luxor, Egypt.

For he fled to Egypt, to the great temples of wisdom there, and was tutored from the time he was twelve years old and beyond until he came at the age of thirty to the Holy Land once again and began to proclaim the great Christ truths of the Great White Brotherhood which had been kept in the Essene archives for centuries.

We want to point out to you, then, that the doctrine of reembodiment was the most important thing that the people could understand. But when it became perverted and twisted in the hands of priests who did not understand it, the people themselves could readily accept the repudiation of it.

The priests actually created a pseudoreligion using the basis of Christianity. They created an idea of hell and hellfire and damnation. They created an idea that would incite fear in the people, who were very superstitious.

And we have to remember one particular thing right now, dear hearts. We have to remember that knowledge was not as great on earth in that day as it is today, that the masses of the people were relatively uneducated, that the priests were educated in Latin and Greek and they were very wise but the average proletarian and even the average businessman did not have an understanding of the great theologies of the times.

Therefore it was quite a simple matter to make the alterations in the monasteries, to burn the scriptures containing the great cosmic truths that were deleted, and to bring forth the newly altered scriptures. And after a couple of decades, most of the people who remembered what had happened were dead.

People did not live in those days as long as they do today. When a person was thirty, they were old. And people who were forty were ancient, very few people living beyond the age of fifty. This is a matter of history. And we realize that this is true. They had many diseases in those days. They began to marry very early, sometimes at fourteen and fifteen. They had their children, their childbearing years came very early. And the men and women were quite inclined toward debauchery, even a worse debauchery than we have in the world today.

I think our modern society, for example, with its particular demands in the labor market, is such that it almost automatically demands that people take a little better care of their bodies. Then, too, we've learned also how to control disease to a much greater degree. We've learned the use of vitamins and we are able to correct many of the errors of the past that were fatal through surgery and various other types of healing techniques.

So we have prolonged life. But that does not necessarily mean that we have enhanced life. Because, after all, what we ought to be interested in is showing the proper use of life. And the proper use of life is very much involved with the theology of the Divine Theosophia. If you do not have the holy wisdom of the Blessed Virgin, the Divine Theosophia, the Holy Mother of Wisdom, and I'm speaking figuratively here, if you do not have that wisdom which is the wisdom of God, you really do not understand yourself.

And in order to get this wisdom, you have to go to those who possess it. If you want to perfect your life in any of the ancient skills, such as artistry, if you want to become a painter, you apprentice yourself to a great painter. If you want to become a sculptor, you go to a sculptor and you ask him to teach you how to sculpt. If you want to play the piano, you take lessons from someone who knows. If you want voice culture, you go to a great singer. If you want to learn judo, you go to a judo instructor who knows what he's doing.

You have to go to people who have mastered their subject proficiently. If you put yourselves in the hands of those who don't know their subject, you're certainly going to wind up as a tinhorn spectacle. You really can't expect that if you put yourself in the hands of an amateur that you're going to really be a victorious person.

And so the masters of wisdom, the masters of the Far East have made a science of the study of the soul, of the study of the human spirit, have actually examined with the most minute eye of detail the ancient writings of the Essenes, the writings of the ancient order of the priests of Melchizedek, the Zend-Avesta and the writings of various secret orders such as the Zend orders, the orders of Zoroaster, the orders of the sacred fire. And unless we have examined many of these ancient orders and are initiated into the priesthood of these orders, we ourselves only have a smattering of knowledge concerning the cosmic truths.

The hieroglyphs of universal truth are actually alive in the ethers, but they may just as well not exist there insofar as the average person is concerned. For the average person is not aware of their existence. And the average person believes in the sophistry of society. They believe in the writings of society as the ultimate. They believe that the educational systems of the intellect of this world, the various universities of this world, have already accumulated all knowledge and all wisdom about the world.

And this, of course, is a most ridiculous fallacy. It results in a person being very limited. Yet the strange thing here is that those who have this knowledge often feel that the people who do not have it are the ones who are limited. But it is possible to have the knowledge of the world, you can have all of the knowledge of the world, you can examine all of the great tomes of the great universities and you can even graduate from any number of schools, and still you will not of necessity have the knowledge of the spiritual hierarchy.

If you want that, you have to go to the cosmic masters. The cosmic masters have that knowledge, and they are willing to part with it. And their price involves concern for the individual and his spiritual evolution. They are not interested in giving you this power, their power, their wisdom so that you can make a display of it before your fellowmen and show them how much you know. They are concerned with the correct use of that power for your own freedom.

Therefore we will proceed. The Master Jesus, then, taught his disciples many things in a great mystery, the hidden wisdom of God. This is perpetuated through Saint Paul and through Peter and the others who went around and taught privately. The true Christian doctrines were not always recorded in the scriptures—the scriptures themselves being the skeletal framework on which was hung the actual central nervous system and all of the other systems of the body politic of the real teachings of the Master.

The commentaries that were actually kept then, and remained a part of the archives of the ancient Essenes and others, contained the unwritten (so to speak, as far as the average Christian is concerned) laws of God. But actually they were recorded in part and they exist today in some of the ancient monasteries in Tibet and in South America.

There is in South America, in a very remote jungle place, a tremendous temple in which are hidden writings so beautiful that they would move the hearts of those who at least have sense enough to heed them. Others, of course, might read them without ever realizing the tremendous spiritual impact that is behind these teachings.

Now, this is what we are talking about. We're talking about the evolution of man. Darwin brought out the evolution of man almost as an anthropoid, that he came forth and gradually erected himself from the status of a dangling or gangling ape until he finally became an upright man and went through the various stages that we know, such as Cro-Magnon man and so forth. Well, this, of course, has been accepted today in our universities and schools as the actual evolution of man.

We are concerned with the spiritual evolution of man, and therefore we are going to present to you a fact concerning the identity of every man. And we are going to say to you tonight that every man was simultaneously, as far as God is concerned, created in the image of God in the beginning.

We avow that first Genesis with its statement, "In the beginning God created the heavens and the earth,"[3] is true. We also avow that the statement, "And the LORD God made man in his own image, in the image and likeness of God created he him; male and female created he them"[4] is a cosmic truth.

But we are going to show you why it is not a truth in the manifest world, whereas it is a truth in the unmanifest world. We understand the use of the words *Grund* and *Ungrund*—the *Grund*, of course, being the created and the *Ungrund,* the uncreated. And when we say the uncreated, we're speaking about the created that is not yet manifest. When I use the word the *Ungrund,* I'm referring to the created which is not manifest in form.

In other words, God created man in his own image. He breathed this image into the soul. He put in the seed, the very heart of that seed that would unfold and produce the rose of true being on the spinal stalk.

The spine, in a sense, was like the stem of the flower. And the brain and the higher intelligence centers at the end of the spinal stalk—the medulla oblongata, the pia mater and the dura mater, the various hemispheres of the brain—all of this was actually intended to resemble a flower, a lotus.

And this was intended to open and unfold the latent spiritual intelligences in man that would enable him to have the power to cast out demons, the power to be able to cast out unwanted energies from his own world, the power to cast out unwanted energies from other people's worlds, the power to restore the sick, to raise the dead, to walk upon the water, to break the bread, to multiply substance, to vanish from people's sight and reassemble one's atoms in a distant place, to project the *ka,* as the ancient Egyptians said, from one place to another, and withal, when the *ka* was projected, to also with the *ka* project the sensory intelligences that would enable the individual to absorb the principles of the particular area to which the person did project—in other words, to travel through the atmosphere with the speed of light and be able to gather information without being present with your physical body.

All of these mysteries were taught and practiced by Jesus and the ancient teachers. They were adepts. And whereas Christianity has given these powers only to Christ, we who are in the know realize that Lord Buddha and many of the other avatars that descended to this planet had these powers also and used these powers. Somehow or other in our narrow Christian ideas and our sectarian ideas we have relegated the Far Eastern masters to the position of being infidels, pagans, and almost anti-Christ, when in reality they were men of beauty and virtue and discipline which itself was extremely valuable and valid.

Now, coming back to the seven days of creation, when God created all things in these seven days of creation and he finished the work, the LORD God made one statement which I want to burn into your minds tonight. And that statement is, "And the LORD God saw the creation which he had made, and, behold, it was very good!"[5]

Behold, it was *very* good! This is the thing you must burn into your consciousness. This is the particular gift of God that will enable you to burn the mayic world before your gaze, to let the piercing glance of the spiritual sight from within you come through your two eyes with their double vision to form the third-eye vision that will enable you to peer behind the scene of the physical, environmental world and recognize at last that you are gazing on naked reality and that naked primal reality is not simple but complex. For all of the complexity of the known world and all of the complexity of manifestation is all the inherent seed patterns that are locked within the physical, mental, psychospiritual world.

They are in the soul of man. They are latent. They are unmanifest. Therefore they are in the realm of the *Ungrund*. They are in the realm of that which is created by God but which has not been ratified or co-created by man.

The LORD God said to man, "Take dominion over the earth."[6] Man has not taken dominion over the earth, but the moon god has taken dominion over him. And what is the moon god? The moon god, of course, is the power that acts on these instinctive reactions, the reactions that are a part of the instinctive mind, the power that acts on the intelligence body of man and the power that acts on the emotional body of man. And when the power acts on these bodies, then, you see, you do not have higher intelligence acting but you have lower intelligence acting.

And therefore man is not living in the spiritual evolutionary world or the spiritual evolutionary life at all. He's living still in the carnal life. And that's what Saint Paul was talking about. He kept saying, "Put off the old man with his weight of sin. Put on the Christ. I die daily."[7] He meant, "I die daily to the instinctive mind. I die daily to the intelligent mind. I die daily to the emotional mind. I live, then, daily in the Higher Mind."

And this idea of living in the Higher Mind is the flame in the chalice. It's the idea, first of all, that such a mind exists. We have to have a creation in our own being that is almost a womb. We have to create a womb. And then in that womb the Holy Spirit comes down. And the Holy Spirit is the flame in this crystal chalice. For you cannot put this holy thing into this carnal intelligence, into this sensual being of man. You cannot put this intelligence down into this instinctive, animalistic world. You have to replace it by a special activity.

No man, the Master said, taketh the new wine and putteth it into old wineskins. But he takes new wineskins and he forms them that he may expressly put the new wine into the new wineskins.[8]

Here, then, is the creation by each individual of the higher evolutionary mind as an embryonic womb chalice in which the flame spirit of the invincible, eternal, living God with a tremendous cosmic reality that he created and saw that was good, putting that good through the power of the descending Paraclete into this chalice that we ourselves have created as a potential of the Christ mind in ourselves.

And unless you do this act yourself—and no one on this earth or in heaven or anywhere can do it for you—you will remain a part of the instinctive, intelligent, dying, mortal mind. But if you open up the gateways of consciousness to the invisible realms that are above, you will not only have the power and dominion over yourself, but you will have the power and dominion over this earth, because the meek shall inherit the earth.[9]

And when you understand this, you will know what it means to be the meek. And I tell you tonight that they are the strongest people on the face of this earth. The odd prophets, the strange people who have been thought odd because the holy teaching itself is so different than the carnal mind can imagine, are the strongest people on this earth.

You can kill them as babies by the sword, as they tried to do in the time of Christ. Herod sent out the soldiers to slay the firstborn. You can do anything that you want to do to stamp out and destroy the cosmic power, but these people will come back stronger than ever and they will inherit the earth.

And those who live only in the instinctive and intellectual mind, those who live only in these things, they will surely perish from the earth because there is no life in the instinct. There is only the power to preserve temporal life. There is no wisdom in the intelligence, for the intelligence itself is only a plastic vehicle, a sort of digital computer system that is able to gather, assimilate, classify, in other words, sort information and then spew it forth automatedly.

That's all people are. And none of that has provided a solution to our free society. And none of that ever will. And we will not be able to unite all kindreds, tongues, and peoples underneath the banner of peace, underneath the banner of freedom, underneath the banner of harmony so long as we are engaged in this fierce struggle with ourselves which is all a part of the fiery yet dying intensity of the carnal mind.

It's like the writhing of a serpent in the pit. It lashes out with its tail. It strikes here and it strikes there. It has the poison of an adder. But it never in all eternity has generated a society free from war, from hatred, from bloodshed, from carnality. It is a *preying* society. It is not a *praying* society that says, "Thy will be done on earth even as it is done in heaven."[10]

And so tonight I want to bring forth to you the understanding that when the divine plan is grasped, the divine plan of the ages, when our souls are able to rise out of their instinctual reactions and intelligent reactions to obtain the Christ mind and the fire, the flame in the chalice, when we are able to enter in to the relationship with the Spirit as we ought to enter in, we are going to come in contact with the masters of the Far East.

And then we're going to understand what is meant by the vicarious at-one-ment, the vicarious atonement. The whole world today is fooled by it. We have great preachers standing up before the television screens with massive audiences, all preconditioned from childhood on to accept the idea that Jesus died for you.

I have never said nor will I say that Christ did not die. I'm talking about Christ Jesus. Christ Jesus, of course, hung upon the Judean hillside. He also was born in Bethlehem. But though he be born in Bethlehem a thousand times, if he is not born in us, his birth there is in vain. And though he hang upon a thousand trees and sheds his blood, unless we ourselves come to understand the meaning of the cross, the meaning of the soul crucified in Matter, the meaning of the soul unfolding itself in Matter, the meaning of the soul interpreting its mission in life, we ourselves are living in vain.

You remember the passage, "And departing, leave behind us footsteps on the sands of time."[11] This is a latent desire in people. People have a great desire to be able to influence society for the better. They want very badly to do it. The world is full of good people—and also of misguided ones.

When I heard Dr. Kenneth McFarland, formerly educational consultant to General Motors Corporation, give his famous address in 1950, "Fathoming the Fifties," I was struck with one particular facet of his whole talk. He said that the world had all these good people I just mentioned to you in it. They believe the right things. They belong to the right clubs. They are for the right things, but they do very little about it.

Today now removed from Plymouth Rock, today now removed from Independence Hall, today now removed from the time of the minutemen that stood guard at Lexington and Concord, we no longer have the struggles of the early colonial days. Our food comes to us in cans. Our religion is prepared on scrolls and almost handed to us to swallow as a pill. Everything is prepared and prepackaged, prewrapped and predigested. The thinking man is dead. We have a few distinguished people who are able to think for themselves and to develop a philosophy in this life—such as Eric Hoffer,[12] even though he came from a group of longshoremen. Yet every one of us is intended to do so.

But we have today a preclusion whereby religious society has formulated a dyed-in-the-wool dogmatic conclusion. "You are born, you must die. If you follow our teachings, you will go to heaven." Where is heaven? Jesus said the kingdom of heaven is within you.[13] And if we don't have it, if we don't find it here, which is our mission, if we miss the boat, then the opportunity of this life is lost.

God in his great mercy will give you another chance through reembodiment, yes. But it will not be this one. And it will mean a longer struggle. It will also mean that you have lived in vain in this life.

We are all a part of instinctive reaction. We are all a part of intelligence. We all have intelligence. We gather intelligence. We all draw conclusions. We have our various virtues and vices. Our freedom will not come through our virtues any more than it will through our vices. For our freedom will come when we are a part of the evolutionary mainstream of the cosmic purposes of God.

These we see cast upon the backdrop of historical scenes that moves like a river. We see the whole thing. We go back to the Garden of Eden. We see the Hanging Gardens of Nebuchadnezzar in Babylon. We watch as they build the tower of Babel. We see the children of Israel exit for the Promised Land out of Egypt. We see the epochs of King David as he kills Goliath upon the hillside. We see the formulation of the wonderful psalms, "The Lord is my shepherd; I shall not want."[14] All of these things, the whole drama of civilization is before us.

Yet today we are not turning out as products in our evolution young men and women who are interested in spiritual conclusions. What are they interested in? They are interested in instant love, instant attainment, instant satisfaction. And this is a pseudocreation of the Madison Avenue advertising crowd, the Hollywood crowd, the moviemakers. These filmmakers have created all these things as a part of the master plot to destroy our America, to tear down our youth, to destroy the vision that we need.

I think it was Ezekiel who said, "Without vision the people perish."[15] But it doesn't matter who said it. It's true. Without vision we all perish. And what I am trying to do tonight is to give you a coup d'oeil, a little glimpse of yourself as a part of the moving pageant of creation. You were there with God when he made this universe.

You say you don't remember it. Your soul has a memory of its own. Your physical memory is tethered to those instinctive reactions that you had from babyhood to the present hour. Your intelligent mind remembers the various experiences you have had. They are part of your etheric record. But you do not remember—of course, you don't remember it—the creation of God. But your soul has it all recorded.

Your soul could today draw forth a reel from every lifetime you've ever lived and project it on the screen and show you every life. And I think if you did see those lives, you would recognize that you have been a part of an ascending spiral of self, that you have been climbing cycled stairs. And whereas people that have observed you only for a short period of time might say, "Those people are going backward. They don't want to do anything right. They don't have any hopes. They're not a very good person. They're selfish and deluded and cruel, vicious, unkind, unkempt, dirty, impure of mind, indolent. They've got every bad quality you can think of."

I want to tell you that people may manifest for a time these qualities. But when they are quickened in the seed of God that is within them, when they go back to that primal seed, "The LORD

God saw the creation which he had made and, behold, it was very good," when they go back to that primal mainstream of their own being, they are going to start to manifest the Higher Mind and the flame in the chalice is going to come down.

And when it comes down, it will not be a sudden conflagration. It will not be instant victory. It will not mean that you're going to be transformed by taking a pill and the minute you take that pill, you're going to suddenly experience the profound knowledge of Zarathustra, "Thus spake Zarathustra," that all at once you're going to be illumined, all at once the universe is going to shake, the ground is going to open, and Aladdin is going to come forth, and you're going to rub that magic ring and the genie's going to appear and say, "Here's everything."

This is eye magic. This is the expectation of man today. They are wanting in their religious experience magic. This is what's behind the phenomenon that says, "Will you accept the Lord Jesus as your Saviour? Don't you want to be saved today?"

Dear hearts, what does it mean, "be saved"? You were created by God in his own image. You have lost that image. We must regain it. Can you regain it by a thaumaturgical act, the utterance of a few words, the rubbing of a magic ring? Are you going to be saved because you do some ritualistic act? I don't think so.

I think that we must rejoin the mainstream of our spiritual evolution in whatever day we broke off that connection. Whether we broke it off in the first day of creation, the second day, the third, the fourth, the fifth, the sixth or the seventh, wherever we broke off our connection with God, I believe we have to rejoin that mainstream of spiritual evolution right where we left it.

We have to begin weaving the garment where we dropped the stitch. And when we pick it up, if we pick it up, and we begin to weave, we begin to knit, we begin to crochet, we begin to put in these missing stitches and rejoin, we're going to flow along. And I don't believe every soul is going to flow along at the same rate.

Some people don't want it that bad. Some people want the world more than they want God.

You're going to get, dear hearts, exactly what you want. So let your desires be understood by you to be the transforming key, the key to transformation. If you don't have the right kind of desires, you're not going to effect the right kind of transformation in your world.

The all-chemistry of God is a gift in your hand. You hold it for yourself. And in a sense, you hold it for your brothers in the world. For every act that you do that makes the world a better place because God lives in you will make the world a better place for your brothers. And every act they do that is constructive will be for you as well as for them. And the same is true of the destructive side of life.

So you see, the animalistic man is not ready for the higher things of the spirit. And what we have had happen is, we have had zealous men and women in the Christian religion who have gone out like Calvin and Zwingli. They have said to themselves, "We are going to make these people do what God wants them to do." And they've brought down the hammer of the law. Did you know that Calvin had people hung in Geneva, Switzerland, in the name of Christ? Do you have any idea the terrific life that these people lived, of forcing people into Christianity?

Well, all you have to do is see James Michener's *Hawaii,* the movie which portrayed the activity of Calvin. It showed how vicious a human being could be under the idea of compelling people to accept Christianity. He became the true Devil's advocate. He created more inharmony in the world and turned more souls into the hell that he proclaimed than probably any man ever did before in history.

And this is what has happened. For hell itself is in this wise, as Omar Khayyám said, "I sent my soul through the invisible to spell some word of the hereafter. And by and by my soul returned to me and said, I myself am heaven and hell."

Resident, then, within your being is all of this cosmic drama. Otherwise you wouldn't be a part of it. It's a case of the shining dewdrop slipping into the sea. You've got to become a shining dew-drop to slip into the shining sea.

You can be unseparated. You can be a part of the world. You can be a part of just intelligence, just instinct, just emotion. But unless you develop the higher faculties of the Christ mind, you will never have your victory.

And when you get that, you can look at a man and you can read his aura on sight. You know exactly what he thinks, what he is, what he feels. You won't tell him about it. You'll be too discreet and too aware of the fact that it's more important that you do him good than that you do him harm.

You will have the power to lay your hands on the sick and they will recover, to raise the dead. You'll have the power to bless and to heal. You'll have the power of understanding. You'll have the power to see into the invisible. You'll be able to see the spirits leave a dying person. You'll be able to watch the soul go out. You'll be able to see the masters at inner levels. You'll be able to exit the body at will and to return. You will even be able eventually to formulate a body out of atomic substance and ensoul it and go where you want to go with that body and appear before those you want to appear before and to dissolve that body at will.

"All power in heaven and earth is given unto me."[16] And I will give it unto whomsoever I will, the Master said.

Faith is necessary in doing all things. We read in Hebrews, through faith they cast out demons. Through faith they overcame this and they overcame that. There's a long list there. It says they were sawn asunder.[17] Do you know what that means? It means they strung them up, head downward and took a saw between their legs and cut them in half. But they never put an end to their faith.

When you understand this, when you understand the power of faith, when you understand the magic of faith, when you understand what it can do for you to believe and to believe the right things, you will understand that we have a world of hope and beauty here.

The facade, the shoddy images that people have, these will die. These will perish from the earth. War and darkness and shadow and sickness and unhappiness, these are no part of the first six and seven days of creation. These are a part of the instinctive, animalistic, human creation. They will die. They will perish. But the kingdom of God will not perish.

And a man need not think that because he is grass, he is going to live forever. He can only live forever if he puts on the wedding garment of the Lord, if he learns the mystery of weaving the deathless solar body, if he learns how to control the centripetal and centrifugal force around the spinal column, to raise it from the coccygeal center up to the spiritual eye where it will then, through the power of the caduceus, develop the wings of the mind that will lift the mind up to proximity to the divine mind. For only when the mind of man becomes one with the mind of God can he actually perform the miracles that will develop in him this deathless solar body.

The deathless solar body is a scientific garment. It was actually taught by the Master Serapis at Luxor, Egypt, and Jesus learned it there. But it's been taught by the Brotherhood through the ages.

You can take your energy and expend it in any way you want to. Go right ahead. You can just waste your energy, but it will not weave the deathless solar garment. And if you read the scriptures correctly, you will find the real meaning in the statement of Jesus when he says, the king gave a great feast. The people came, and some people were there without a wedding garment. And what happened? The master said, "Friend, how comest thou hither without a wedding garment?" He says, "Take this unprofitable servant and cast him into outer darkness."[18]

Now, some people say, "Well, God is so merciful." Of course he's merciful. He's too merciful to those who have already attained their perfection to go ahead and invite the devil into heaven. He doesn't want Mephistopheles to be hobnobbing with those who have already won their victory.

And there is an element of mercy in the universe that people here on earth should understand. God separates the righteous from the unrighteous. And we ourselves are a part of the sifting process. We function as God. And we decide by our acts, in fact, exactly which way we are going. He isn't interfering.

You can listen to Billy Graham. You can listen to Oral Roberts. You can listen to the great evangelists that are on television. You can go to the tents. You can go to the churches. You can study the various philosophies. And every single one of them will ultimately come to the same place, where you are lost, you're going to Hades unless you accept their brand of theology. And if you accept it, and you can meet all kinds of people who have, you do not find that these people are necessarily living the life or following the pathway that the Master trod.

It's not an external thing, dear hearts. It's an internal thing. It's an internal activity that enfires the soul and brings him back to the evolutionary mainstream.

The evolutionary mainstream, mind you, this is what we're talking about. This is what it's all about. It's bringing yourself out of yourself, rising out of instinctive mind and intelligence, rising out of instinctive emotion, getting into the higher planes of the mind, developing these. When you can do that, you will then have attained.

Now this is what we teach here. This is what we teach. This is the way we explain the law.

September 14, 1969
Colorado Springs, Colorado

CHAPTER 6

Penetration, Focalization, and Control of Consciousness

First, I want to make clear that we are dealing with what can be termed a *dispersion* in the universe itself. And the illusion of space and time is probably actually a myth. In other words, you start with a photon of light and you may build a sun out of that. And you will have probably a *Grund*, and then you will have to have some space into which to project your *Grund*. You can call this *Ungrund*. So you have the realm of the created (the *Grund*) and the realm of the uncreated (the *Ungrund*).

We recognize as our scientists of our world have said that the universe may be like a balloon and somebody is blowing it up. The illusion of space would vanish in the curvatures of space. And after all, how important is it that we understand that in its vast macrocosmic scale? But what we are interested in is understanding the consciousness by which we understand everything else.

Each of us individually is given by God a consciousness. The consciousness God has given to us is really our own because he gave it to us. It is no more his. It belongs to us. But in a very strange sense, he still has a mortgage on it. Do you understand that at all?

It comes from him and it eventually is expected to return to him because he gave it for a purpose.

Why did he give us consciousness in the first place? He gave it to us so that we could acquire. And what is it he wants us to acquire? He wants us to acquire understanding. Did he or did he did not say, "With all thy getting get understanding"?[1] He said that and he meant it. And therefore, in the sense that man has free will, the Father gave him a consciousness which he can bend to his own liking.

It has been proven that individuals can think very bad thoughts and do very bad deeds. Witness the conspiracies of the Machiavellis or the poisonings of the Borgias. Down through history we have seen men like Cardinal Richelieu, and we have been astounded at the strange level of their thought which could in some way or other unite one moment with God and the next moment with the evil forces of the world. We've seen this also in the late Rasputin, who could turn around and reach out and take what he wanted from the world and then when he wanted to be pious he could look up to heaven and pray and, lo and behold, a person would be healed.

This has always been very difficult for man to understand, especially in the light of the fact that the Bible says, "Mine eyes are too pure to behold iniquity."[2] I think, then, all of you should understand that God never, ever thinks iniquity. Only man, through his misuse of the free will which God gave him, thinks iniquitously.

Well, where does he think? He thinks in his consciousness. And because there really is only one consciousness, it being polarized according to different vibratory rates, there is a simultaneous preoccupation already of space by the various consciousnesses of man.

In other words, Marguerite Baker there, she thinks she's thinking all by herself. Right alongside of her, we find Dr. Olivia Bryant. And she's also thinking—Dr. Octavia, didn't I say that? I meant Octavia, excuse me. I don't know what's wrong with me that I seem to once in a while get these tortoises and hares mixed up. Anyway, I knew your name. I went to India with you. I still do know it.

There they sit together and they both have minds. Now, maybe one would be in Los Angeles sometime, and one would be sitting over here in Colorado Springs. But in actuality, it wouldn't make any difference whether they were in Darjeeling, India, or in Colorado Springs or where they are. The mind is simultaneously occupying almost the total of macrocosmic space at the same time that it occupies the total of microcosmic space, because there is an interchange between the macrocosm and the microcosm—and don't you forget it.

Honey child, you are reaching out and influencing the whole universe by your thought. And that is why the Tree of Life in the midst of the garden is guarded by the flaming cherubim.[3] God had to retreat behind the sacrosanct realm of infinity in order to preserve the order and purity of being there. But to man is given this portion of the sacred fire that is a spark of the divine intelligence that does fill and influence the whole cosmos.

Please don't think that somebody practicing witchcraft in England or Texas or Louisiana or Haiti cannot influence the whole world. But please don't get some kind of a crazy idea that a man or woman invoking light anywhere on earth cannot also influence the whole world. And because light is stronger than darkness, light will ultimately overcome and light will rule everywhere and darkness will fall.

In connection with spiritual darkness, one of the forms of spiritual darkness, which I have always incisively found to be the most evil of all, is that miserable spirit of gossip, which goes out into the world. I believe that there is nothing more malevolent than for people to try to turn other people against each other. I believe this and I believe that is one of the causes why we have so much density in the focalization of consciousness.

When you start to take a divine seed thought of truth into your consciousness and you are going to meditate on it and you are going to send it out into the world, do you know that it is actually in many cases challenged by the universe, put to a trial to see whether or not it is a thing of value? And the universe either accepts what you send out or it rejects it because of its inherent characteristics.

So try to make your matrix in focalizing your consciousness powerful and honest. Don't just try to make it powerful. A lot of people try to make it powerful and that's where they strain their own power aspect and their love aspect and their wisdom aspect. Everything is strained about them because they don't understand what is actually taking place.

People ask me, "Where do you get the energy from that you can stand up there for so many days and talk to us and all of this?" Well, the energy comes from God and to God it returns. But it is because basically I have certainly an honest heart toward everyone on this planet. I believe with all my heart that my wife is like this also and most of our staff are this way, and I like to believe that most of our students are this way also.

I have found through the years that the unfortunate thing that has often happened with people is that rather than become constructive, they have become destructive and sought to find fault with someone. That's why I rather laughed at that tortoise and hare bit, you know, because the other night after I had taken the dictation from Meta on the first night of the conference and I had been through all of the different sessions with you, I happened to be just a tiny bit tired and unconsciously I switched that. And you know it's very easy to do that. I heard the late President Kennedy do the same thing. He was a pretty smart man and he just got something all balled up one time when he was talking in Washington. So I realize this can easily happen.

Well, I was kind of glad that it happened, because it was almost a perfect demonstration of the fact that human nature would probably remember that more than they would some of the good things that I've said. Isn't that true?

You know, people say, "He got mixed up." Well, the main thing is not to be permanently mixed up. We can all get mixed up or muddled once in a while in maybe an expression, but to be permanently mixed up is something else. The guy or the gal that can mix you up permanently, they're the one you want to watch out for. Do you see what I mean?

So when we deal with the penetration, the focalization of consciousness, these are the factors. Space itself is charged with the bric-a-brac of human thought. It is also charged simultaneously with the constructive thought of the masters of wisdom. And this is what probably provides the conductor through space for the good thoughts. It's a matter of affinity.

When you have good thoughts, remember they are always going with God. *Vaya con Dios,* go with God. That statement, *vaya con Dios,* is rather interesting because I took Latin in school and I found out that there was a Latin word, *via,* and that to me denoted the flow or the way to go. *Via* is the way. And that is Latin. What is that?

Student: *Via* is a road also.

MLP: Oh, I know that. And so the road or the way or whatever you want to call it is out here. And you have to realize that something has to travel over that road. Now, this is a myth in human consciousness, because when we took an airplane from Santa Barbara, California, and then landed eventually in Bombay, India, on the other side of the world, we thought we were going somewhere. But in actuality, thought doesn't have to go by airplane or jet. Thought can travel on its own thought waves just the same as radio and television broadcasts travel all over the world. So the thought waves of human thought can actually travel anywhere.

A man taking LSD can go on a trip where he contacts either discarnate or even incarnate entities from the opium dens of China. Do you understand what I'm talking about? People can send their thought waves anywhere. And they don't have to take LSD to do it. That's the beauty of it. They can do it better without LSD because they are more in control. If they take a drug, they may be in a form of trance state where they go out, but who are they? They're a balloon drifting in the wind. Any force that they contact in the astral realm can mold them.

What we really want, then, is to get people to understand that they, through God, can learn how to penetrate the densities of the world. Supposing you send out a good thought, and you've got another guy out here thinking a bad thought, that is the focus or force of density in the human world mind that causes all these problems to the penetration of your thought. And there are two ways you can get by it. One is to neutralize it and the other is to increase the power of your own thought.

If you make your own thought more powerful, you can penetrate the density with it or you can neutralize the thought and cause it to relax its own intensity so that you penetrate it with less power. So all of these different laws governing penetration of consciousness are active in the world.

There is a word, I believe it's in German, *weltschmerz,* world pain. Do you people, any of you, ever feel the pain that is going on in Poland right now that the great Master spoke about a while ago? Was it last night or was it this morning?

Student: The Great Divine Director.

MLP: The Great Divine Director. You know, I'm only a listener so I sometimes do not hear or record these things until I hear them back to my own consciousness. I'm awake but I still don't always remember everything. I don't think you do either.

So the point I'm trying to make is, do you ever feel the world pain of people that are not necessarily part of you? Well, I contend that in this drama of penetration and focalization of consciousness, without meaning to do so, we often tune in, with the radio of our own mind and being and the radio of our own soul, on a lot of little dramas that are going on in the world.

I think it is very important to be able to have the proper concentration so as to be able to tune out as well as to tune in. Every once in a while I have letters written to me on obsessional insanity, and I want to discuss this with you as part of this lecture. I have people writing to me saying that ghosts, hobgoblins, witches, black forces, negativity, dreams of death, all kinds of horror problems are coming to them, and they want to know how they can get rid of it and asking for The Summit Lighthouse to help them. Most of these people, in fact I think all of these people, land in the healing chalice.* Many of them respond immediately to our treatment. Some respond partially. And I've had one or two that don't respond at all.

The factor of human karma must be taken into account. Jesus did not, contrary to popular opinion, heal everybody that he contacted and everybody that contacted him. There were those he did not heal for the simple reason that their karma demanded that what they had done to others or to life should be returned to them first.

I remember one of the dictations given in Washington, D.C., that particularly was close to my heart. It said that according to the decree of a certain man's karma, he should have been born without arms and without legs, but by the intercession of the Goddess of Liberty, he was born with arms and with legs, but he could not use them.[4] At least his image was not marred. He didn't look so terrible.

Do you remember thalidomide?[5] A lot of women took that, and they had children without arms and legs. So this is not something that I'm dreaming up. It came from the archangelic realm, and it clearly pointed out that karma has an effect on people.

I want to assure you and I want to guarantee you in this lecture that many people you meet walking down the street with terrible problems—I've seen some problems so horrible that I hate to even think of them—are actually the outpicturing or manifesting of human karma from past ages because of the wickedness that those people did in the past. And this is the karma that they are bearing *with* the mercy of God. Think of what it would be *without* the mercy of God.

---

*I.e., written petitions for them are placed in the healing chalice. These petitions are consecrated and burned at the conclusion of the Wednesday evening healing service.

I believe that we have enough love and beauty in the kingdom of God to warrant our following the consciousness of God and penetrating the density of humanity and our own density with the Mind of Christ. But I want to point out to you that there are many forces in the world that are actually vampire forces that want to steal your energy and plot to take it from you. Whenever you start to penetrate the world mind, they do not like it. Because if you penetrate the world mind with thoughts of Christ, thoughts of God, thoughts of love, thoughts of harmony, thoughts of peace, you are going contrary to the machinations of the people that want to control the world.

Pavlov, the Russian scientist who developed the system whereby he would ring a bell and then later on put a testing instrument on the salivary glands of the dog, would be able to induce saliva or salivation in the dog's mouth by ringing the bell without even giving the dog any food, thus beginning the first principle of psychic brainwashing.

Everyone should understand, then, that you have to contend with many minds whenever you set about the business of working for God. The only way you're ever going to be able to master it, then, is to be able to get a lot of help from the higher realms. I think the Great Divine Director pinpointed that this afternoon when he said we should evoke the angels.

I think many times we try to do it alone. We try to go it alone. And I think many times we prematurely try to project thoughts out into the world. Remember, just as you are trying to project thoughts out into the world, there are hundreds and hundreds of people trying to beam thoughts to you. And they don't have to know you in order to do it.

For example, behind the Iron Curtain, there are any number of what have been termed by some of us as thought police. These people are particularly acting on behalf of the socialist regime. And they constantly beam to the minds of people here in the West that they don't even know thoughts about socialism and the preference of the Soviet Union over the American way of life.

Now, at first you'd say to yourself, "Well, this is a very horrendous thing. How in God's name can people accept that?"

You also look at some of the guys that are married to some of the gals and you wonder how in the world she ever accepted him or he accepted her, don't you? And all you have to do is go down the street, and when you see some of them walking together, you will wonder real hard as to how they ever accepted each other. I sometimes think there's an element of horror in people where they actually enjoy being married to something so opposite to themselves that I really can never quite figure it out.

Well, the main idea, then, in this penetration and focalization lecture on consciousness is to first make your determination that you're going to go to God and get the matrix. And the matrix will usually fit one of the thoughtforms of joy, peace, love, harmony, friendship, wisdom, and the various constructive thoughts. So you get the matrixes of these thoughts and then you make the determination that you're going to expand it into the microcosm.

Now there is a book out—I have a copy of it upstairs, and if I had the time I'd show it to you—which deals with the macrocosm and the microcosm from a very interesting standpoint. It starts out showing a girl sitting in a rocking chair in Amsterdam. She's sitting there in a rocking chair by a big, stone, U-shaped building. And first you see her only. Next slide, from up in the air, you see her sitting in the yard and you see the building.

And then you go up higher over Amsterdam, you see the streets. And then you wind up where you're way up and you see The Hague and all the different areas all around, into the North Sea and everywhere. And then after a while you go up so you're covering half the hemisphere of the world, and you can still see that dot down there that you know is that girl.

And then pretty soon you go up and you see the world in space and then you go out further and you see the planets. And then you see the whole solar system, and then after a while you see the galaxy.

And then it turns on its side and then after a while you see the galaxy from a distance. And then you see the whole universe and then you begin to see other island universes. And you keep on going on and on and on until you've gone into infinity and after a while you're in a whole world that's a sea of white stars. They're all sun systems and universes, and there's no differentiation at all.

Then you start turning the pages and you see the girl sitting in the rocking chair. Then you see she has a ring on her hand or something. And you go down and the first thing you know, I think there's a bee sitting there or a fly or something. And then you go down a little lower and you see the cells. And then you see the bloodstream and you keep on going until you get clear down to the atoms. And then you begin to go into the nucleus of the atoms. And you go down the other way.

And the idea is that man has a microcosm of selfhood. He has a miniature world all inside of his own physical body. And he also has an outer world. So when you start to penetrate yourself with ideas of health and godliness and beauty and joy and peace and harmony between people, you have to draw enough energy according to the particular segment of space that you want to contact. If all you want to do is contact yourself, well, that takes so much energy, you can learn to use it. When you want to contact more people, you put out a little more energy.

The big problem is that people don't think in terms of infinity. They think in terms of the finite. They say to themselves, "Well, that's all the energy I've got." Bunk. You've limited yourself. You have all the energy that God has. All you have to do is learn to use it. And if you're going to use it constructively, you have to recognize that even God would encounter these obstacles of thought if he were to start to penetrate substance with the energy. So you're no different than God is. You get my point?

People put up these negative walls. They put up these negative barriers. And do you know what some of these barriers are? What you call hardened opinion. I don't believe in that.

I believe that anybody can change. If Adolf Hitler were sitting in the other room and he really wanted to find God today, I wouldn't care about his karma. I wouldn't like that, but if he wanted to find God and he came to us and said, "I realize I've done terrible things in the past, I want to find God," I believe that we could accept the possibility of change in him. And I believe that if it was Judas Iscariot, we could accept the possibility of change in him.

Why don't you try accepting the possibility of change in yourself when you start to understand how to project your consciousness out? First of all, change your own consciousness. Work on that for a while until you've got your own consciousness and your own house in order, then start sending out world thought.

Don't start sending out world thoughts at a time when you're also in a state of chaos, because if you do, you're going to transmit that chaos along with all the other things you are. In one way, you are already doing that. But when you don't make the conscious effort to do it, you don't use so much power and therefore you don't effect so much penetration of the world thought. Do you see what I'm trying to drive at? This is a very sound principle. Instead of sending out the world thought prematurely, send out the thought to produce the godlike manifestation in yourself so that you won't be bored.

You know something? I have people come to these dictations, I have people that listen to these dictations all over the world. An awful lot of them like them, but there are some people that get bored with them and turn them off halfway through. And they say, "Oh, let's do the 'Hail Mary' or let's do something else. We've listened to this dictation. We've heard enough of Jesus. Let's turn him off." And this happens.

I have people come here on a Sunday night when there isn't anything more important in the whole universe than this teaching. They come here at about 7:30, and by 8:30 they're ready to go home. I let them go about nine, but that extra half hour really pains some of them. So they don't come back anymore. Others tell me that this is the most interesting study they've ever had. And I believe it is. I think that our sermons are better than most churches in the whole world.

But you know something? They are geared to one hour, they're one-hour people. And it's very hard for them to get over the idea of one hour. Well, how else are they ever going to get anywhere unless the teaching is given to them? Oh, they might go over to India to some yogi. But you know what time they get up over there and start their mantras? Four-thirty or four o'clock. Well, you think we have sessions. They have sessions every day over there in their ashrams. That's how they get to where they're going. I think it's about time that we get where we're going, too.

So we have the focalization, the penetration of consciousness. But let's penetrate the hardness in our own hearts. Let's ask the love of God to come down and saturate us. Let's ask the wisdom of God to saturate us. Let's help God along a little bit. Let's think with him. Instead of resisting him, let's understand there are a lot of forces that want to keep us out.

I'm going to tell you one law to close with on this lecture. It's the law of decrees. When new people come in here and have never heard decrees before, they may not understand them. This is a many-faceted thing I am going to tell you. I think it was this lady that was studying and practicing witchcraft who said that we sounded like a Black Panther meeting here. Well, I don't think most of you know it, but the Black Panthers, I believe, made a study of our decrees before they ever started their work, and they use decrees constantly in a negative way, in reverse, because they know the power of decrees.

Now, Mrs. Booth, are you here?

Annice Booth: Yes, I am.

MLP: What did you hear from the Black Panthers that were chanting on the streets of Hayward, California?

AB: On the day of Martin Luther King's funeral, they had a demonstration chanting. "We've got the power, the power." I don't want to say it as they were. And then "Get off the street" to each white person they saw. And their rhythm was the same as ours, but the power was absolutely—

MLP: Satanic.

AB: Oh, it was terrible.

MLP: Terrible power. But they also use that [chanting rhythmically] "We've got the power. We've got the power. We've got the power. Get off the street. Get off the street. Get off the street." Instead of saying, "Beloved I AM," they were no doubt, you know, saying other things.

And you will hear chants like this: "Police, go home. Police, go home. Police, go home, go home, go home. Police, go home. Police, go home. Police, go home, go home, go home." Well, you see—yes?

Student: How about these whistles that the Japanese use when they get into rhythm?

MLP: Well, it's all energy, you know. And when it's in rhythm, it's harder.

I'll explain to you one law of rhythm, which has to do with marching troops across a bridge. Every time they come to a bridge, they're always put at ease and they're not marched across. They go across the bridge, you know, in a dismissed state.

Why is that? You know what would happen to the bridge if they went across in rhythm? It'd be destroyed. The walls of Jericho were torn down, back in the time of Jericho, the same way, by the priests marching around the walls of the city.

A violin string can also break a crystal goblet. And a woman can sing at a certain level and do the same—did you know that? [To an opera singer in the audience:] I believe you could.

Well, I want to get back to this law of decrees. The moment a new person comes in the room and they listen to you decreeing, right away they come in with entities. Now, practically every human being on earth has entities at one time or another in their life. They're like the barnacles on a ship. They are there. Most of us don't pay any attention to them. You don't pay attention if you have a wart somewhere on your body, do you?

So the people don't understand that these entities talk to you. And when a person comes here for the first time, the entities will say, "Look at those silly people. Oh, they're silly. This is a ridiculous nuthouse, a nut factory. Why, whoever heard such a thing as people making those decrees? Doesn't it say somewhere in the Bible, 'And the heathen will repeat vain things over and over and over'?"[6] Well, it does, you know, but I don't think these are vain things. And this repetition is perfectly valid, you see.

But you know what happens? If the new people keep on listening to your decrees and if they start to decree, their entities will get out. The entities will have to leave them. So before the entities have to leave, they try to make the person get out, so they can stay at home.

When you deal with the penetration and focalization of consciousness, then, these people are never actually penetrated by divine ideas. There is no focalization of the primal sanities of Nature, as Walt Whitman said, that are in their thinking. They don't reason. They go up here to Colorado College and they study for four years to be something or other, maybe they have their B.S. degree. And they come in here and in one hour they're ready to walk out, even in the midst of a sermon.

Did you know that on Sunday nights I have very few decrees here for the sake of the public? And even a real good sermon, they're ready to walk out. They don't want to hear the truth. They come and they listen and they go away.

This organization is probably more attacked than any other because of its decrees. But we are not going to stop decreeing, because that's what brought us here. That's why we're here, because the decrees are fulfilling the needs of our soul. Why, for heaven's sake, the subconscious is literally littered with all kinds of bad ideas. We give these decrees and we straighten ourselves out, realign ourselves. We free those energies inside of ourselves. We become powerful beings. Almost everything has been done here through decrees. All of us have benefited by it.

How about you, Jeffrey?

Jeffrey: Yes, indeed.

MLP: When you came here you were far different, were you not? Now they sit in here, these boys, and they whip up a storm with Astrea till eleven o'clock at night, working hard.

You know what the boys did here? They really touched my heart. A group of the new boys that were on twenty-dollar salaries, they started tithing, giving ten percent of that to the masters. Wasn't that a terrific thing? They had a bowl of money sitting over here that they had put together. Well, it really touched my heart. I was moved by it.

So you folks see that there are a lot of things involved in Summitry, more than you ever dreamed of. So please try to remember to straighten out the microcosmic man, you. And remember, it isn't going to take forever to do it. If you set your mind and heart to it, I would go so far as to say you can go a long way in 1971. Probably by July, a lot of you who have never done this before will be ready to start projecting into the world thought.

Spend about six months projecting into yourself. Let the first half of the year be devoted this—not exclusively, those of you who are already trained, but those of you who are starting out. Those of you who are already qualified, begin to do both. Project into yourself and then simultaneously get the messages from God that you can send out into the world, meditate on the world thought, you see? Send out love and help to these people and the banner of freedom, as the Great Divine Director said.[7]

This will end my lecture on the penetration and focalization of consciousness.

January 2, 1971
Colorado Springs, Colorado

CHAPTER 7

Thoughts Are . . .

We should recognize that we are not merely a conglomerate of bones, flesh, and blood, "as," Christ said, "ye see me have."[1] In other words, "Henceforth know we no man anymore after the flesh."[2]

Most of us, through familiarity with the orb of vision, will always develop a response to the stimuli of vision. If we see someone approaching us, we recognize them by our sight. But what is it that we see of the individual? What we see is merely the same thing that we see in everyone that we meet except we identify a different pattern. In other words, we recognize a different person. But the real person is seldom perceived through the ordinary vision.

"Henceforth know we no man anymore after the flesh." So what is it, then, that we really probably are perceiving in a human being when they approach us if we have the spiritual eyes to discern? It is the inner structure of man. But underneath this inner structure of man individualized is God. And if we look at God in a man named John Jones or we see God in someone called Shelley Jones, it doesn't make any difference, do you see? Because God is the same in everyone. But what is it, then, that we see structured within man?

It is the use of thought. Two thoughts are manifest. The first thought is the thought of God, and this, in effect, is God individualized, per se. But we are not concerned with this, because God is the same in all. What we are concerned with recognizing is individuality. This is the structure of man's use of thought. God's use of thought produces the spirit of the Universal in all, and it is the true common denominator whereby we may see a similarity in us all. The differences that are compounded are compounded through the use of thought.

Thought is ours, as it is God's. In other words, if we have the components to produce fire, we have the flint and we have a stack of straw, what is it that ignites the straw but the spark from the flint as we strike it. This produces a flame and the flame consumes the straw.

Saint Paul said, many, many centuries ago on Mars' Hill, "Ye men of Athens, I beheld here an altar to the unknown God whom ye therefore ignorantly worship, him declare I unto you. God that made the heavens and the earth . . . " He went on and then he spoke of that God as some of the poets had said in that time, "Ye are his offspring." In other words, "Him declare I unto you."[3]

And he went on to say, "God that made the heavens and the earth dwelleth not in temples made with hands." So the structures that house God in reality are the things that are made without human agency. Yet, in effect, we are all architects. *You* are an architect! And you are drawing a blueprint whether it is the haphazard creation of a child playing upon the rug with blocks, or whether it is a mature individual creating a blueprint for a city, a traffic pattern by which people will find it easy to move about, or mapping out areas of the brain where dangers or infection lurk that must be expurgated by the scalpel of the surgeon.

All things that we do of a material nature, all things that we do of a spiritual nature, and even the idling of the mind, all things are the result of correct thought or incorrect thought or idle thought. Boredom is produced because of a lack of human interest. Why a lack of human interest? Because a state of almost autohypnosis is produced, or because of external communications of psychic energy from those who intend to malign the human race, whereby our minds or brains in their hemispheres become polarized to the state of non-thought. In other words, we become bored, we lose interest in the vitality of God.

And why is this so? It is because we do not understand the correct use of these two phrases, "Resist not evil"[4] and "Resist the devil and he will flee from you."[5] We must correctly divide the Word. We must break the bread of life. We must recognize that if we take our thought energy, and we constantly maintain a state of on guard—in other words, we are always on the *qui vive,* we're always standing defensively with sword in hand ready to thrust—if our energies are totally engaged in the defensive maneuver, we probably are losing out a great deal on life. Because correct thought requires the relaxed state, the state of peace.

Hence both statements are absolutely correct. There are times when we must be on the defensive, we must resist evil. There are times when it is best not to engage our energies in even recognizing evil but rather to stress the absolute indomitable power of recognizing the all-power of God, the power of goodness that created the original, the pure, the pristine pattern of life, not only for this planet but for the universe.

Somehow or other man has a tendency, of course, to identify with his home, with his locale, with his wife, with his family, with his friends. We become identified with centers of being, the centers of other people's being, their life. And we think that because we incorporate individuals into our life that we are identifying in a stronger way with life.

I remember something my mother told me and I remember something that various aged people have told me, that they had come to the place where all of their school chums, those they went to school with in the elementary school, all of the people that occupied their hometown that they knew, in fact all of their friends had passed on, and they sat alone. And now they did not have the self-same interest that they formerly had in living, because their associates were gone. And somehow or other the acceptance of their own passing, which they had resisted before, now was possible to them and they sat and waited to die.

This shows, then, how we have a tendency not to identify with the universe, with the ongoingness of generations, but rather to identify with those that we hold near and dear. I am not advocating that we should turn against those that we love—no. But I am advocating a sense of identification with the ongoingness, hopefully, of the world and the positive thought that we must send out into space as a means of hallowing space in order to create in our world the great tender realities that God has already placed within us. For we are alchemists, one and all. It is up to us to evoke responses from the world.

Today most people are victims of reaction. The action of others affects us and we identify with what people do to us. We must become prime movers of destiny, not just the moved, for we are not the checkers or the chessmen upon the board. Instead, we are the movers if we will take dominion over the earth.

The masses of people today are like sheep going up the gateways to the slaughterhouses. They are victims of mass movements, of mass thinking, and they do not have the alchemical freedom which the masters intend those who are truly free to have, to be, and to manifest.

Thoughts are. And the structure of our thoughts affects us more than we can know. For example, let us take an individual who finally grows weak and discouraged fighting the world's thought about him or her. I want to bring this out because it is a very important part of your future life if you will let it be.

Did you know, for example—and I experienced this for myself—many years ago I worked for a man whose name was Wright, and he was never wrong. And so, I really never had a great deal of fear of people nor did I fear circumstances. And so one day a matter came up that it was necessary for me to go to his office. And I went into his office and for the first time in my life, I was amazed to find myself stuttering, "Y-Y-Yes, M-M-Mister W-W-Wright." I was stuttering.

Imperfection was manifesting in my world. Where did it come from? At that time, at first, I was more or less oblivious of where it came from. How could this be, that I, to whom my mother always said had the gift of gab, could now find myself speechless before this man? And he had a little mustache and he was very suave and very distinguished, Mr. Wright. And there I sat shivering in my chair and wishing that I could sink down through the floor. Why?

Well, I found out. And the reason was Mr. Wright's thought of me and Mr. Wright could not be wrong. I was accepting the overcoat, the patina, the garments of his thought. And I noticed, time after time, whenever I entered his office, I had the same experience—until I learned to overthrow, to dethrone, to kick out Mr. Wright's wrong thought of me.

The people of the world have what we may call an inadvertent hypnotic effect on each other, and they learn how to do it. Yesterday morning, when I was making a television film for one of the local stations, the gentleman who was interviewing me said that he was able to guide the conversation by the hypnotism of his thought. No, he may do it with some people. He did not do it with us. And I'm not boasting of this. It is simply that God has said that we should take dominion over our *own* world, not over the world of others.

I do not think it would have been proper had I elected to try to dominate Mr. Wright, even if Mr. Wright was wrong. It was up to me to dominate the image of myself, to assert by thought the kind of a person I wanted to be—to be a follower of God, yes, but not God as an insipid, antiseptic image of an old man in some section of the universe whose long, white beard, painted by a long-passed-away Leonardo da Vinci, should somehow or other create an image of God as though God were feeble and helpless. In reality, God is all beauty, all life, all wonder, all joy, all reality and the avant-garde transcendent manifestation of the selfhood of every person, not just myself.

What a wonderful thing, then, it is to be able to obey the injunctions of Jesus Christ and to recognize that we have a responsibility at times to resist the form of evil that comes to us in order to enthrone in us someone else's image of what we are rather than God's image of what we are.

"Now, it does not yet appear," the masters tell us, "what we shall be." But it goes on to say, "When he shall appear, when we shall see him as he is, we shall be like him."[6]

And so, it is essential that we recognize our own limitations about God, that we realize that we are affected by our limitations of God. Our ideas of God may be immature, infantile, prattling. I'm not saying that yours is, I said ours may be.

The point is, we have to be capable of growing up spiritually, of maturing, of being able to hold lofty concepts of God. We must recognize that we may transcend or rise above those concepts of yesterday to understand that God that is a spirit has provided a vehicle through which we may express, and that of more importance even than the physical vehicle, the part of man that can exercise and demonstrate physical mastery is the mind of man that is identifiable with the mind of God, that can state with the Christ, "All power in heaven and earth is given unto me,"[7] and I will give it to whomsoever I will.

We must recognize that the will and the motives of the will are paramount and of great import in our establishing a forcefield of what we determine is the will of God around ourselves, holding an openness in spirit, asking God to help us in our own envisioning of what thoughts we wish to share with him.

Getting back, then, to the thoughts of God, it is important that we understand in a deeper way the nature of God and the ability of God to let us mature, to let us grow up in Christ.

Many people have felt that Christ was only the man who lived as Jesus two thousand years ago, without understanding the joint-heirship that is possible to all of us. As a small boy, I used to ponder on this. I wondered many times, "Why did God create, according to the patterns that orthodoxy brings to us, one man and make him the doorway to all life?"

Later on, of course, and I'm sure many of you have understood this, the Universal Christ appeared. I was able to see that God had one image in which he created all men and that that image was actually the Christ image. And then I understood the scriptures in John where it says, "All things were made by him and without him was nothing made that was made. In him was life."[8] And so we recognize the statement, "Before Abraham was, I AM."[9] This takes us back to the latent image of God that is placed within us for photographic development.

Do you understand what I'm talking about? A camera, a simple little thing like a camera in which there is placed film, perceives through its own lens-eye system an image. The image is transferred by light to the film, and then if you carry that camera a thousand years before developing it, when it was developed, that camera print would be the image that was taken one thousand years ago or two or more.

So we have to understand that when man was created in God's image, it was the placing upon the film of consciousness of a latent image. And the development of that image belongs to us, and that development is an ageless process, and is not necessarily one in which the first are assured of being the last. For Jesus said, "Many that are first shall be last and the last, first,"[10] indicating that physical time is not necessarily the guarantee or assurance that we are going to develop that image first.

So what is it that really counts? It is the determination and the motivation of our hearts which indicates our whole intent to be all that God intends us to be. Our thought must become congruent with God's thought. The triad of the Holy Spirit, of the Father, the Son, and the Holy Spirit, must become congruent with our body, our mind, and our soul, and our whole being. We have to let the wholeness of ourselves become the allness of God, and this is really a process. It is a process whereby Christhood is attained.

It is naturally attained as a product that can be truly stamped "Made in heaven." Yet this product evolves from the plane of this earth where we find ourselves. So thoughts are. And in reality, all of the people that we meet are products of their thoughts.

I want to touch, then, briefly upon what we call "the idling of the mind," which can be used as an interval to create and to take dominion over the earth when what precedes it is a directive from the conscious motive and will of the individual. If you determine that a thing shall be so and you let that saying, as Christ said, "sink down into your ears,"[11] which means enter your whole heart, permeate your body, your mind, and your soul, it is absolutely possible that that thought can be in manifestation in a moment, in the twinkling of an eye.

I will cite an example for you that I think you deserve to hear. Several years ago in the state of Virginia I was quite high up on a ladder just about dinnertime. The rung broke and I found myself hurled with almost the speed of an automobile to the ground below. My body hit the ground with such force that my heart lost its rhythm. Not only did my heart lose its rhythm, but I felt the gush of warm blood flooding all over internal organs, and I knew within myself that I was intended to die from that fall.

I said one thing. I said, "Lord Christ, I know I have really seriously injured myself, or so my senses report. There is not time, and I know it, in order to plead with you, for I know that you want me home." I said, "I *demand* in the name of Almighty God that every electron, every cell, every part of my being shall be made whole this instant, and I demand that it remain so and that I suffer no effects from this fall."

In the meantime, my heart was finally gasping for its last breath, you might say, but I kept on, and I affirmed absolutely the perfection of God. Within three minutes I was on my feet. I walked in the house. I sat down at the table. I ate my evening meal. I said practically nothing. And I want to tell you today that I have never suffered any ill effects from that, neither was I sore nor did I have any bad effects in my system. I maintained the perfect health of the Christ consciousness through the motivation, intent, and determination to do so.

Do not, then, sell yourself short or sell short the capacities and potentials that lie within you. You have, by the power of the divine thought, a most magnificent power that really is greater than all the physicians of the world. You have the good physician. And quite naturally, if you obey his laws, if you affirm his perfection by the actions you do every day—and I'm sure we all, when we get out sometimes in hotels, motels, and things that you run into along the road that masquerade as bistros, places you can eat, I'm sure that we all have created indiscretions, as I have, too, and I admit it, but not through free will but through circumstances—if we will try to eat right, to think right, to live right and to be right, it will work and we will manifest the kingdom of heaven within ourselves.

Now, I started to tell you something about the idling of the mind which you have heard of before. It is this. The idle mind is supposed to be the "devil's workshop." I have never quite been able to figure out why it isn't God's. But I rather think that the reason this is so is because God is busy always thinking.

You remember Jesus made a very interesting statement: "The Father worketh hitherto, and I work."[12] So somehow or other, whereas the concept of the meditator, the man sitting in padmasana, in the lotus posture, the man just thinking about God or meditating upon him comes to mind in many cases as being the supreme. I think that in reality, even though the meditative posture not be assumed, that man can, if he wills it so—and I say if he *wills* it so—he can enter in to the great powerhouse of God's consciousness without necessarily looking like someone that is meditating.

I remember several years ago being in the home of an East Indian who was a disciple of a great guru, and we were getting ready to have some chapatis. There was a young lady there, a rather tall young lady, who had really participated in all of the aspects of yoga—and I am not picking on yoga, just stating this fact because it was so humorous. Somehow or other this young lady, who was quite tall and stately, decided that it was very important that she be noticed by others.

Many students do this; they become self-conscious in assuming any form of meditation, even if it just be to sit in front of other people. I experienced a similar thing in one of the ashrams that I attended many years ago. I was sitting there meditating and I happened to open my eyes, and lo and behold, all the very advanced spiritual people, *very* advanced, were looking at me. And so I was aware of the fact that they weren't watching God, they were looking at me.

And so this woman was very, very self-conscious, and as we looked at her, she had a case of fluttering eyelids. Unless you were to see this for yourself, you could not imagine it. Whereas you might see someone winking at you at a certain speed, she was going about ten times that fast, and both eyelids were flickering up and down. It was very difficult for me to keep a straight face, and I imagine you'd have had the same trouble as I did.

Many times people become involved in externals, you see. And so, an idle mind can be the devil's workshop, and sometimes people imagine that the mind in meditation should be a complete blank, that they should just stop thinking and sit there, and then open the door, "Open the door, Richard." But you just don't know what's coming in when you do that, and people become victims of all kinds of thoughts.

And the reason for that is that many people do not understand the flight of the bumblebee. I'm going to tell you what I mean.

In other words, they don't understand that half the world is sleeping most of the time. And there are a great many people in different parts of the world who are sleeping the sleep which we call the "drug sleep." Their consciousness becomes a vehicle through which mass entities act.

Do you remember when Jesus came upon the disciples, and he found there was a boy there possessed with a demon? The disciples were trying their best to exorcise the demon. It almost reminded us of the sorcerer's apprentice. They were trying to really get rid of this demon, and the demon wouldn't go.

So Jesus looked at them and cast the demon right out. And then they said, "How did you do it?" And he said, "Well, this kind goeth out only by prayer and fasting."[13] And we have to understand that only by what we will call obsession can people actually let into their world not only the seven bad demons that were in there before and then cast out, but they can let in sometimes seventy times seven. They just become filled with mass entities.

I'm not boasting now in what I say, but by God's grace I have the power to see entities, and I can see them on people. I remember one time going into a certain psychic's home, and this psychic had probably around five hundred entities in the room in which he worked. He was a chiropractic doctor, and I use lots of chiropractic and recommend it—it's a fine thing. But this individual was a little different.

The whole room was just filled with around five hundred entities, and they were mounted on the wall like you see deer heads and fish mounted on a wall. He didn't actually have physical things there, but these were living entities that were almost in the dead state—they were hanging like barnacles on a ship.

You can imagine the level of the vampirism that was in those entities. They would sap the energy of the people. People would come in there to feel better, to take a treatment, and then the entities would turn around and vampirize them as they were going out the door.

Their latter state would be worse than their former.

These things exist all the time. People go into an airplane and they take a seat, and they don't seem to recognize that the type of person that sat there before may determine their comfort for the entire flight. And the same is true of a bus or a car.

This is one of the reasons why we maintain a Greyhound bus that is fitted out with our own beds. All the facilities that we need are all right there. We can eat, cook, and sleep twelve people and travel all over the country. The gasoline tank holds enough gas to take you seven hundred miles, and then you can refill. So you can travel a major portion of the day without ever filling up with gas. We have air-conditioning, telephone, sewer, electric lights, our own power plant and all of these things.

Why do we do it? We don't do it for luxury. It's a matter of not having to sleep in beds in which other people have slept the night before and for all the nights before that since the time the hotel was built. It's a matter of being able to stay in our own vibratory action. And I certainly recommend it if it's possible for everybody. It's a good system.

If you can't do it, what do you do? You certainly use that power of right thought in order to create an environment that you want to feel comfortable in. And this is a right thing. You should not just sit there and allow the leeches of the vibrations of someone else to sap your energy so that you arrive where you are going almost in a state of despair. Instead, you should exercise dominion over your world. Do you see the point? It's a very important point, and it's practical and it works and we've tried it again and again.

Do you know what a deep-dish telescope is? These are the kind of telescopes that look at the stars, like you saw in those pictures this morning. Deep-dish telescopes are able to get radio signals from far-off stars and bring them down here where they can be amplified and astronomers can get a picture of what's going on. This requires great sensitivity.

Both Elizabeth and I are highly sensitized individuals, and it is possible that if people sleep in the room where we are that entities can come through them because they're sleeping. That's why I advocate that we don't have anybody sleeping in here. Do you understand? It's really quite a problem. We have to keep people awake.

I remember one time I was in Los Angeles and I was in a desperate situation because there was a woman that had a lot of psychic energy that was the wrong kind of energy. And so she parked right in the front row—and she insisted on the front row, mind you. I could have understood it if it was up in the balcony, but in the front row. And she had to go to sleep.

So I finally in desperation seized the American flag, and I went over there and I pounded her on the toes with it and woke her up. And she looked at me and said, "What's happening?"

I said, "You can't sleep in my meeting. If you want to sleep, you're going to have to go home, go to bed."

So I brought the flag back. And she said, "I've been sick."

I said, "Well, maybe you should be at home and be in bed, then. But I don't want you to sleep."

Because what happens is that a lot of times an entity can come in, I don't say every time, but it can come in through a person's consciousness. And then because this living human being is acting as a focus for that entity in the very room, because of my sensitivity, this may very well break up my ability to minister to the people who come to hear me—because I'm very dependent on attunement with my God Presence. But so are you. And this is where a lot of people don't realize how much their happiness depends upon their contact with God.

You know, there's an old saying that goes like this, "If diving into the sea in search of a pearl you don't find a pearl, the fault lies not in the sea but in thee." And so if we would stop to realize that much of our happiness and our enjoyment of life and our advancement and our progress depends upon our receptivity rather than just the speaker, we would understand not only generation but regeneration. We would understand that we have a right to tune in with our Divine Presence so that we can appreciate what's being done.

In other words, if I tune in with God, and I bring God down into my consciousness, and God synthesizes and spins out the cocoon of words, those words would not, even if they were charged with the keys of hell and of death, if they'd give you the victory over hell and death, unless you use those keys, they will not work. You can carry them around as an ornament. You can pin them on your dress or on your suit or put them in your pocket. But this will not help.

The correct use of the keys to the kingdom is what really counts. I am absolutely convinced that the masters have again and again given us in the *Pearls of Wisdom* keys to our spiritual identity. I'm convinced that the book [*Climb the Highest Mountain*], for example, contains thousands and thousands of keys. I am convinced by the fact that I have seen individuals ascend through the teachings of the masters in The Summit Lighthouse and I'm sure in probably many other organizations. I don't specifically know of them, but I do know that it has worked through our organization—not through the physical organization but through obedience to the precepts of the masters, obedience to God. So if those keys are there and they work, it is up to us as individuals to become a little bit more determined in correcting our world.

Several years ago I was fortunate enough to hear Dr. Kenneth MacFarland, who was then the educational consultant for General Motors. The man talked for four hours without stopping. And when he was through, the audience was begging for more. So I was convinced at that time, and I still am convinced, that it is possible to spark and inspire a group of people and literally, in many cases, to make it possible for them to toast their shins on your fires.

I don't find anything wrong with that, providing individuals can come to the realization of the fact that they have the same stimulus within themselves and then if you can inspire them to start using it, because then the greatest joy comes. If it comes as a result of inspiration from the outside to the inside, this is fine. But it cannot always be guaranteed to happen, because we do not always sit on the coattails of someone that is capable of providing the stimuli.

So what is more important, then, the ability to just listen or the ability to be able to generate and regenerate within ourselves? I think it is the ability to kindle thought—in other words, to kindle the divine thought in ourselves and by the bursting forth of this thought to begin to realize what and who we are.

And when we do, when we begin to generate this thought and to regenerate it in people, it is not too long a time before the whole atmosphere of the room becomes vibrant. It becomes vital. It becomes an outreach of God to man. And even to the city, to the walls of the community, there is an extension of the divine ray of man's right thought about himself. Thought is a powerful activity. Let's see just how powerful.

Let us now begin the process of examining how the warp and the woof of creation was interwoven by divine thought. We can do this through, of course, inductive reasoning and deductive reasoning or through syllogistic reasoning. We can go all the different routes. But what we want to do in this case, I think, is to start from the physical evidences that are apparent to our eyes and then move inward until we see how the lifewaves of God's thought are really the substance or the energy by which all things are compounded or composed.

Here we are. We have a living organism, our own body—and I think it's probably best that we start with our own physical body. You have a beating heart, and your heart is beating with God's energy right now. The drums of life are moving and flowing, and because they move and flow, you have consciousness. You would not have consciousness if it were not for the diastole and systole of the heart, for the ebb and the flow of the tides, for the dark and the daylight—in other words, for the negative and positive energies, the yin and the yang. You would not have this unless the law was outworking in your being. In this case, it is the law of abundant life.

And so your heart is beating. But like all parts of your body—the brain, the bone, the hands, all substance—the heart is composed of little tiny cells. Some years ago, *Life* magazine photographed one of these cells and blew it up to the size of a huge page and we were able to see what looked like a miniature city, almost a Buckminster Fuller creation, the geodesic dome, as it were. Vast physical enterprises were going on within the city of the cell.

We see that the cell itself is quite complex. The cell is actually like the brick of which a building is composed. But you all know that the grains of sand compose the brick and many other things including the substance of the mortar. So the cells exist, and in effect, they are working side by side with all of the other cells of the heart.

But if you actually go below the cellular level into what we call the atomic structure, you are going to find, as all of our young people know and most of the older people know, the cells are composed of atoms. Of course, because we can't see a physical atom, we have a tendency to more or less disregard all of its implications.

But in reality, the scientific laws and the laws of nature put it all together and it works. And because it works, it is important to us. It may not be necessary that we understand how it works in order to have it work, of course, but it does probably help our native curiosity. We would like to know how things work.

So we come to the point of the atomic structure. And there, of course, we have the electrons within the atoms and we have the center of the electron with all of the forces that are revolving around it. And we can keep going down.

It's almost like that picture of a little girl holding a mirror. Did you ever see the pictures that used to appear back in the 1800s— I imagine some of you have these picture books in your attic—where a little girl was standing there holding a mirror? She has beautiful hair, it's very long, and she's holding this mirror in her hand. You look into the mirror and what do you see but the little girl. And you see this girl holding another mirror in her hand, and then that mirror is holding another little girl and another mirror. It's the same girl. And this goes back into infinity.

Well, you come to a point where after a while it seems there is no basis for going any deeper. So what then? When you come to what seems to be the ultimate little amount of substance that you can identify, what is it that actually controls life? It is what is called by our scientists "mind stuff." Think of that, and see how thought is the basis of creation. But whose thought?

We read that God is a spirit. And so somehow or other as Shakespeare wrote, "This cloud-capped domain and all these spires could pass away and vanish into thin air."[14] And we have to recognize that if God withdrew the support of his thought from the physicality of the world and the universe, the whole universe would then vanish away. Even though we might be right here, we would vanish away with it from a physical standpoint. Yet, because we are a part of God, we would not really disappear. We would be right where God is, and we could say, "Where thou art, I AM."

So that Being and Be-ness are very vital parts of our being, because through Be-ing and Be-ness, we attain immortality, and this is the immortality of God. In effect, man's existence in God is not dependent on his goodness or his evil, on his achievement or his nonachievement, upon whether he manifests dark or light. I want you to understand this. It is not dependent on that.

But I'm talking about God's awareness of man without man's awareness of God. You could be sleeping and still be a part of the universe.

Do you understand this? Whether you're sound asleep or dead, it doesn't make any difference while you're sound asleep or dead, because you will still be a part of God. And the sinner as well as the saint has this because all things came forth through Christ and came forth from God, or from Spirit, into the womb of Matter—including our bodies, our science, our human logic as well as our divine logic.

But what is it, then, that is so vitally important? It is our self-awareness, our awareness of the fact that we are. God may be aware that we are, in whatever form that may be. But we need to be aware of life. And through our awareness, we will find a divine unity manifesting in our life.

This is the required synthesis that we all must achieve. Christ had this. He looked up, he raised his hands, and he said, "Father, I thank thee."[15] And it passed through the untrammeled universe. It absolutely wiped out impediment. The very thought, "Father, I thank thee!" penetrated through substance.

Do you see how powerful thought is? Thoughts are.

God bless you.

September 2, 1972
Atlanta, Georgia

CHAPTER 8

The Use of Thoughtforms in the Expansion of Consciousness

I think we have to recognize the geometry of God, and the geometry of God is in the available thoughtforms—the trapezoid, the square, and the various symbols that have been used in some of the ancient fraternities. But we have to recognize that there is some validity in the use of these thoughtforms in the expansion of our consciousness. Now I'll try to show you how this works.

Down through the years, we have had various dictations from the masters that relate to thoughtforms. One of the masters once said, for example, "You people have a consciousness about the size of a thimble when you should understand that you can expand it to the size of a barrel—or bigger."[1]

What are we doing but actually envisioning the hoop of the thimble, the circle itself, and the depth of the thimble—the size, the dimension of the thimble? And we are expanding it from the thimble to the barrel.

Basically, then, geometric forms can be utilized according to the size of familiar objects, and we can qualify them with greater dimension. If we want to increase the capacity of our mind to receive, we can envision the thoughtform of a cup, a goblet, a chalice.

The moment you think of a cup, you may have a tendency in your mind to associate the cup with a little cold water you're giving "in my name," you know, as Jesus said.[2] You think of the giving of something to someone else. So this in itself is an expansion or an extension of your own ideas, through the symbol of the cup, into the lives of others.

But let's change that cup now and put a foot on it and make it into a chalice. Immediately you think of the purification of the Holy Spirit, the descending dove coming down into the cup, you see. And you begin to feel that it is almost like a magnetic flux. It's a flux of light—the bending of light rays into the cup to take the form of the cup. And when they bend there, we suddenly get the idea of the accumulation of light rays. In other words, the laying of one light ray upon another—like a patine.

You know how you take something and you will coat it with gold—gold plate it? Well, that's overlaying or putting a patine of pure gold over our object. In this case, the object of the cup, we are going to cause light—because it is descending from the Presence in the form of a dove—we're going to cause it to bend in the chalice. And then it piles up, you see. The light rays just keep overlaying and overlaying and overlaying and finally they increase in density.

But of course, when you think of light, you think of illumination. So in reality, you don't think of density, but still it is the density of light. But light doesn't have any density. You see, light has illumination. It has lumens. So we realize that we can cause light mentally to accumulate at a given spot.

The personal application and value of the use of thoughtforms in the expansion of consciousness relates to the human heart because the heart itself has within it a chamber—and it is a chamber of great beauty. And so we see that one can have chalices within chalices. One can have geometric forms within geometric forms.

Consciousness itself is actually constrained by thoughtforms.

I want this understood by people. It is both constrained, restrained, and expanded. You can do with consciousness a great deal by creating thoughtforms which relate to the geometrizing of God. It's a sort of cosmic trigonometry. It's a magnificent thing. It's a cosmic calculus. It's a form of the divine mind being used for expansive purposes.

I think probably the idea that a human being contains enough "spaghetti" inside of him—if I may use the term "spaghetti" rather jokingly, such as blood vessels and nerve paths and various other cylindrical networks, arterial cardiovascular networks, and nerve networks through the body—that if you took all these out of one human body and put them together, you would be able to go to the moon and more just on the strength of the length of these noodles that are inside of us, you see.

So we have to recognize the ability of mentally compressing objects into a very small space. In a way, we are a little jewel box, physically speaking. But we are also a little jewel box mentally. We have a great deal more room in our jewel box from a mental standpoint than we do from a physical standpoint. But at the same time, when you involve yourself in the expansion of consciousness by thoughtforms, you have to recognize that the first step is to bring the thoughtform into consonance with your physical formation so that it becomes rational to you.

If you do not deal with a rational thoughtform, it's like going ahead and having a nebulous cloud out here in space. What is it but a cloud of steam? You try to define it. You try to name it. You try to duplicate it in thought and feeling, and you cannot do it.

But, you see, when you deal with familiar objects such as your physical body, you can relate the fact that a thoughtform is being brought into your physical form. And then—by the power of the mind, which has the power of expansion—you can take it out of the body and put it anywhere you want in space. Actually you are attracting to that thoughtform, then, the various emanations of your consciousness itself. You are creating an extension in consciousness which later becomes a method whereby you can expand the mind and being of yourself.

So you start out with a chalice. It's not very big. It's just a little cup or a glass around the heart. But you suddenly begin to decide that you are going to invoke the Spirit of God into that chalice. Well, someone may have some idea of the right and wrong of all this. They say, "What right do I have as an individual to invoke the Spirit of God into my chalice?"

You have every right, because God gave it to you in the beginning. He said, "Let us make man in our image."[3] He made you in his image. He made you in his likeness. He created you to be the authority in your world.

The biggest problem today in all of the whole human race is the fact that people do not want to take authority in their world. Instead of taking authority in their world, they allow other people to literally push them around with different ideas. Fads. Somebody over in Paris decides they're going to have long skirts, "maxi-skirts," this year. So they go ahead and create the maxi-skirts, and the whole world, practically, follows the Paris fashion fad. And the same with the mini-skirts and everything else.

So we have to understand that we have to take dominion over our life, and we have every right to do it in regard to these thought-forms. You are then doing what God commanded you to do. He said, "Take dominion over the earth."[4] Well, he wasn't talking just about the physical earth. He was talking about the earth of yourself, too.

What does it say in the Bible? It says, "And the earth standing in the water and out of the water."[5] What's it talking about—"In the water and out of the water"? It's talking about a human baptism, you see—someone standing in the water and out of the water.

You have to understand that the geometrizing of God is the methodology of God. God has methods. If you will ever look under a microscope very carefully, or if you'll ever study cytology and the makeup of the various cells of the body and different cells of rocks and matter formations, you will realize that there is a natural geometry in the Lord's creation of material, of matter itself. And "matter" really means *mater* (from the Latin), or "mother." And, of course, our physicians have given this name to various parts of the body—like the *dura mater* of the brain and the *pia mater* and so on. So we have to understand all this.

Now, here we are creating mentally a chalice around the heart. The value of that chalice is purely a starting value. It's valuable as a point where you can begin your expansion of consciousness. You can go out and suddenly decide you're going to drown yourself in a chalice so big that you can't even imagine it around yourself. But it has to be relevant to what you can imagine.

You cannot make an infinite chalice—now, can you really? It has to be in the known universe. You have to deal with known objects, so you start out with the physical. You make your chalice bigger and bigger and bigger and bigger—and one of these days you come to the point where you can actually mentally decide that you're going to be within a chalice as big as the earth. And so you do!

Now, you may elect, instead of standing in a chalice, to stand in a pyramid or a cylinder or a square, a cube, or any other geometric object. And these thoughtforms can become the means of the expansion of your consciousness.

I particularly want to warn the people that no one who is interested in tethering themselves to reality should indulge in this to the extent of more or less living in a world of fantasy or delusion. These should be controlled experiments in consciousness, and you should be careful to engage in them only for a limited period of time—because I'm going to tell you about the lever. I'm not talking about the rising of the king of France. I'm talking about the lever that is the lever of relativity.

In other words, when you start these mental doings, you are starting a process in the macrocosm that is occurring now first in the microcosm. You will not be able to create that infinite chalice we spoke about. But your God Presence can. And the pattern for these doings must, according to cosmic law, occur from your level. You have to be the authority for your world.

So by the creation of these proper thoughtforms and the endowment of yourself with the desire to produce these states of consciousness that are representative of an expanded awareness, you have to make these forms and then release them into the Universal.

I recommend and I advocate holy prayer before doing so. I recommend protection from mighty Astrea so that you are not in any way being invaded by astral entities. I recommend care and consideration in the creation of these thoughtforms. And I recommend that after you have created them as large as you desire at a given time, that you then turn the thoughtform over to your God Presence for amplification.

Why? Because your God Presence has now received the mandate of your own authority to create. And whether you're awake or whether you're asleep or whether you're doing something else, your God Presence will take it up.

Do you know what that means—to "take it up"? Do you know the greatest healing that can occur in the whole world, for example, occurs when the God Presence does it? You in your human self can do nothing. When Jesus said, "I of myself can do nothing. It is the Father in me which doeth the work,"[6] he was making the statement regarding the transfer of authority by the dominion of the human will to the divine will and the power of the cosmic lever of relativity acting for man in the name of God. Do you see?

It is an involved process, but I have tried to reduce it to words that can be understandable by you. I personally have done a few things with this most effectively. And I know that it does work.

I suggest that you confine your early experiments of this nature to the more simple form, because a great deal depends upon your own standards of morality, decency, and the elimination from your world of conflicting images. By eliminating conflicting images, not filling your mind with all of the crud (if I may use the word) of the world and then expecting that you're going to start in and mix up this heavenly elixir with a human idea—it will not work as effectively. It may work a little, but I would be careful.

I would first try to purify the consciousness with the violet flame. I would have the highest motives in my doing, and I would make these determinations, and then I would work in the field of expanding my awareness and consciousness by the use of thoughtforms.

These thoughtforms also may include such objects as wings. I have spent a great deal of time with the thoughtform of wings. And I find that this is most valuable for elevating your consciousness. In order to have wings, I suggest that you use Beethoven's *Ninth Symphony*, for example, the Grail music from *Parsifal*, by Richard Wagner, "The Ride of the Valkyries," or some of those high-quality classical renderings which are very inspiring and elevating to your consciousness. The *Lohengrin* music is also very good.

You use this music and then you envision a pair of wings, for example, on an hourglass, and you see the wings raising the hourglass. The idea is to elevate time into its proper use. And how better can you use it properly than to understand that God, who is eternity represented in the rising, is also magnetized, or drawn, into your image and then transferred to you—because you have the authority and because you have given that authority to your God Presence to act for you.

Without your mandate, without the mandate of prayer or the mandate of your decrees or the mandate of your desires in some manner voiced to the Spirit, there can be no manifestation. Basically, this is what was known long ago in some metaphysical movements as treasure-mapping. But this is by far a more advanced method of doing it—dealing with geometric figures and thoughtforms.

Now, as I've said before, there are all kinds of thoughtforms that are valuable to pregnant mothers, for example. These thoughtforms are particularly valuable if they will try to trace mentally the lines of some of the great Grecian statues so that they can bring these lines into physical manifestation. This is accomplished through first carrying the thoughtform up to their Christ Self and then to their God Presence—through their mandate, through their desire—and then calling for the perfect form to be brought down into their womb and utilized as the matrix which is then carried out by the body elemental of the mother and the formative elemental of the child.

Now, those who understand our work in detail will get a little more out of this, I realize. But I can't this afternoon try to expand on this to the extent of drawing maps of our whole work. So I must, of necessity, confine myself as I have to the explanation involving thoughtforms.

I want to deal also with color in regard to our meditation. Let's say that we have created this chalice colorless. We've created it in black and white. It is possible for us to embellish the thoughtform by the use of correct color, primarily pastel colors such as the beautiful pinks, the beautiful violets, the beautiful soft pastel yellows. All of these colors actually can be drawn mentally within the object of our thoughtform.

You may say to me, "Well, wouldn't the black and white be enough?" No. Because the black and white in reality is to a certain degree involved with the nature of the gray ones. While the white is all right, the moment you put any black into it at all, you are going to dilute your whole situation. You'll dilute the whole formula, you see. So I suggest that rather than use black, you use colors. Even in the formation of what you would consider to be the black and white lines that make up the form of the chalice, I would suggest that you actually use color rather than use black as the demarcation line for your subject.

I want to bring in another factor here which is extremely important in the use of thoughtforms, and that is the quality of tone. Now, after you've created, we'll say, a beautiful violet-colored chalice in the ethers, involving either the heart or the heart chakra or even the third eye or any other part of your being, you can qualify that with tone. And by "tone," I mean you can cause the object itself to appear, as an object of pink glass, as though you took a metal rod and caused the glass to vibrate so that it will emit a tone.

In other words, we are endowing our thought creation with the quality of a solid object and we are giving it the quality of creating a musical tone. Do you see what I mean? You can do this with any object having a geometric form.

Now, it is always desirable that we call for such a tone as the high C vibration, for example. The idea is that if we get the right tone, it will vibrate according to certain laws of the universe that are very, very secretive and very involved with manifestation. This science of intonation is a part of the "hidden wisdom" spoken of by Paul as the mystery of God. So I'm not permitted to give you the full structure of what you can do with tone in connection with the mind. But I can say that in this mental picture you can use tone, which gives a further solidity to your object from a mental standpoint, and thus whatever you send out will return to you. So, by this law, if you don't use the quality of a tone in your thought creation, you are going to lack something of value to yourself.

The more reality you can put into the mental image, the greater chances you have of this object materializing—not necessarily in the sense that you're going to bring forth beautiful little glasses that are going to drop from the Universal, as Baird Spalding described. This happens to be one of the steps, however. But I'm talking about improving and expanding awareness and consciousness through guiding your thoughts along these geometric lines, which is one of the first steps that you're going to have to take before you can use the creative abilities that God has given you.

Later on you can use this in symmetry such as the molding of sculpture. You can actually mold and sculpt, if you wish, using these principles. But I think that the person who begins to work first in the realm of mind and form and cosmic symmetry has a better chance of executing this in the world of form than the person who does not.

I recommend to all of you who are interested in these experiments that you engage in them for a limited time rather than a maximum time. If you do engage in them a maximum time, you may find that you will be subject to potentially harmful influences. But by using them just for a short time, like five minutes once or twice a day, you'll begin to condition your mind and your spirit and your being to your creative abilities.

And these creative abilities will come out in all of your work. You will begin to understand how to use your physical senses in an improved manner. You will understand that you are working with the fingers of the mind and with the creative ability of the mind through the use of these thoughtforms, and later you will transfer your sensory awareness to your fingertips.

This means that you will be able to have an expanded awareness in your lower consciousness (as well as in your higher consciousness) and increased sensitivity in your analyses of conditions and things and people. You will find that you can, with greater ease, pick up on vibratory patterns and that you will be less subject to the mental manipulations of various people who are using witchcraft and various forms of black magic against you, for example, or against anyone in the world, because you will be stronger for using these images. Through the creation of these thoughtforms under God's direction, through your I AM Presence, you will find that you will have greater control of your creative aspects than you have ever had before.

Now, don't expect this control to manifest immediately. It may not do so for a period of three or four months. But if you keep building into your consciousness your valuable experiments in the use of thoughtforms for the expansion of consciousness—purely for the use of good—you will be strengthening your mental body and your creative faculties.

I recommend to you, then, that you try this—but don't make it a god to yourself. This is only one of the creative aspects of life. There are many.

So now you are dealing with a tone, you're dealing with a color. In our recognition of the use of these creative faculties, a great deal is to be obtained. Man is actually preparing to enter into his own divinity. In reality, he was made in the divine image. This is one way he can return to that pure image.

What a silly thing that people are stressing all of this "in sin did my mother conceive me." Well, condemnation really is a tool of the forces of evil and it is not to be used by the spiritual aspirant on the spiritual path. He should not use it against others or against himself. Condemnation is stultifying. It prevents a man from actually realizing what things are all about—what is real about himself and what is illusory.

So I think maybe, just out of the interest of further enhancing your creative ability, I will give you a little skit that I sometimes do for the benefit of some people.

They'll come up to me and they'll ask me a question and they'll say, "Do you know this?" or "Do you know that?"

And I'll say, "Well, not knowing with any great degree of certainty, I therefore hesitate to respond to you, fearing that I might thereby prevaricate and suffer dire calamity, which has naught to do with the indubitable angelic acclamation of the ineffable austerity of the approaching woes, or the incontrovertible inexhaustibility of divine providence. By now I hope that your sufficiency is quite suffancified, because any more'd be a vulgar superfluity."

This is the sort of thing that really doesn't do anything for you, but it probably entertains you a little bit.

So I want to bring to your attention that creative ability is possible through the use of geometric figures. And I also want to take up the spiral because this is a delightful mechanism.

We are dealing now with the circle, or the laws of eternal cycles.

We can create a golden cycle. And then we can attach this cycle mentally to the next cycle. The way to do it is with the spiral—then you have a natural flow, you see. You have no interruption if you do it with circles.

Can you imagine piling circles one on top of each other like a bunch of dinner plates? You begin to wonder, after a while, if they're all going to fall down. So instead of that you just connect them in one beautiful flow—and it's a spiral staircase that leads to the stars!

Well, you know, you would be absolutely amazed when you begin working with these figures to realize that God used geometry so wonderfully to illustrate to humanity their own natural abilities to scale the stars in creative thought—because this is very practical. Through these exercises, uneducated men can suddenly become educated. Why? Because we are dealing with the automation processes.

I think most of you are familiar with the Russian scientist Pavlov and the "conditioned reflexes." It was a matter of placing sensing devices in the mouth of a dog to register the saliva. Pavlov found that by ringing a dinner bell and then feeding the dog, he could measure the saliva that would always come whenever the dog would be fed. Well, later on he took away the food and rang the bell and he still got the saliva. So he began to understand the matter of conditioned responses, you see.

Now unfortunately, the Pavlovian theories have been used in a negative way by Lavrentiy Beria, who used to be with the NKVD, or the Soviet secret police. They used it in a wrong way as a hypnotic device to manipulate and control political prisoners in times of war and to influence people in various nations where they could use these principles against them. But this was a very limited thing.

That was only a first step for man to understand the spirals of the cosmos and the controls that can be actually used by us for our betterment—to help ourselves and also to guard against the influences of other people who have nefarious ideas, who don't yet understand the principles that God has given us of "live and let live."

We have no right to try to influence anybody else against their free will. God doesn't practice it, does he? But we have every intent of practicing for ourselves the taking of dominion over our world and the developing of our own creative ability.

If we don't develop it, somebody else isn't going to develop it for us—are they? Do you believe they are? They can't, can they? It's impossible. We have to develop it for ourselves. Each of you will have to follow these experiments.

It's like the dead language of Latin, for example. You have a scholar go ahead and learn to speak Latin. Well, you say, it's a dead language. Who wants to speak Latin? But the mental gymnastics involved in the speaking of Latin prepare him for the understanding of almost every other language on the face of the earth, and they give him the ability to think properly.

I think we should understand the need to make ourselves do these things just the same as we eat our daily bread. We've got to become a well-rounded person, a person who is able to utilize the mechanics of the Spirit in the creating of form.

I happen to believe that even when you come to the point of your ascension and you come to the point where you have risen to be, more or less, a god of another solar system—did you hear what I said? I said a god of another solar system. You. Yes, you. That's who I'm talking to. As the Psalmist said, "Ye are gods."[7] Somewhere along the pathway, if you're going to be "children of the Most High," you've got to master all of these things that deal with the control and creation of form and substance.

And form and substance is very important to Spirit. Because Spirit created it for a reason. There is a raison d'être to that, you see—to the creation of substance. And actually what we're trying to do with these thoughtforms is to give you a creative power and a control of your own life and your life energies.

It's a pantomime that eventually will become a very effective means of helping you to grow spiritually. Yes, it could be used negatively. But if you do that, you'll pay and pay and pay. So I pray to God that nobody will ever use it in a negative way but just use this knowledge to try to take your first toddling steps in dealing with energy from a higher level.

God bless you and thank you for your attention.

April 10, 1971
Colorado Springs, Colorado

CHAPTER 9

Instruction on Evoking the Illumination Flame

M indful of the fact that the great central problem of the earth tonight and in this age is perhaps the dispersion of ignorance in the world that passes as knowledge, we must consider the need for calling forth or evoking the illumination flame. This flame has the power to strip the mind and being of man of the misunderstandings that are like an arrow shot that don't make the mark. And therefore we are able through this flame to understand when we have not scored in our thinking, in our realizations, when these realizations fall short of the mark of reality, when these realizations are distortions of the original and true plan.

And so what we need to do, then, is recognize that wisdom is not mere words. It is the ability to communicate the eternal knowledge of the Father to ourselves and all mankind that passes all understanding of the finite world.[1]

We may reduce matters to a formula to be accepted or believed, but a formula that is without the actual inherent patterns of deliverance is actually meaningless to the individual because it is not practical. And so, we are not interested in a montage of mere symbols that have no translatable meaning or reality to ourselves, but we are interested in those symbols that are transmitted to us by the Presence, by the Christ, which will fulfill the need for spiritual transmutation within our consciousness.

So as we do this decree, "Golden Flame from the Central Sun," let us realize that we are not invoking unreality or impractical manifestation. We are invoking a flame that has within it the tangible and inherent power to change mortal thought and feeling, to change the very principle of understanding within ourselves, so that when the divine matrix is lowered it is not, then, communicating to us an uncertain sound,[2] but it is communicating to us a certain sound and the realization of how this may be applied in our world—or, in the absence of the possibility of actually using it as an application consciously, of how we may accept the inner workings of the flame so as to produce inner wisdom or comprehension by creating within ourselves the matrices of wisdom, which then become the means by which we will understand not only physical things—physical wisdom, knowledge of words, semantics, all these things—but also spiritual things, which will be inwardly interpreted as they pass through this matrix, which is actually a foundation of Christ-reality. Do you see?

So let us give this decree with this thought in mind. And let this be a calm, knowing decree that will evoke that flame, with no mortal feeling that we ourselves are actually acting, but that the flame and the beings to whom we call are doing it, and they are fulfilling the fiats that we make. And there is no question that these fiats are being fulfilled. In the calm knowing of this, then, you see, we are able to actually experience the release or fulfillment of our invocation.

January 28, 1970
Colorado Springs, Colorado

GOLDEN FLAME FROM THE CENTRAL SUN

In the name of the beloved mighty victorious Presence of God, I AM in me, Holy Christ Selves of all earth's evolutions, beloved Alpha and Omega, beloved Helios and Vesta, beloved Great Central Sun messengers, all cosmic beings, powers, activities, and legions of Light, the beloved God and Goddess Meru, and all who serve Illumination's flame, beloved Guru Ma and Lanello, the entire Spirit of the Great White Brotherhood and the World Mother, elemental life—fire, air, water, and earth! I decree:

> Golden flame from the Central Sun, (3x)
> Expand thy Light through me today! (3x)
> Golden flame from the Central Sun, (3x)
> Transmute all wrong Illumination's way! (3x)
> Golden flame from the Central Sun, (3x)
> Direct our youth into action God's way! (3x)
> Golden flame from the Central Sun, (3x)
> Illumination's flame, fore'er hold sway! (3x)
> Golden flame from the Central Sun, (3x)
> Illumine the earth by Christ-command! (3x)
> Golden flame from the Central Sun, (3x)
> Thy beauteous power I now demand! (3x)

> Take dominion now,
> To thy Light I bow;
> I AM thy dazzling Light,
> Golden flame so bright.
> Grateful for thy ray
> Sent to me each day,
> Fill me through and through
> Until there's only you!

I live, move, and have my being within a mighty pillar of Illumination's golden flame from the heart of God in the Great Central Sun and my very own individualized Mighty I AM Presence, beloved Alpha and Omega, beloved Helios and Vesta, and all who serve God's victorious golden Light radiance which blesses and heals, illumines and seals me and all mankind forever in the Light of God that never, never, never fails.

CHAPTER 10

Developing Ascended Master Love

Now first of all, before we even go into this subject very thoroughly, let us ask ourselves this question, "What is divine love?"

"Oh," you say, "it's very simple. It means the love of God, and God is love. I've heard this since I was a little girl in Sunday school, that God is love. It's very simple." But let us now ask you this question, "Is it really as simple as people say that it is?"

I think it may be simple, that is, the idea of divine love, but apparently people have different ideas of just what it is. And therefore it is not simple in the sense that there is no common denominator in the minds of most people as to just what divine love is. People often feel that any love, any feeling of kindness toward another person or even toward themselves is divine love. Some people feel that love for Nature is divine love.

Now mark you well, I did not say that it was not. I did not say that divine love was not love for Nature. I did not say that divine love was not love for your fellowman. It may well be all of these things in the right perspective, but I am sure you will agree that divine love must be more for the simple reason that God, the Creator, is more than the sum total of the parts of creation.

In other words, you have man made in his image,[1] the scriptures report. Fearfully and wonderfully made,[2] our senses report to us, for as we examine the fabric of our physical body, the way it functions, we realize that it is a work of art in itself. The inbreath of the atmosphere, the exhalation of impurity, the constant re-energizing and recharging of the body by the intake of food and air and water, these speak to us of divine love because divine love has wrought well in our body. And today we're living in a time when people identify very much with their body.

Others, of course, who are more polarized along the line of the intellect are perhaps more inclined to identify with the mind. And they think that their mind is very wonderful, and of course it is. Still others are more inclined to identify with the power.

That's why we're going to talk on developing these three aspects of God—developing divine love, developing divine wisdom, and developing divine power. We have placed love first because love is the fulfilling of the whole law.[3]

When we begin to ask ourselves just what divine love is, we see that it is much more than just a feeling. And perhaps we should start, then, by saying what love is not, that is to say, what love is not exclusively. It is certainly not just a feeling. And if it is just a feeling, it is the greatest feeling there is anywhere in existence. But it is not just a feeling. Divine love *activates* feeling. It animates. It inspires. It makes you feel good.

But divine love, strange as it may seem, can sometimes make the human feel just a little uncomfortable. You remember that Jesus said, "I am not come to send peace on earth but a sword."[4] So there we see a strange statement. He talked about a sword. How can a man of God, the Son of God, talk about a sword and say he's not come to send peace on earth but a sword? We ask ourselves that question. And we have the answers before us, all around us, but many times we are not aware of the answers. We see the answers, but we do not see them.

That which makes the human comfortable may not be divine love at all. But that which makes the soul comfortable may be divine love. In other words, we cannot say that divine love is tons of vegetables or food. This is the harvest season. We cannot say that divine love is just a lovely home to live in. We cannot say that divine love is just a wonderful education or a great deal of money or many friends or a good husband or a good wife or fine children or a good reputation, although all of these things are desirable.

These things can be the product of divine love. But let's be honest with one another. People have a good home who have no belief in God whatsoever. There are millions of people who do not believe in God that live in good homes and wear good clothes and have nice-looking children and drive nice cars and have status and a good job and security, and they say they're very happy. But they do not have divine love because they have no love for God whatsoever. They'll admit this. They don't even believe in God.

So we see that if we look at the outer and say that this is divine love, which it really is, but to be divine love it has to touched from within—the golden tone to this picture, the pink tone, to be "in the pink," the blue tone that gives you that expansive feeling from the wild blue yonder, you know, to Almighty God, the infinite power. All of this starts within and then works out.

Let us ask ourselves again and again, what is divine love? We might even drop the "divine" for a moment and ask ourselves, what is love? I think that most people believe that love is a feeling that they have for someone else and that is all it is. But Jesus and Saint Paul gave us a great deal of insight on divine love. Jesus said of the commandments, "A new commandment I give unto you, that ye love one another."[5] And he also said something to the effect that if thou shalt love the Lord thy God with all thy heart and thy neighbor as thyself that you shall fulfill all of the commandments.[6]

Somehow or other, if we look very closely, we find that divine love and divine law are very close to one another. The Law of God by which he framed the universe is very close to divine love.

You know the place in Revelations where it states that God measured the temple so many cubits this way and that way.[7] This, of course, is the architecture of the New Jerusalem. *Jeru* is "new," and *Salem* is "peace." And so we read in that, "the new peace." The ever-new peace of God is brought about by the architecture of heaven. And the architecture of heaven is reflected in law. And law is love, and love is law.

Unfortunately, somewhere along the line, our emotional body has become entangled, and so we have come to think of divine love as a feeling. It is a joyous feeling, we say. And we identify with the feeling of love, just as men and women identify with the good feeling they get out of prayer rather than the subject to whom they are praying.

It is one thing to enjoy praying. However, I must in this lecture give you the honest facts, because we are going to show how to develop divine love—but in order to develop it, we must understand what it is and what it is not.

People actually enjoy praying. Some of the great yogis in India have said that people enjoy meditating on God because they get such a good feeling out of it. And actually, a lot of people enjoy not being burdened with any responsibility whatsoever, and therefore they like to feel that their religion becomes a haven, a refuge for themselves where they can escape from the world. And divine love to them is a haven, a place of refuge, somewhere they can escape from reality.

Now, I don't say that reality is out here in the street. That is a very unreal condition. Certainly it is not the love of God in manifestation. But at the same time, we must have discrimination to see what is coming up through the tree, because the scriptures read, "The ax is laid to the root of the tree. And every tree that bringeth forth or beareth not good fruit shall be hewn down and cast into the fire,[8] for the fire shall try every man's work of what sort it is."[9]

The fire will try the work because only the good can endure and only divine love can endure forever. You cannot perpetuate anything that is less than divine love. And we can deceive ourselves as religion has done and as religious people have done for centuries. Again and again we can trick ourselves into substituting a feeling or a sense for a reality from within, you see.

God is reality. God is truth. God is light. And the love of God is the love of truth and the love of light and the love of grace and graciousness. It's much more than that, but it is the love of love—but for its own sake, not for the sake of the person who is the lover. This is the love that one feels for the beloved that exceeds the love one feels for oneself. And this is the love which God has given unto us, each one of us. He has loved us with a greater love than he has loved himself. And he has taken the substance of his being—body, mind, soul consciousness, and comfortable identity of perfection—and he has poured that out lavishly upon mankind in an unworthy state in order that they might, through learning to love this grace which he is—this power, this wisdom, this love which he is—through emulating it, that they might become godlike, that they might be formed in the image in which he created them.

Man is not manifesting the life of "in the image of God created he him." Man is manifesting an image of his own creation, which stems from a lack of divine love and an externalization of selfishness. But men are not aware of that selfishness. They think that they are selfless. Again and again we find man creating laws which he then lives by, and he believes that these laws which he has created and lives by are God's laws. These laws have become translated through his mind and feeling into a reality which is not congruent or does not correspond with the reality that others have, and thus there have been schisms and splinters and divisions all over the world from the very beginning of time, created in the name of religion and in the name of God, whereas there is but one reality, and this reality Jesus declared. This reality Saint Germain declared. This reality Morya declared. It was this reality that Morya searched for when he came as Melchior to the feet of the babe, the Messiah. And it was this reality that gave the elixir of life to Saint Germain, that that enabled him to endure century after century—because he drank of the cup of true divine love, which endures.

Nothing can endure forever except that love of God. All else must pass away, because the moment you drop down to become a lesser object than perfection, you immediately drop into what we must call "transition" or the realm of change. And that is all death is. Death is not real. Death doesn't really happen. If it does, then every night when you go to sleep you die, as Saint Germain has pointed out in various ways. Saint Paul pointed it out, perhaps the best way, when he said, "I die daily."[10] And so people do die daily. They die to conditions that they are unhappy about and they die also in the sense of passing away from consciousness in the hours of sleep.

Now, then, we are beginning, I think, to see a little bit of what love is. Love must be the fulfilling of the Law. And the Law must be the fulfilling of love. They must come full circle together. Somehow or other, we have interpreted the Law as harsh. But I think it would be a far greater deprivation if the Law did not function. Supposing that the sun decided not to come up some day. Supposing the sun decided it would violate the law of the cycles and it would remain— of course, you know and I know that the sun doesn't come up. The earth turns on its axis. But you see, supposing the earth decided to stop right there somewhere in space, and it wouldn't turn. What would happen to the side of the earth where there was no sunlight? And what would happen to the side of the earth where the sun continued to bake and bake and bake? We would have freezing cold on one side of the planet and we would have Sahara Deserts on the other and people would be baking and burning up. And all of our air-conditioning systems would not cool the planet.

What would happen to the cycle of photosynthesis if the Law did not function properly? What would happen to the plants of the world? They would die. And when the plants did not live, what would happen to the atmosphere as man continued to pour out carbon dioxide and the plants did not consume it and so it accumulated upon the planet?

The circulation of truth is very important because there are not too many people that really understand truth in depth. They understand surface truth. Certainly, if I meet you out here, and you come in this yard and, as you're walking in the yard I say, "Oh, there's Marie Smith"—supposing this is someone that I know or that comes here. And I say, "Isn't that wonderful? I'm so happy to see her." And I rush out and I grab both of her hands in mine and I say, "Oh, Marie, I'm so happy to see you. It's a real delight to see you." And she exchanges the same pleasantry with me. People observing may say, "How loving and kind these people are! How loving and kind the people are at the Summit!"

Well, this is a casual observation. You will find this type of love expressed many places in many churches. You may find that even in concerts or among musicians and doctors or at medical fraternities. You may find it everywhere. The outer expression of divine love, of love, is that what it is? Or is it but the outer expression of the niceties of life?

Now, certainly we don't frown on that. I approve of warmth and friendship and kindness and these external conditions, as I am sure you do. But there is a great deal more than this surface type of love. This type of love one person once referred to as "ooshy-gooshy." That was the word that one person that I know used to refer to the type of love that bubbles over, it's effervescent on others. I think it's nice to see effervescent people. I personally like them, but I also like people who are restrained, as well, because they're both manifesting the type of feeling that they feel is all right for them. It is their bearing that is manifesting.

But what is most important is what is happening inside of the person. If the love of God, then, is not exactly the externals but is an internal action of the givingness of God to us, and our love of

God means the givingness of ourselves to him, how does it affect our relationship with one another?

I would say rather profoundly, for this simple reason: that if you and I are giving ourselves to God without reserve, and he is giving himself to us without reserve, then we would be very kindred spirits. And we should be most harmonious by nature and internally with one another, but not necessarily exhibit all of this in our surface relationships.

I'll give you an example. Supposing that we were running a dairy farm here and all of you ladies were taking care of the goats and the men were taking care of the cows and I was working for the owner of the farm, I was the overseer. I would send a group of the girls out to clean the goats and take care of the goats and milk them and bring the milk in and the men out to take care of the cows. And then you people would begin having a high old time out here in the barns and on the way to the pasture and you'd begin wasting time, and you would be doing things that would defeat the purpose of the farm. If I was the overseer responsible for it and I would come up to you to discuss this, would I then say to you, "Oh, you did a wonderful thing," if you were actually wasting time and not doing your job properly?

I don't think I should at all, because as the overseer I would have the responsibility for the whole establishment, and I would naturally have to speak to the sub-overseers and then, if necessary, to the whole group to see that the condition that would be wrong would be corrected. And if necessary, if all of these people were truly supposed to be following God, I would not necessarily have to speak to them with absolutely ooshy-gooshy type of language.

If necessary, I could straighten them out with a very sharp word, because God is not responsible for man's wrongdoing, but man is responsible for it. And we, then, if we are in positions where we are overseers of one another, we would have to deal with the human, and the human is sometimes rebellious and sometimes stubborn, and therefore we might express a word of sharpness, certainly not to God, but to the human. And this would not be out of order at all, but someone looking on might say, "Oh, I think that's terrible. They're not expressing divine love."

Well, divine love would not let the wrong type of action go on again and again and again with no correction whatsoever of that actionm, because this would be producing the conditions that make for transition. In other words, these are dying conditions. Anything less than perfection has to be changed sometime, somewhere. And even the law of containment is a definite law of love if it's handled properly. "Whom the Lord loveth he chasteneth," I quote, "and he scourgeth every son whom he receiveth."[11]

What this means is that the ego of a person may be corrected or curbed or scourged by God either directly through conscience or through circumstances in life, but this does not need to interfere at all with divine love. In fact, it reinforces divine love—if it's properly accepted, if you accept the word of your teacher.

Supposing you have a schoolteacher. In fact, I can go back to my Latin teacher. She was probably the meanest school teacher that I had, yet I learned more from her than any other teacher I ever had because she made me work. And I was just a bit frightened of her. But I one time had a talk with her in private and I learned that she was really a very loving person underneath it all.

During World War II, I served under a Captain McVicker, who was of reputation the type of man that is very severe, and almost the entire squadron was completely afraid of this man—their whole being was filled with fear. I had a private interview with him, which I sought, and he assisted me in finding my way out of a very difficult problem, as a father would with a son.

And I said to him, "Captain McVicker, you are a priceless person, but you're not at all the type of man that people think you are."

He said, "And don't you ever tell them that I am not that. If you do, I will certainly really become that for you. I want you to keep my image very severe, for I am finding it very helpful in controlling the people." And this is often true in life, that some of the people that we might have a little rough spot with turn out to be our best friends after we get to know them, if we are willing to accept.

In developing divine love, then, I would like to point out some of the ways in which you can do it. First of all, Jesus said, "Thou shalt love the Lord thy God with all thy heart." Then the first law is to realize who the Lord thy God is.

The Lord thy God is certainly not external, but is the true Being of man, the true Creator of man, the true I AM Presence, in other words. And what is the I AM Presence? Notice that *I AM* is tied to the word *Presence*. And *Presence* denotes eternal reality—not temporal reality but eternal reality—because it deals with omnipresence, everywhere present forever.

I AM denotes that your being is tied to that, certainly not your earthly being, for before you came forth from your mother, you first came forth from God. Therefore you didn't begin to be as a baby in this embodiment, but you were long, long, long before that.

So the I AM Presence or Be-ness or Being, this is where you must pay your allegiance. You must recognize that this is something that, while it may be outside of yourself, is also within yourself. You see what I mean? The threefold flame of that Presence is anchored within you. It must conform to the Chart of Your Divine Self, because the Chart has the pattern, you see. No matter how we try, we can never get away from the pattern of the Chart. It's accurate. It's correct.

So we must turn to God and recognize our Presence, our I AM Presence, as our God. But we must realize that the individualized I AM Presence is the symbol of the I AM Presence from the Great Central Sun, the universal I AM Presence. And that is our God, the God of very gods.

You see, you have the I AM Presence individualized. And that is the focus of God for you, the divine image. Then you have the source of your own I AM Presence, which is the God of very gods, the universal one I AM Presence from which all I AM Presences are projected through mighty light rays from the Great Central Sun.

So we must understand that we're dealing with reality and with permanent reality. And we must understand, in order to develop love for this permanent reality, that this permanent reality has no part of error whatever. And we must develop the feeling of being very impersonal with ourselves if we're going to develop love for this I AM Presence. We can give no quarter whatever to the human of ourselves if we're going to develop love for the Mighty I AM Presence, if we're going to develop ascended master love.

Our own human is the first one we must deal with rather than deal with someone else's human. And I'm going to tell you at this point exactly what happens in the student body in almost every religion, in almost every organization, including our own: practically everybody begins to practice some form of criticism or condemnation or judgment against someone else's human before they start taking care of their own.

This is very, very natural. But if we take care of our own human first, our very attitude will be so charged with ascended master love that other people near us will feel that this is not an action of our human, but they'll feel that it is an action of the universal law and the universal law of love. And therefore you will get far less resistance or resentment from people if you're acting from that plane, you see. And you will be developing ascended master love and retaining it, because your motive is what transfigures you.

I'm going to tell you something that may sound a little unpleasant, but it's important. There are a lot of people in positions such as I am in right now—lecturers, ministers, speakers, teachers, and even chief laymen in many religions—who enjoy correcting other people. They get a charge out of finding flaws in people. They are happy about it. If you didn't have some sort of fault that they could pick on, they wouldn't like you too well. They like to correct you and they look for these things because it gives them an opportunity.

This is wrong motivation to begin with, because it is deriving plea-sure from evil. And it is completely an enemy of developing ascended master love.

So right motive is the feeling of being the great giver to the God who is the greatest giver. In other words, you recognize your I AM Presence in this development as the greatest giver that has ever existed or ever will exist now and forever. And then you determine that you are going to be just as great a giver to God of yourself as he is of himself to you.

This creates a divine balance because God will never be outdone by you. And the more that you give of your love to him, the more he is in debt to you. And he pays his debts so promptly that you just keep right on gaining his love, which is infinite, in your finite state. And he keeps on getting more of you. And what he does with it is he changes it into more of him and sends it back to you.

And then, you see, you function from the plane of right motive, and that's the ascended master motive. Motive is really tied with motor, isn't it? Motor and motive, it is the force that drives you. The force that drives you, then, is divine love. In all of your doing, "with all of thy getting, get understanding."[12] And in this case, with all of thy getting of God, see that you give this same spirit of God to others who are your brothers. And this motive will change the whole picture.

I have functioned from this motive, I'll be frank with you. And I have walked up to people functioning from the divine motive. And I have found that there are still people that will become angry when you correct them, even though you are functioning from the divine motive. And this is a case of where you have to love yourself properly. You cannot be swayed by the human of any other person at all. But that doesn't mean that you should be aloof or rejoice in the fact that the individual has not responded properly to you or to your ministration. God does not. So in developing love for God, you must be as God is.

There was a man, I think his name was Sheldon, a minister who lived many years ago, who wrote a book called *In His Steps*.[13] And one of the mottoes of the book was, "What would Jesus do?" And the businessmen in this story pasted this motto or engraved this motto in their offices, and they applied this to everything that they did. The mayor of the town, when he had to make a decision, would ask himself, "What would Jesus do?" And then he'd think very carefully as to what Jesus would do if he were holding the same job that this man had. The whole town was transformed by that one slogan, "What would Jesus do?"

Jesus is one of many ascended masters. And so there's nothing wrong with saying, "What would the ascended masters do?" when you come to deal with any situation. And in the development of ascended master love, you must ask yourself, "How would the masters develop their ascended master love? How do they develop ascended master love themselves?" The masters are still developing it. They have told us themselves that God is infinite. They have told us that after the ascension, they still go on and on and on transcending whatever they have of attainment and attunement. Therefore we have to admit that there is infinite possibility.

So the question is a worthy one, "How do the masters develop ascended master love?" And now we come to the prime point here, and that is the activation of right vision. Vision has been referred to again and again. "Without vision, the people perish."[14] Now, the wrong concepts about the world and about Nature and about one another can cut us off so that we are living in a world of our own making. We are not facing reality at all.

I know that I have stood on lecture platforms here and there in different parts of the world, and I know that I have gone with great love into cities where I have prayed valiantly for the people by God's grace. And I know with all my heart that I have sought earnestly to do God's will for different people, and I have had in the audience occasionally, quite rarely but occasionally, people who have said that they had never seen anyone that came closer to resembling the devil in embodiment than I did. The reason I'm telling you that is to show you that this was the definite opinion of one person in one city.

I have also had them where they glorified me and singled out some member of the audience or someone that was associated with the activity or some other religious leader and came to me and said that they were the devil in embodiment.

Well, I have checked into many of these conditions quite closely, and I have found out that there are a lot more good people that are trying to do well than there are people that are trying to do ill. And most of the people who do ill are misguided people. But the fact remains that they have the wrong vision, and therefore it is important that we get the correct vision about the masters in order to develop the love that the masters have.

One of the qualities that many people admire in the masters is their domination, supposedly, over outer conditions. I'm supposed to walk over here and just disappear in a puff of smoke. This is what we call the sense of the miraculous. They feel that the masters could do that. The masters could go over here and disappear and reappear at will, and they are in love with this idea for themselves because their imagination is stimulated by it. Perhaps when they were little children, they played at this game of "I'll go over here and disappear," and it gave them a feeling of elation—but it's an egotistical feeling.

I know that I shunned this attitude for many years. In fact, if I may be permitted this reference, I didn't know who I was in a previous embodiment when I started my studies under the Master's direction. I had no knowledge of any of my embodiments at all. And so I said to the Master one time, "You've never told me who I was. I don't know anything about my past lives, and I'm not going to ask you to tell me. When you get ready to tell me, you will. And if you never tell me, I'll consider perhaps it's a wise thing or you would have told me." And I just simply dismissed it from my mind and I left it in God's hands. I did not probe it.

Then one day, the Master began to reveal one embodiment. And I was rather pleased and I thought, "Well, that's really amazing, very amazing." Well, then he revealed another one. And you know, in a very short space of time, I had seven or eight embodiments revealed. But you know, at the time he revealed it, it didn't make too much difference. I had outgrown the idea of that as being too important and I had gone on to other ideas. And I think the vision that I held was very important for me, as I look back over it now, the fact that I was willing to go on whether or not the Master pleased my human by revealing something that would make me feel that I had been someone either important or unimportant, famous or infamous.

You know, one is never sure whether they were incarcerated in the Bastille or whether they were walking along through the wheat fields with the Master. We all like to feel somehow or other that we were on the Master's side, not on Pilate's legions' side or perhaps the centurion who drove the nails through his hand. We don't want to see that kind of picture. Yet certainly that kind of a person needs salvation, don't they? They need it worse than the people who were walking alongside of him, and God wants them to have it.

So perhaps, however, it would be a good thing, in the moral climate in which we live, which has exterior righteousness emblazoned in people's being but feels that what they can get away with is all right—perhaps it would be just as well, then, if we didn't know all of our past embodiments, especially the infamous ones, because if people knew that we were not someone that was good or beautiful or famous, they probably wouldn't feel too kindly. How would you like the idea of Judas Iscariot sitting in here? Some people would be very uncomfortable. Of course, they wouldn't mind at all if Saint Peter was embodied in the flesh and sitting here. They might think that would be fine.

So what we must do is get away from our changing person in developing ascended master love. This does not mean cruelty.

It does not mean the impersonality that is cold or unthinking or unfeeling. It means a dedication to a higher image of ourselves. To develop a higher image of ourselves is to open the door for ascended master love, and we cannot mold it in the contemporary image of our friends.

We cannot mold it in the contemporary image of even the ascended masters in past embodiments before their ascension, because they made a few mistakes. In fact, Jesus himself told me. He said that if he had it to do over again, he would not have used the thongs in the temple and kicked over their tables. He would have spoken out, but he admitted to me that there had been a certain righteous indignation in his being at the time which prompted him to do it.

He quoted to me one of the old scriptures. He said, "The zeal of thine house hath eaten me up."[15] He was zealous for God. But he said, "Could I recommend today that you who follow after me should go out into the world and kick over these people's tables and overturn them? If you did, you would be incarcerated in prison and you would not be able to go on." And he said he got away with it in his day because of the followers he had. And the moral code and the code of that day was a little different than it is today. He was revered as a great rabbi and a great teacher and he got away with it. Today, of course, Jesus would have been locked up in Queens jail or in Bellevue in New York if he'd gone down the streets of the boroughs there and started kicking in the established business places.

I remember I was with Elizabeth one time up toward Rochester, New York, and I saw a car dealership up there that is occupying a church. They had taken over a church building, steeple and all— I think the bell was even in there. And they had on the church lawn huge signs for the car agency. I said to Elizabeth, "You know, this is one of the times I wish that I had the power to disappear, because if I could, I'd go in there and I'd start kicking things around, and I'd tell them, 'You've made my Father's house a house of merchandise.'"[16]

And then I'd disappear. I wouldn't dare to have them after me, because they'd lock me up."

And this is true. You couldn't get away with it today. But the Master showed me that he himself would not recommend this type of conduct today. Let all things be done decently and in order. Doesn't mean you can't abhor the things that are evil. Doesn't mean you can't speak out against them, but you have to do it in a proper manner, in what we call a Christlike manner. Without vision, the people perish. We must be transcendent about this.

The masters will be the first to admit that crudities of the past were refinements of the past. In other words, today we would consider some things crude, and yet they were the refinements of that age. Some of the refinements of today will become crudities of a future age, perhaps.

We must remember, then, that in developing ascended master love, the vision must transcend itself.

And it is not, then, just a feeling of good, but it does produce a feeling of good. It really does. But it must be more than the feeling. It must be a tie to the Presence in action through us. It must be a conscious tie, because that enhances it all. But we must understand what the Presence would do. We ought not to be blind to what the Presence would do. We must call for a revelation of the Presence.

I remember one time when this organization first started, I said to Master Morya, "If only I had a million dollars, if only I had ten or fifteen people that I could depend on, on the staff, if I only had this or had that, oh, we'd do wonders."

I want to tell you something. I have learned that the mere acquisition of dollars in itself is not nearly as important as learning how to spend that money to get the best results with the money that you have. And the masters started me out with pennies. And then the pennies became dollars and dollars became tens and the tens became hundreds and the hundreds became thousands to be used for his work. But I would not have known how to handle it at the beginning. I wouldn't have known what to purchase. My sense of values would have been wrong. And I've learned an awful lot over the past few years—when a dollar should be spent for advertising, how you can use it wisely.

For example, take this property at Beacon's Head, this very house here. We would spend three times what we're spending for this house if we were to go out and have Elizabeth and I live separately as a lot of pastors do, live in our own house and then have another building for the church, and then have another building for the printing press somewhere, an office building, you know, and then have another building to house the staff or have them living off somewhere else separately. We effect a tremendous savings. In fact, it makes it possible, and we have a much better place here, you see. So wisdom comes in many ways.

And also the people—I would not have known what to do with the people. It's a very strange thing, but you take the development of a business form, a record, the record-keeping parts of an organization like ours. This is fantastic. You can ask our staff. They'll tell you that it takes years to develop a certain system. These things are valuable factors of anything, even God's business. And it takes time.

And therefore the development of ascended master love takes time, but that's all we have. We have eternity, and we might as well start right and keep on going right. And one of the things that helps, then, to develop ascended master love is a sense of peace about it all, not a sense of flurry and hurry. But don't let that peace become the kind of thing that some people do.

Now, little Sean was taught by Tom Miller to say the slogan of the year, "Peace with honor." So he came down to have his dinner the other day and sat there and his mother was serving peas and he looked up and he says, "Peas with honor?" So you see you can actually have a certain amount of savoir faire on a thing like that. You can even have your peas with honor.

You can develop ascended master love about all these different things and be right-motivated, not wrong-motivated. There's a right way and there's a wrong way to do it all. And I'm sure that God will speak in the heart to us if our motives are pure. So let's have peace about it all, but let not that peace become the type of peace that is complacency.

Let's not be complacent and say, "Well, I've always done it this way." I talked to a man the other day who is connected with an organization that he knows—at the time that he spoke to me he knew it—he said he knew it was tied to the false hierarchy. They were imitating the ascended masters but they were not practicing it. And I said to him, "Why in the name of God do you stay in anything like this when you know what we are standing for?"

He said, "I started with them and I don't like the idea of change." Well, there's going to be an awful lot of changes wrought inside of all of us before we attain perfection, unless we're already perfect.

Now, if you're already perfect, and I'm already perfect, we don't need any changes. You can't change perfection to anything higher than perfection. You might be able to have divine transcendental-ism—God may improve himself, in other words. But at the same time, once you get up there into your ascension, you can't improve on that.

And we're not up there yet. We're down here. Whether we're here to teach and we're already perfect but we're just teaching per-fection—that's the only reason we're here—we all like to think that. We like to say, "I'm one of the guardian spirits, you know, that are down here." Everyone wants to be someone important—as at the masked Halloween ball that they had in Chicago. They called it a reincarnation party. Everyone came dressed as they were in their last incarnation, and they were all kings and queens. There were no common people there at all.

But let's face it. We're not kings and queens and we're not all knaves. We have very, very splendid people in the activity but we must learn to face the reality of ourselves. We must learn to capture the divine vision of what we shall be. I think it was Saint Paul who said, "Now we see through a glass, darkly, but then we shall see face to face. Now we know in part, but then shall we know even as we are known."[17]

And it is important to realize that the *then*, "*then* shall we know," is the key. And it also can be asked as a question, "When?" "Then" or "when," you see. When is the then, in other words, that this is going to happen? Now, of course, right now—the eternal now that is the same yesterday, today, and forever, the divine I-mage, the magic of the I AM Presence. And you as children of God must capture the vision of what divine love is and then outpicture what you see.

This is going to change. It won't all be understood at once. The masters have admitted that understanding has evolved. And what does "evolve" mean? It means "e" for energy (and this is almost always true universally) and "volve" from "revolve," which means to turn. Energy to turn. In this case, it is energy to return back to God from whence you came. It is the evolvement, the evolution, the turning of the soul within the field of energy so that it is moving forward toward the goal appointed by Almighty God.

And you can't be what you can't see. If you can't see God, you can't be God. Therefore the whole thing is the vi-son, v-i-s-i-o-n— the victorious I [eye] son—to realize that you are the son of victory rather than the son of defeat, to realize that your purpose is the purpose we stated first, the purpose of ascended master love. That is your purpose. Be specific. Make yourself identify with the purpose.

Today people identify with ethnic groups. They identify with creed. They identify with race. They identify with family and cir- cumstance, poverty and wealth. They identify with even feelings of fear or feelings of false security.

I don't know if you know it or not, but there are a lot of cults today in the religious field that actually encourage people to become ostriches. They want you to keep your head down in the sand and affirm over and over, "There is no other reality but this or that."

We are a hundred percent in favor of affirming divine reality.

But you have to have the discrimination that Christ had himself when he looked at the fig tree that was barren and said, "Let no man eat of thee anymore, ever again."[18] If you can't have discrimination to know the difference between good and evil, how in the world are you ever going to eschew evil and cleave to that which is good?

You have to know in yourself and in other people what is good and what is evil. Otherwise you might join the mescaline cult. Maybe you'll turn around, start taking some of these drugs that are going to give you hallucinations of floating around in the Mayan realm down in South America or floating around having visions and psychic experiences and beautiful colors, you know. They don't tell you about all the other side effects and the changes in personality.

I talked with a woman out in the West, and she said, "Everything is good." I said, "Yes." And then she went on to cite some more and she said, "That's good." And I said, "Yes."

It reminded me very much of the story I heard several years ago about the Chinese and Japanese having a war and how the Chinaman was in his laundry and the Japanese man came in and said, "We had a big battle last night. We killed four Chinese for every Japanese that was killed. Don't you think that's wonderful for us?"

The Chinaman says, "Yes. Very wonderful."

A few weeks later he came in with his shirts again. "We had a big battle. We killed three Chinese for every Japanese. Don't you think that's good?"

"Yes. Pretty good, pretty good."

Came in a little later, he says, "We killed two Chinese for every single Japanese that was killed. Don't you think that's good?"

"Yes," he says, with a big wide grin. "Very good. Pretty soon no more Japanese."

That's the way it is with some of these people, you see. They try to create the illusion that everything is good.

This woman told me this after I'd had a very galling experience.

It was a case of being invited to a party where I was supposed to be honored because of the work I'm doing for the masters. And I found that instead of being honored, I was being dishonored through attempts to involve me in human argument. I was asked questions which I tried to avoid about other people and other organizations that I did not care to discuss, and then I was condemned for it.

The person came back to me and said, "Oh, I think that's good. I think it's wonderful." "Well," I said, "I don't think anything that is discordant is wonderful. I think everything should be handled with God-control and with divine love."

And this is exactly what I am talking about today, developing divine love.

I think if you really practice divine love, there's something in your feeling world that you're a different person than those who just function from the plane of ego or ideation because they always feel that they are the doer. And this is another thing in developing divine love: Stop trying to feel that you are the doer of good, but become imbued with the idea that God through you is the doer of good, and then watch very closely that you apply to him for wisdom. Do you see what I mean? Apply your heart to God for wisdom to see that, as Morya wrote a man recently (in a private, confidential letter—I won't tell you who the man was), and at the very end of the letter the Master said to him, "I pray that the light that is in thee be not darkness."[19]

And that's the whole thing. Develop ascended master love by being the great giver, giving yourself to God, and being the great receiver by receiving from the great giver, God, all that he can give to you.

Be at peace about all this expansion. Be right-motivated. Don't be motivated in your relationship with others by things that are going to make you feel fat and pompous—you know what I'm talking about—but humble, contrite, and generous of heart. But don't even let your generosity become inflated by a feeling that because you have done so much for someone that they should be eternally grateful to you. You should be eternally grateful to them for providing you with an opportunity to do something, because if you didn't do anything, if you didn't act, you would never get there. We have to act and act and act again and again, because our victory is attained by a series of actions whereby God acts through us and fulfills his Law.

I run into people who say a statement that is a complete antithesis of what President Kennedy said.* They ask themselves, "What can this organization do for me? What can God do for me?" There is a complete cult of people today in America who actually flourish on the idea of prosperity as being first. They have actually put God behind and prosperity first. And they believe that if any of you people are not manifesting abundance of wealth, that this denotes a lack of spirituality. Sometimes God gives a great deal of wealth to people so that they can do a great deal of good with it. And then again, he tests the same people in another embodiment with a certain amount of lack so that they learn how to handle themselves and learn about how the other half of the world lives.

You have all these conditions. We are not judges of one another. We are brothers of one another. And in developing ascended master love, we must be mindful of our responsibility to purpose in whatever circumstance we find ourselves in, not to think, "What can God do for me?" but "What can I do for him on earth?"

It follows as the day the night, that when God himself sees you thinking how you can spread his work, spread his Word, make the world more beautiful, love nature more by appreciation of nature, study to show thyself approved unto God, so that you can understand more, that God is going to shower more wisdom upon you. God is going to bless you. You are going to develop ascended master love. It will not be a light that is within you that becomes darkness,

---

*In his inaugural address, January 20, 1961, John F. Kennedy said, "Ask not what your country can do for you—ask what you can do for your country."

but it will be a light that is light and gives light to other people. And then God will be glorified in that.

We can't do it from the human level, but we can try.

What I'm trying to say is that in the absence of spiritual guidance from on high . . .

Let us develop a situation for a moment here. I'm going to come back to that and I'm going to use that. Let's develop a situation. Let's say you meet Joe Smith out here, and he comes to you at the Stratford Motor Hotel and he says, "I have just joined the Summit and I want to know how to get out there to Beacon's Head. Can you help me?"

Let's say that somehow or other, you just don't like his looks at all. You say, "Well, that fellow doesn't even belong out there in the Summit. He's not dressed properly. He doesn't have the right manners. He looks to me like he's just a little bit goofy. I don't think I feel like telling him about how to get there or anything. I certainly don't want him in my car and to ride out there. Why, he doesn't even smell to us as if he took a bath this morning." It's quite a situation. Everything tells you something against Joe Smith.

Now, how do the masters regard this whole situation? What would the masters do in this situation? He wants to know how to get here. What's going to happen to you if you take him out here? Is this an opportunity or is this a time to be persnickety about it all and decide that you're going to?

Now, supposing you go to God. This is what I wanted to get at more than anything else. You go to God and the masters and you ask for guidance and the heavens are sheer lead. You don't get any answer at all. You say, "Dear Lord, help me. I want to know what to do with this thing. And help me quickly because he's standing here now and he's asking me. What shall I do? I don't know what to do."

In the absence of a reply from heaven, what do you do? When you're developing ascended master love, now, and you don't hear from God as to how to develop it and you ask and you don't receive on the instant—maybe he answered you but you didn't hear it—what do you do then, now? "What do I do now, Mama?"

You know what you do? You rely on the highest understanding that you have of what's right and wrong, don't you? You go by the things that you've been taught. And you make your own decision and then you abide by it. And if you feel that Christ would turn the man down—and you perhaps remember Dostoevsky's story about the leper, how this leper kept coming to him and the man didn't want to have anything to do with him, and he was told to embrace him. And toward the end he finally wrapped his arms right around the man and drew his leprous face right up to his and kissed him. And at that point he turned into the living body of Christ right in his arms. It's quite a story.

But the whole idea there is that you have to be the one to go by the Word of God when it's given and compare the word that you get with also the reality that you know, because once in a while, the sinister will come in on a curve.

I want to point out that it is very important that one learn to define what God is, what love is, and then to learn to distinguish in human situations and in life situations what is acting in your world. And then let God act. Let divine love, let ascended master love act through you, and that is the best development there is.

It's like the little private out in the battlefield. He says to the officer who is dying there, "But sir," he said, "I didn't go to West Point."

"I tell you," he said, "I'm making you the captain. Here's my uniform. Take my hat."

What's he going to do? He's commissioned on the battlefield. And that's the whole idea. You're commissioned down here by God —you're commissioned. It's the great command. "Go ye therefore into all the world and preach the gospel to every creature."[20] The commission from the masters is given to us to be emissaries of divine love. We can't get away from it. Maybe you say you're not as thoroughly trained as you'd like to be. Maybe you sense some lack in your world. What difference does it make? The master says, "Look, I'm giving you the commission now. Go and be that which I am." And in this case, the best way to develop divine love, the best way to develop ascended master love is to act the part of the master.

It's just sort of a vicarious at-one-ment, being in the framework of what a master would do. What would the masters do right now in this case? Begin playing the role of the master. Don't feel that it's a desecration. This is the final point I want to make. Play at being God, if you will. It's not a desecration. But don't deceive yourself when you play at it. Know when you're playing and when you're serious. You understand what I mean?

In other words, if you are acting the part of an ascended master, don't do it with pride. Don't go out there and try to impress somebody. And don't do anything in order to make yourself pompous or feel big. Do everything to make the universe big, to interpret the greatness of God to others, and you will automatically grow spiritually and expand and expand and expand and expand because you can't do it phonily. You can't do it by being a phony. You can only do it by being exactly the reality that God is.

The world is full of phonies. The only trouble is that most of them don't even know it. Ignorance is bliss. They'd be right with you. They'd be right here today. They'd be standing shoulder-to-shoulder with the masters if they knew better. Don't feel that you're superior to them. Feel grateful that God has given you this opportunity—as I do. I feel grateful. I don't feel I'm one whit better. I say, "But for the grace of God, there I would be."

And you know, if you will continue to feel this way, you will have so much light ultimately that it will rub off and rub off and rub off on these people. And more and more of them will start coming. "What have they got? They've got something. I know they've got something. There's something different about them. And it's quite wonderful."

We hear from the hotels at different times. They'll say, "You have such a nice group of people." At the Dodge House hotel they used to tell us what a wonderful group of people we had: "There's something different about your people. They're so friendly and yet reserved and they're courteous and they're just grand people. And they seem to have something. What is it?"

Curiosity? It attracts. And ultimately we ourselves as an organization expand.

Ascended master love will do it. Nothing else exceeds it. But it has to be real ascended master love. And that's why I opened this talk and started out asking what it is, what is ascended master love, because people have so many ideas about what it is that I felt it was very important to define it.

October 21, 1965
Vienna, Virginia

CHAPTER 11

Purity of Heart

We have all heard it said, "The pure in heart shall see God."[1] And so, with this in memory, most of us embarking on the spiritual path from the very beginning have recognized the value of purity of heart, because purity of heart is like unto a mirror of perfection. Purity of heart is like the perfect glass that reflects exactly what it sees because it has the silver applied to the back of it and it is true in its reflective quality.

The moment we create even a slight aberration in purity of heart, we change the base of the pyramid of life. The slightest aberration in the base of the pyramid manifests as crookedness in the apex. We need, then, from time to time to come to a place in our own thoughts where we true our worlds, where we true the mirror to make certain that it is reflective of God.

I believe that many people have gods made in their own image and in their own likeness. I do not think that the fact that people do this is of necessity what they intend to do.

We want, then, to speak of purity of heart and purity of mind and purity of being and refer to this great cosmic mirror we all must create to reflect the image of God as the most important ingredient to true divine seeing. And the trueing of our mirror is essential because if we do not keep it true, we are going to have warp in our manifestation.

Ours is no ordinary activity. The Summit Lighthouse organization from its very earliest inception has been founded upon progressive revelation, whereas most organizations are founded on dogma. There is a vast difference between dogma and progressive revelation. Dogma means that we have theorized and accepted our theories and systematized these theories and written them down and professed that "this is what I believe," whether or not we have actually proven it. And most of dogma cannot be proved to the satisfaction of the total universal man.

But progressive revelation can be proved if man will qualify for it. The whole problem, however, in this matter is that unless the mirror be true, what you see in the mirror may be only an anthropomorphic god, a god made in your image. And unless you have traversed the path far enough that the image that you wear is the image of God completely, you still have a considerable potential of human error in your thinking. It is, then, the grace of God and the grace of God alone that keeps us true and pure.

So I believe we should seek for this purity of heart which is the totality of the vision of man. The total vision must be purified. That's purity of heart as I see it.

Purity of heart does not mean that you just have your little heart down here washed, because you can't get at that heart with a physical body. It doesn't mean that you should just have a feeling, a situation where you feel good. And why do you feel good in many cases? You feel good because the sordid memories of something or other that you did against the law have been buried. They're buried in that merciful subconscious, which swallows them up, hoping to eventually transmute them. And you feel a little better because they're buried. It's like the murderer burying his mistakes and feeling that as soon as he's buried and covered over the last shovelful of earth, that he's taken care of everything.

Submersion of our inequities is not of necessity a guarantee that we have a pure heart. Submersion of our inequities means, very simply put, that the memories we have of any sordid doings whatever that we have ever done have been submerged to the level where we don't see them anymore, and out of sight, out of mind.

The question, then, comes to mind, are we supposed to sit and review and mull over all of the wrongs we think that we may have done in life? And the answer, of course, is no. I do not hold against the concept of burying these problems. Even though I seem to speak against it, I do not hold against it. But I would like to point out that this multitude of sins that people have had in their past lives and in the present life—and even in this moment, for that matter, we could still have sins of thought—ought to be submerged, because it is not proper that we should concentrate upon them.

And why is it so that we should not concentrate upon them? Because they will always engender self-condemnation. Therefore what we should do is continue to invoke the flame of transmutation and call upon the law of forgiveness. We should do that every day. Let God through his sacred fire allow what we call the penetration of the sacred fire to go down into the subterranean regions and burn out of our consciousness the cause, effect, record, and memory of all conditions that are unwanted, undesirable, and impure in our lives. Let God do it. This is important. And we must have faith in his forgiveness.

One of the biggest tricks of the enemy in existence is to say to our mind, "You know, sometime, somewhere you did something wrong" and resurrect the memory of this wrong. Then when the wrong comes back, condemnation returns, and with condemnation comes inefficiency in functioning as a true spiritual being.

Man no longer functions, then, as he ought to function. He not only fails to transmute his wrongs but the wrongs that he revives in memory may become revived, then, in activity because he may say to himself by reason of excuse, "Well, I'm beginning to think that

272   DISCOURSES ON COSMIC LAW • 1

I did this or that wrong in the past and so maybe there really isn't any hope for me." And that is the most stupid thing any person can do. It is utterly stupid because Christ has said, God has said (it's all the same), "Be ye perfect."[2] We are supposed to be perfect—but the perfection has to be in the perfection of God.

I wanted to bring this out because purity of heart is something that a lot of people fail to really understand. Purity of heart is a condition of reflecting the heart of God in our own lives. It has nothing to do with good and evil in ourselves. The good and evil in ourselves will both melt away when we reflect enough of God. That's what is meant by the statement that God made concerning Abraham the patriarch when he said he would not impute sin unto Abraham because he was a man after his own heart.[3] In other words, he wanted the purity of the heart of God. And this shows that it has nothing to do with good and evil.

People are always inclined to think of their great goodness, and this creates almost a sort of a fraudulent panacea of self-righteousness that just simply fills the consciousness. People get filled with the idea of how good they are because they did a few good deeds, thought a few good thoughts—and the same with evil.

Good and evil are bad, both. Did you hear what I said? I said good is bad because the "good" that we're talking about has to be repudiated by man. "Why callest thou me good?" the Master said. "There is none good but one, that is, God."[4] We have to understand this.

It is a matter, then, of *mirroring* the perfection of God in our life. That is the pure in heart, because then you can see God and God is good. But this goodness is not the goodness of man. It's the goodness of God captured in the pure, pristine purpose. Do you hear me? The pure, pristine purposes of God.

October 31, 1971
Colorado Springs, Colorado

CHAPTER 12

Waves Upon the Sea

A Lecture Inspired by the Seven Chohans

The message of this day is old, its fragrance ever new. The understanding of the mysteries of life even today are perceived through the veil and the few remain the repositories of the wisdom intended for the many.

Light supersedes darkness. Light and life are synonymous. Purity is the nature of God. Eternal forgiveness is in his domain. "As I live, saith the LORD God, I have no pleasure in the death of the wicked."[1] The nature of man as the image of God is life, truth, and understanding of the way.

Energy is all derived from the Great Source, the generator of all that lives. All light comes from the one Great Generator of life. And, as in the old-fashioned Christmas tree strings with which we are familiar, the circuit of life is always just that—a great circle.

We all, spliced into that circle and joined to the connections, are thus connected with the One Source of life. When men are separated from that circle of life by the change called death, it is as though they were spliced out for the moment from the circle, and the circle again joins together, so that it can be rightly said that all upon earth are manifestations of the One Life.

Because life is dual, the mystery and the mysteries of life are hidden from the wise and the prudent and revealed unto babes. It is, then, so simple and yet so complex that we are often disturbed because of its simplicity at one time and disturbed because of its immensity and complexity at another time. God has not intended it to be so. The way and the message were intended to be made plain.

Through actual malintent, the pristine teachings of the LORD God have been distorted again and again by the mind of man. Many well-intended people have misinterpreted and distorted the purity of the teachings so that today the world is a hodgepodge, a variety that is not the spice of life but the bane of life. And we need, today as never before, the clarity and the purity and the radiance of the divine plan as it went forth in the beginning as the Word. The Word, the sound of OM, AUM, Amen, I AM, and all of this is identifiable with the reality of that which we call being, which identifies with consciousness.

We borrow and we receive from God a portion of his consciousness. There is but one ocean. And out of the ocean there are many drops. We are all one drop of the ocean. Qualitatively we have within us all of the beauty, the rainbow radiance, the celestial light, the heavenly wisdom, the divine power, and the divine love that abides within the full consciousness of God in the Great Central Sun.

Men ask, "Where is heaven?" They ask, "Where is hell?" Jesus said, "The kingdom of God is within you."[2] Jesus was a master. He attained his victory over death. He showed the way as many other avatars have done. For God has not only one son, but many sons that he desires to bring to his own heart. We are all sons of God as we accept the message of our own divine reality.

The fogginess of consciousness, the befuddlement of man, the confusion of dogma and doctrine, the impurity of men in act and deed have all kept men from perceiving the reality of truth, because the crystal-clear lens through which we must perceive truth is our own consciousness. Therefore we must not be so foolish as to criticize the realities of life simply because we do not understand them. We must not try to substitute our own limited understanding for the mighty understanding vouchsafed to the Brothers in White, the masters of the Great White Brotherhood.

We must recognize that the spirit of truth is abroad in the earth today. But the spirit of error is also abroad. And wherever the Spirit of God goes, there also go the sons of Belial. And those ordinances which are not of God are just as much in action today as are the activities of God insofar as man goes.

However, the kingdom of God is infinite, and that infinite kingdom, represented by the angelic hosts, is very real today. Angels exist. And they do assist mankind. In addition to angels, elemental beings, who are the gardeners of the LORD, dwell with us below to assist nature in her manifestation. Throughout the world there is the broad and vast radiance of hierarchy.

But like a giant broadcasting station whose power is infinite, this radiance of hierarchy goes through our bodies, brains, beings, and minds, but does not register with us unless we are in tune with it. We become in tune with it through consonance with divine ideas, through the purification of our hearts. But false dogma, false concepts, prejudice, pride, and human reason are the distortions in the lens of the mind which prevent the actualization of the grace of God in our hearts.

We need, therefore, the humility of purpose which will enable us to see the clearness of the Christ essence as our own. Jesus said, "The kingdom of God is within you." And the kingdom of God that is within you is the most priceless treasure—the pearl of great price—that any man, woman, or child can ever know or own. To possess it is to possess divine understanding.

And this is a city that sitteth on a hill, a radiance that cannot be hidden because it is of God. Abraham Lincoln said long ago, "You may fool all of the people some of the time, you can even fool some of the people all of the time, but you can't fool all of the people all of the time." And therefore there is always a remnant in whom there is the essence of faith, who understand that grace cometh not by man's words alone but by the Spirit of God, and that grace and truth and mercy exist today in the world with all of its darkness and shadow, its warfare, its confusing elements, and its own warp of distortion.

Let us, then, understand that the Brotherhood will give us to eat no more of the divine manna than we are capable of digesting. Of course, tonight we have here with us some who have not attended this conference until this evening. They are not aware of the step-up in the vibratory action of the room, of the class, nor do they, perhaps, have the knowledge that was given to us through the class. And I say this with my tongue in cheek, for I have long ago learned to reckon with the fact that there are always wiser men and wiser women than myself. And so, I look to the God within each individual and extend the welcome of the Great White Brotherhood to everyone who cometh here for the first time, that they may understand that this is not an ordinary activity.

This activity was founded by one of the great masters of the Great White Brotherhood. This has nothing to do with race or with color or even with creed. It has to do with the white light, the halo, or nimbus, that surrounds all who become one with God. This activity is a manifestation of one of the brothers of the spiritual hierarchy of this planet, the guardian spirits who watch over, under divine direction, the affairs of men and rush in to seal and heal the breach in human affairs whenever they can. They have no power to interfere with the free will of man. And therefore they must always act when they are invited. They are real. They are genuine. And they work with the Lord and Master Jesus together with other great masters of the universal consciousness of God.

One of the great fallacies in human thought and reason is that because there is but one God, there can be but one Son of God. This was never the divine intent. The one Son of God—and there is an only begotten Son of the Father—is the universal Christ spirit, the Logos that "before Abraham was, I AM."[3] This second person of the Trinity existed, then, in the consciousness of God from the beginning. For God is a Spirit, and the Spirit of God sent forth by the power of his own cognition and majesty the Son, or the radiance of himself, the Solar Logos, the universal Logos, the Word that went forth and by its vibratory action shook all things into manifestation. And therefore all things are a manifestation of the mind-stuff of God.

This universal consciousness, this light, this *emanation* (energy *manifestation*) of God is the only reality in the universe, the only begotten of the Father. This great reality exists in every human heart and is the Holy Christ Self, the mediator between the earth man and the heavenly man that is above each individual. For God has said, "I will draw nigh unto you if you will draw nigh unto me."[4]

If we understand this, then we must be receptive to the great creative intelligence that gave us birth. We must recognize that it is a lie fostered by malintent upon man to create the illusion that there is and can be only one son of the Father. There is only one begotten Son and that is the universal Christ.

Jesus was a manifestation of that and demonstrated for all time that resurrection which he so ably represented in his Palestinian mission. However, we today have the same opportunity that he did, and in his own words we may draw the recognition of this truth; for he has spoken saying, "He that believeth on me, the works that I do shall he do also; and greater works than these shall he do; because I go unto my Father."[5]

We must recognize, then, that each time a universal soul who has attained to his Christ stature goes back to the heart of God, he carries with him the richening of his own earth experiences. And thus the Godhead gains in transcendence and transcendent power. And the power of infinity is itself multiplied because man has served the divine cause. The sons of God are like the waves upon the sea, like the sand by the seashore, like the stars of the heaven innumerable.

We all exist in the consciousness of God in the divine image. If it were not so, he would have told us so, because he clearly stated, "So God created man in his own image, in the image of God created he him; male and female created he them."[6] If man is made in the image of God and his likeness, there is no higher.

How, then, could there be one son above the other? How could one individual, per se, stand above the other except through the use of opportunity, for God is a God of justice, and when men serve him and devote themselves to him, he honors their efforts. For it is written that every jot and tittle of the law shall remain in effect. It is also written that whatsoever a man doeth he shall receive the reward for that which he doeth.[7]

If God, then, who is a just God, giveth his reward to men, it must be because of their recognition of his love and his light. They must understand that his service is the service of the king. They must understand that to serve him is to be crowned by attainment. They must understand that he has the authority over every lifestream upon this planet. They must understand that he is willing to bestow power to man as soon as man demonstrates his readiness to receive it.

But God is no fool. Men are fools when they fail to accept his laws, when they think that sins can be forgiven without some recompense being made. And therefore the right of remission of sins in itself is a spiritual grace and spiritual gift. When men remit the sins of another, they remit them and lift the balancing action of those sins temporarily, holding them in suspension until the lifestream can make the necessary cosmic adjustment.

One of the reasons why other teachings have gone forth is because the sinister strategies of darkness upon this planet have desired men to think that their sins could be so easily forgiven and blotted out that men would then take license and liberty by reason of this and go forth into the world of form and hate their neighbor, with a sense that this would be with impunity. In reality, this is not true, for every act of man stands before the eye of God, and there is nothing whatsoever that men do of either good or evil that is not itself brought immediately to their own individualized records. And this is the justice of Almighty God.

One of the strange things that has happened upon this earth is that the spirit of darkness has also gone abroad upon the earth, and it has gone abroad and influenced men in the very areas of their salvation. Therefore, many of the so-called religious organizations of the world, ignorantly and not in malice but in a sense of not knowing and by reason of entanglement in the skeins of dogma, are caught up into the concept of the forgiveness of sins as something that comes to men simply for the asking. They do not understand the difference between the forgiveness of sins and the justification of man's iniquities.

Whatever a man doeth, whatever his iniquities are, these iniquities must be balanced. We cannot commit acts of thievery, we cannot steal, without returning to life that which we have stolen, in many cases with interest. Therefore when the thief comes and says to someone, "Will you forgive me? I have stolen your purse." The one may forgive him, and he may say to the Father, "Father, will you forgive me? I've stolen his purse," but it is required by the law that the purse be returned to the one from whom it is taken with every coin and cent of the realm placed therein. You see, this is the justice of God.

But the forces of shadow have desired to create the illusions of the senses into the churches and religious activities of the world in order to give men a false feeling of security that they can go out and do wrong and then say, "I'm sorry." It is well to say I'm sorry, and much better than not to say it, but certainly this does not absolve mankind from those things which are the justice of God.

The Great White Brotherhood has always known this great truth. But it has been exceedingly difficult, because of the counsels of the world and because of the teachings of the world that men have honored from the time they were children, to show them the great truths of the Brotherhood. For when God sends forth one of his servants to the earth as an avatar or a son of God who desires to teach mankind and pour forth the love of the Father as well as the wisdom of the Father, men are often caught in the snares of their own thoughts of dogma. And they decide that that one is, in reality, rather than being a true prophet of God, false in nature and proclaiming the essence of false dogma.

Therefore, men continually sag in the quicksand of all that has gone before, historically speaking, in religion and they do not understand that the power of the one God is everywhere with the wisdom and the purity of his intent. Because of all of this, men stand at the crossroads of life and they cry, "Whence, whither, and how?"

The answers are in the ascended masters' consciousness. It is not possible for men to immediately grasp it all. We can only say, Be alert! Be alive! And look you well to that which you believe. For this world, while it belongs unto God, is also your world, your inheritance, if you can have the meekness of heart to develop the strength of character and divine idealism to understand that the search for the true and living God must go on, fostered by a desire within you. You must spur yourselves to seek out and to find that truth which, though it be as simple as that which a child could learn, has become complicated in the processes of life.

I shall say no more on this subject now. I shall close the door upon it. But I pray that those of you who are receptive to the light which God is will open the doors of your hearts and ponder well upon these thoughts. For they are not my own, but they have come from a higher source.

March 26, 1967
Colorado Springs, Colorado

CHAPTER 13

The Accent Is Love

E veryone in this world needs to have love. We see love manifest primarily, I think, the kind of love that we're talking about, through the love of a mother for her child—although to a young man or a young woman in the prime years romantic love, married love, the love of a sweetheart seems to be paramount in the consciousness. I doubt very much if people at that age realize the role that the glands of the body play in this form of love. However, I think we make a great error if we think it is all a matter of glands. It is more than that. There is definitely imbued in the consciousness of all people by Nature itself the magnificent feeling of wanting to identify with someone.

The reason this is so is that God never created any of us—I said, *any* of us—alone. We were not made singly. We were made dually. Very few people, however, in the world are aware of this consciously. They are driven by this factor to seek a mate. "God created man in his own image, in the image of God created he him; male and female created he them."[1]

Does this not strike you as passing strange? Well, it isn't. It's real simple. It references the nature of God. "God is a Spirit: and they that worship God must worship him in spirit and in truth."[2]

But did you ever stop to realize that the Spirit itself was androgynous in nature? I believe it is the Mormon Church that teaches that God is physical. And this was quite a shock to me when I actually was exposed to this teaching. They teach that God has a physical body like you and I and apparently no bigger or no smaller and that he exists somewhere and actually sits there in the universe. This is what was reported to me.

Now, I myself do not embrace that tenet except that I hold that God is physical in us, that he was physical in Christ. And I read in Colossians, "For all the fullness of the Godhead dwelled in him bodily."[3] Therefore, if it dwelled in him bodily as the great exemplar, it is possible for this God to dwell in us bodily also. And it is wise and well that we assume the role or at least consider the possibility of it. It is a grave error for us to cast ourselves into a mold, which I think is deceitful, that we can never be any more than what we are. We can be the fullness of the Godhead bodily ourselves. Otherwise we would not have a joint heirship with Christ.[4] If you're a joint heir with Christ to the realities of God, then you have to be able to obtain it.

So, we have to recognize the meaning of the word *androgynous.* Androgynous, of course, refers to both masculine and feminine qualities existing simultaneously and usually in balance in any person. In one sense of the word, then, you're all familiar with a hermaphrodite. And you realize that a person who is both male and female is a strange person, or so considered by humanity, and yet actually all of us are in one sense of the word androgynous.

There are certain physical characteristics that will bear this out. Not only that, but the androgynous nature of man usually works to a sixty-forty balance. Men are usually balanced sixty percent toward the masculine and forty percent feminine. I would really dislike to see a man who was without that forty percent or thirty percent feminine side. (And you do occasionally find this imbalance in women, too.) Women are also balanced: sixty percent feminine, about forty percent masculine. And once in a while it gets kind of fifty-ish. And you've seen it both ways.

You know, love is a many-splendored thing. Love is not just one type of love. There's not just romantic love, married love, maternal love, paternal love, filial love. There is such a thing as divine love. And then there is a love of Nature. There is actually a love that is based on desire and desire alone. And in this case, desire love always becomes angry if the beloved does not react as intended. Do you follow me? Love where it is purely desire wants something from the other person. And unless it gets what it wants, it becomes quickly angry, because in reality it is not in love with the person at all. It is in love with its own desire.

So we have to recognize desire love as a thing apart from genuine spiritual love. There are very few people on earth today who really understand the nature of love or even understand their own nature. When we come to the point where we can understand our own nature, we can probably do a lot of things to correct our attitude toward love. You also would be quite amazed to know that there are some people who say they are in love with God when in reality this, too, is only desire love. I'm going to tell you why.

All the way back to the old tribal customs and the earliest beginnings of primitive religion, man has expected from his shaman, his priest, or whoever he has looked to for spiritual guidance the answer to his problems. He has expected religion to provide solutions to his problems. But many times he does not recognize the key which was so beautifully illustrated in the teachings of Jesus, "Daughter, go in peace; thy faith hath made thee whole."[5] Do you understand that? Thy faith hath made thee whole.

Well, everybody says, "Thy faith hath made thee whole." But they don't put the accent in the right place. "Thy" is where the accent should be. "*Thy* faith hath made thee whole," which again brings the whole responsibility back to ourselves. The accent on love, then, must develop in us an awareness of what love is, and if we understand what love is, we will understand that love is God.

But this becomes too nebulous to most of us. We say, "Well, what is God?" God is a spirit. So we say a spirit is love. But we still are face to face with the divisions that we have made of ideas. We divide ideas just like you break bread into little hunks. And sometimes when you see the crumbs lying all over the table, it doesn't look like the whole loaf anymore. And this is true. So we have to understand a little more about love. And I want to quickly take it apart and put it together.

As I see it, genuine love is always the greatest giver. There is one reason why people do not actually give themselves to God or to one another without reserve. And that is, of course, in the case of one another, they have so many times given themselves to people and been hurt by it that they have reached a point where they hesitate to give themselves lest the person will turn around and rend them. You know what I'm talking about? You give yourself to somebody. You extend your love to a person and it's unrequited. It's unreciprocated. And of course, in the cases of where we expected something in return, we don't get anything in return, and so we feel very disappointed in that, too.

Love, then, of course, has to be very delicately balanced. I'm not going to say "like a Swiss watch," because some of the Swiss watches I've had lately have not always behaved, either, although they do make pretty good watches. But love has to be balanced. We have to be aware of ourselves and of other people. We have to be aware of their limitations and our own limitations. Now, I don't mean to dwell on them. Don't sit here and say, "Aunt Minnie has limitations." Don't sit here and say, "I've got limitations." If you do, you're actually limiting yourselves where you shouldn't. But be aware of the fact that limitations exist in this world of form. And it is important that you understand that people cannot measure up to something that they have not yet attained to.

If you don't believe it, go to a gymnasium. Go to one of these poles, those of you who can still broad jump, put the bar across and go out and jump over it and then raise it a little higher. After a while you reach a point where you can't jump over it. Isn't this right? Well, that's your limitation. But you may go out tomorrow after you've been practicing a while and you may raise it a little bit. And this is how the great athletes actually finally attain.

So I think that one of the problems with all of us is that sometimes we expect more of people than they are able to give. They all have a capacity. And I think one of the greatest problems in the world when you're dealing with love is that everybody thinks that everyone else has as much love as they have. But many times they don't, and sometimes we fool ourselves and what we call love is not so much love as it is expectancy.

It's expectancy, and when the expectancy is not fulfilled, then, you see, we are disappointed and what we have called love quickly turns to hate. We many times turn to develop hatred of that which does not respond as we think to what we think is our love. And this is what Jesus said, "Search the scriptures, for in them ye think ye find eternal life and they are they which testify of me."[6]

All right, then, love is God. But let's put another *o* in it. Love is good. This means the state of being in perfect balance regardless of what the other fellow does. Don't expect anything of anybody and you won't be disappointed.

Several classes ago, a very nice young couple—well, they're not so young but I'll call them young—they came to Colorado Springs at Elizabeth's invitation. She called them on the phone and said, "Are you coming to the conference?"

And these people had had a lot of trouble and they'd written to Elizabeth and she wanted to try to help them. And they said, "No, we don't have the money," very sadly.

"Do you want to come to the conference?"

"Yes."

"Well, can you get to the conference?"

"Yes."

"Do you have a car?"

"Yes."

"Do you have the gasoline money?"

"Yes."

"Well," she said, "if I were to permit you, and make an exception for you and give you your food in our kitchen with our staff and we allowed you to sleep in our gatehouse, we made a bed for you, would you come?"

"Oh, you bet! We'd come."

So they came. And we were out at the hour they arrived. They came to the gate. They were admitted by our new executive secretary who was raised in South Africa and educated in London. And she talks something like this. She'd say, "Oh, I'm so glad to see you," you know. So she came to the gate with this accent. And she greeted them, said she was so glad to see them, and Mrs. Prophet would be back a little later.

Now, these dear people, to tell you the truth, to them that accent represented a high-toned person, a person who was a swell-head, a person who thought they were better than someone else. And when she told them that they could come to her apartment and that they could have her bedroom there because Mrs. Prophet had felt that they would be more comfortable there than in the gatehouse, which was true, they quickly got into their car and thanked her and said they'd see Mrs. Prophet in the evening and immediately left home and went back several states away without ever coming to the class, as angry as mad hornets. They were so angry that they could hardly see straight. They got home and they finally cooled off. Elizabeth wrote them a beautiful letter and said she knew that something had happened. And of course it did.

But this was a case of where the accent was not on genuine love but it was on expectancy. Now, if these people had had recognition of the great magnet of Almighty God—and I want you to connect with this idea right now. I want you to see God's love as a magnet. If you connect with that magnet and feel the power of that magnet and it stays with you strong enough, none of these problems of false expectancies will cause you to become disturbed and to lose your self-control.

You're living in an imperfect world. And the only reason it's imperfect is because the accent is *not* love, but the accent is expectancy. And therefore most of the reactions of people are caused by these false expectancies. And if people keep on becoming responsive to reaction, they develop pathways through the nervous system and through the psyche of man that eventually become uncontrollable forces in their own world. In other words, they cannot govern themselves.

So when you recognize the magnet of God's love and do not make it a function conditioned by human conduct, then you are able to master your world in an entirely different manner than when you are always expecting something from someone and they are always disappointing you. Oh, you'll still have problems. Who doesn't have problems? Everyone has problems. You'll have some problems, but the wonder of it all will be your reaction to your problems.

You see, even in serious illnesses, there is a recuperative period that is needed by the body even after the cause and core of the illness is removed. Don't think, then, that the minute you see truth that it's going to heal you immediately or free you immediately. The Bible says, "You shall know the truth and the truth shall make you free."[7] It doesn't say, "You shall know the truth and the moment you know the truth, the truth is going to make you free."

And this is where people really get into trouble. They think that because they go ahead and harvest the wheat that they're going to sit down the next minute to the table and eat the loaf of bread. The wheat has to be ground. It has to be refined. It has to be processed. We have to shape it and mix it with water and yeast. And then we have to permit it to grow in the bread tin and expand, and then we set it in the oven and a certain amount of time elapses before it is baked. Otherwise we have half-baked bread.

And that's exactly what we have in the world today. We have half-baked people because they have not waited for themselves to develop in accordance with the metaphysical and spiritual instructions that they have been given. They have the most valuable instructions in The Summit Lighthouse that can ever be given anywhere on the face of this earth, and many times the whole problem is a matter of digestion, a matter of assimilation, a matter of practice of the principles. After all, we are not karma-less people. We have karma. We've lived before. We've had experiences before. And some of us will live again. And we'll all live forever unless we lose our soul or become a castaway through losing our identity with God.

So then, let us recognize that the most important thing we can do is to put the accent on love but be sure that it is on love and not on something else, because most of the time what we are having that causes all of our problems is little, old habits of me, mine, and ours, in some cases, that go back to our babyhood. And if we had brothers and sisters, perhaps we have more of this than if we were raised alone.

This may surprise you when I say this, but people who were raised alone many times do not develop as much along the line of possessiveness as those who were raised in a family where they would share everything. Now, some people will say, "I think it'd be just the opposite." But it really isn't because, you see, when you're raised alone, you get everything you want as a rule, that is, your parents give you all they can give you, whatever that capacity is. And you receive all these things and you probably are not disappointed in love. You're loved a great deal. But where you have a child who is brought up in a larger family where they have to share, they learn more about sharing, and I think at the same time there is more rivalry created there unless the parents are very wise and do an awful lot to guide the young child.

In other words, regardless of whether I'm right or wrong in my statements—and this lecture doesn't hinge on that—whether I'm right or wrong, the important thing here is that there are childhood influences regardless of from where they come. And we all are victims of these influences. And we have to learn to reeducate the mind, reeducate the consciousness, and put the accent on God, good, which is love, and is never subject to human conditions.

Thank you.

March 26, 1970
Santa Barbara, California

CHAPTER 14

Perfect Love

O ur lecture this afternoon is "Perfect Love." Love itself is supposed to be perfect, so someone might think that it was superfluous to put the word "perfect" before love. But the Bible states that "Perfect love casts out fear,"[1] which leads me to believe that the writer is definitely trying to make clear to our consciousness the nature of love, that love is many things to many people.

We have filial love. We have the love of children for their parents and we have the love of parents for their children. We have romantic love, the love of a man for a woman or a woman for a man. We have self-love, the love of ourselves for the things that we like to enjoy, the things that we like. And self-love is very active in this world today.

Many years ago I was obsessed with the idea that self-love was all wrong and that it should be killed and that the love of God should be substituted for it. Now, I'm not going to tell you that I'm going to repudiate that statement, but I certainly would modify it. I think that self-love is necessary, to a point, until we have replaced it with divine love. But I think that there are degrees of self-love as there are degrees of all kinds of love. I think love is always modified by the degrees of our devotion for the type of love we wish to manifest.

If we wish to manifest love for our neighbor, this is, of course, not self-love. It's a social love. We love society. We love people. But much of love seems to be the result of the feeling that we get out of it. In other words, we desire to love because it makes us happy to love.

A long time ago, when people were—and they still are—giving large donations to churches, a woman decided after she'd given several thousand dollars to the church that she was going to ask it back. (That wasn't us.) So she asked it back. They wouldn't give it to her. So she got a lawyer and she sued the church. And when the lawsuit was filed, the jury was drawn, case was held and the decision was handed down.

And this is what the court said. They said, In the matter of eleemosynary gifts we hold that the gifts are given and the benefits are given more to the donor than to the donee. And so the legal mind and the mind of jurisprudence decided that there were more blessings in giving than in receiving, thus confirming the scriptures.

So we see there is a type of love that actually enjoys the fact that it can love. And in a way this is related to the self. Some people, of course, will hold that any time we receive a benefit that this makes it selfish love. I don't think this is completely true at all. But I think that we always have to watch the degrees and the motives behind whatever we do. If we have expectations of return and we give only because we expect return, it may well be that we are selfishly motivated.

Therefore, when we start to ponder the nature of perfect love, we must realize that perfect love is the real love of God because, as I see it, God does not seem to derive any great specific benefit out of all that he does for mankind. I think that his is the most unselfish love of all. He takes his energy, his creative mind, and everything that he has and is, and he gives it to human beings to work with. And in return he is reviled, cursed, denied, mocked, and scoffed at. He is "despised and rejected of men."[2] And in the God-is-dead theory that recently has been popularized by some of our theologians, we find the proof of the fact that the Creator is not really thanked for all that he has done for man.

Now, I think sometimes, when I really meditate on this, that the reason he is not thanked is because we have not yet really appropriated his intentions. We have misappropriated his intentions. The great givingness of God does not seem to be properly rewarded. And I think that this is because man is yet in his infancy and that perfect love has not actually done her perfect work because we have hindered the perfect work of God by our ignorance, our unbelief, and our acceptance of mortal fallacy.

Human fallibility is at fault, then, interfering with the progress God intends for the race. I think another problem involved here is the fact that we are always prone to condemn ourselves or condemn the Creator. When we condemn ourselves, we are in one sense condemning the Creator, too. And yet, where does the fault lie? We cannot actually go to the Godhead and say, "Well, Father, you made the world such a lousy world that we can't get anything out of it." That wouldn't be true at all, would it? On the other hand, we can't begin to besmirch ourselves as the handiwork of God too much or we're really desecrating the divine intent there, too. So we walk a razor's edge in a way.

And I think that perhaps at times, and I really think this, that blame and condemnation are perhaps the greatest impediment in the world and the greatest cause of the perfect love of God not manifesting. In other words, I am trying to say to you today that if we would stop condemning ourselves, stop condemning God, stop condemning the universe, stop condemning our job, our teachers, our government, and stop condemning in general—just stop it completely—and recognize that we are living in a glorious opportunity, and then ask ourselves just what this opportunity is, that we could well answer it and say, "Well, the opportunity is to express perfect love."

If we would start doing it instead of just talking about it,

I am convinced that we could make our lives, our government, our job, our church, our home, our school, and even Nature a place for the expression of perfect love, because it would begin to express first in ourselves.

Most reactions that occur in the world that bring about resistance movements and rebellion are the result of fear. People are afraid and in their fear, they lash out at the nearest object of their disaffection. So in psychology we learn, too, that paranoia and even schizophrenia is really the result of traumatic fear, dominant fear, fear that becomes obsessive to the point that something has to give. And usually what gives is the mind. The mind divides itself in two because that's the way it can deceive itself. When it divides itself in two, one part of the mind says, "Now, I have to acknowledge this." And the other part says, "I won't acknowledge it." This is a dichotomy.

A tragic happening occurred in a trip from the East Coast by a lady and her husband. They had some children, too. And they were driving along. She was at the wheel and her husband was asleep in the back seat when the car crashed head on and she was killed. The children were alive and uninjured in the car, and he was in the back seat without his shoes. When the ambulance came and the police, he got out of the car and they found him wandering around in circles.

And what did he say? "If I could only find my shoes, everything would be alright." "If I could just find my shoes," he kept repeating, "then everything would be alright," over and over and over again— because the mind that knew that his wife was dead and knew about the tragedy went to sleep. And the other mind, the false mind, came out and told him that if he could only find his shoes, everything would be alright. And this is a little bit illustrative of the dual mind and how it sets up a split pattern.

Several years ago, one of the people that we had at our headquarters, who subsequently left, being unfit for cosmic service, on Monday gave me a check for a thousand dollars and on Friday betrayed me. I asked Saint Germain, "Why?"

Saint Germain said, "You are dealing with a split personality." This woman, when she was very young, had a romance and as a result of what happened in that romance, she decided she would hate men and never marry, but down deep inside of her she still had a yearning to marry and still liked men. So one side of her was attracted to men, and the other side was absolutely in a state of despising men.

The Master told me that this dichotomy had never been healed. And one day Dr. Jekyll would work in her, the Dr. Jekyll of the good little girl that was very, very good. And then on another day, the Mr. Hyde would come out from his hiding place and he would act. And so this unfortunate state of circumstances existed to plague this poor woman. And had I never had the instructions of the Master, I would have remained probably to my dying or ascending day in a state of confusion about why in the world she would give me a thousand dollars one day and turn around and betray me another day. The personal aspects of this are of no concern to anyone. I only cited it as an example.

We then come face to face with the idea of self-condemnation in a matter of perfect love. We have mentioned condemnation of others. Some people justify self-condemnation on the grounds that they deserve to condemn themselves. We hold that no one deserves to condemn themselves, because self-condemnation is equally undesirable with condemnation of others. It is unprofitable.

But we wish to say that the discriminating Christ mind always knows when we err. And it is not wrong for us as divine seekers to recognize when we make a mistake. There's a difference between recognizing when we've made a mistake and condemning ourselves. Some people go so far out on this no-condemnation bit and this speaking evil of no one, they want to become like the three monkeys: "See no evil, hear no evil, and think no evil." This does not mean what most people think. And I want to make this very clear.

In the matter of perfect love, if love is to attain the majority of its perfection, it has to have the quality of Christ-discrimination. And it must be able to recognize the mistakes of itself as well as the mistakes of others, and there is no problem in this as long as we do not reach into the area of condemnation.

However, if I were to be asked or consulted on this whole matter, I would say that I would think that people could have more discrimination towards themselves and less toward others, and then they would be better off. In other words, I think minding our own business in the lives of others is very important. I think that unless we're consulted or asked, we should let people paddle their own canoes—with the exception of those who are teachers and are specifically ordained to bring forth truth. These people are supposed to do it. But the average person today is not supposed to interfere in their neighbor's business by condemning him.

I cannot object to praise. I have never seen anyone harmed by praise providing the praise came from a sincere heart and was indexed by genuine appreciation. If people have appreciation and they tell other people about it, these plaudits are often spurs of great joy. They're joyous spurs. When people are told that they've done something nice or that someone appreciates them—and I don't care who it is, you tell your neighbor this, you say to friends you meet that you're glad to see them—these things generate a little oil that smoothens life's pathway.

Now, some people come along and say, "Well, why should we just pass out the oil? If they deserve to be condemned, let's condemn them." I repeat, no one deserves to be condemned, for the simple reason that evil acts themselves are their own condemnation. People are quite wise until they start being foolish and deceiving themselves by tricking themselves with a double mind, where they try to tell themselves that it's not so.

As one of our brothers and sisters in this group once told me, "Say it isn't so." Just saying something isn't so does not alter its structure at all. We cannot and ought not to be ostriches. We ought to be realists and see just what is going on in the world and in ourselves. But it's a real funny thing that people will see evil everywhere and condemn it and stub their toe over the littlest bit of good that's anywhere and not recognize it. This is also the nature of us all as people.

But I want to emphasize this afternoon that I think that a very, very small percentage of the universe is bad. I think the majority of the people are good—good in their intentions, good in their resolves, good in their concepts of destiny, what they would like to be. The yearnings of the soul, gilded as they are by the divine framework, sort of carry through the whole fabric of life. And I think that Nature is good and also the stars, the sunset, sunrise, the sweetness of the scent of flowers, freshly mown hay, the babbling brook, singing birds, and the hopes of heaven. I think, as Robert Louis Stevenson said, "The world is so full of a number of things, I'm sure we should all be as happy as kings."[3]

But "should be" and "are" are two different things. I am convinced that most people, in their despairs, despair most about little things. Large, ominous ideas and illnesses and things like this, these sometimes come unawares on people, and they take these in stride much better than they do the little things that seem sometimes to threaten so much, but actually are often nothing more than bogeymen—because there is a great deal of happiness in the world that shows that the perfect love of God is a leaven working in society.

I've had conversations with Master Morya. He gave us quite a talk this morning. That talk was not intended to smash or blast your hopes but to show you, in a way, that heaven is laughing at the ridiculous situations people put themselves in because if heaven does not mock them, human beings might take these things seriously.

And we are convinced that this age, regardless of what happens to it, is going to pass into history. And we are convinced that if we don't get it now, ultimately this world is going to get her golden age. What we would like to see happen is have it happen now while we're here, you see. That's the whole thing. And I don't think we can blame ourselves for desiring to see that perfect love.

After all, in one way all the ages past have been stairsteps, and now we come to the landing place. From the time of Christ, from the foundation of the world, mankind has tried to move toward a parliament of man from the standpoint of the divine idea, certainly not from the idea of Nimrod who built the Tower of Babel,[4] not from the idea of one world, from the standpoint of these one-worlders who want to go ahead and just unite people together—like I was talking about the idea that union is like tying two cats' tails together and throwing them over a clothesline. It's not a matter of union; it's a matter of unity.

We want a one world, alright, and so do the masters. Morya pointed that out in his *Encyclical on World Goodwill*. But we don't want one world at any price. The reason we have different nations, different churches, and different philosophies is that they fit the needs of different people. Everyone isn't going to be able to accept our philosophy, simply by reason of the fact that they are so much dyed by the dyed-in-the-wool concepts of orthodoxy that they're as good as dead. They won't change. They've made up their mind to it. They'll tell you this.

I think there's nothing worse in the world than to waste our time trying to change these dyed-in-the-wool people. There are an awful lot of people in the world, and many of them have no church, no philosophy, and no sense of direction. We get them every once in a while when they respond to ads in *Fate* magazine. They write in. They don't even know that a Bible exists. Some of them have never heard of Christ. We are tutoring some of them in the things of Christ. And these are Americans.

We have learned of people where the mother and father never mentioned God in the home and they never knew anything about God. And it may come as a great surprise to you to know that Mrs. Christel Anderson, who was our first secretary, scarcely knew the Bible and was raised more or less along the line of practically no religion. Christel was always interested in our quotations of scriptures from the Bible because she herself had no training in the Bible.

Many of our people are, of course, Christ-oriented from an early Christian home. And when they find the teachings of the masters and understand how those teachings enable them to fit together, like the pieces of a jigsaw puzzle, the many mysteries of life, they are extremely grateful for it. And they should be. We all should be, for I think basically that perfect love has synthesized the many philosophies and religions into a complex whole that is very orderly and sweet.

But I think the most important thing for all of us to have this afternoon is the understanding of how to acquire perfect love. And I fear that the acquisition of perfect love is related to the attention and to energy, both. If, as the Russians have now said, they have discovered that time is energy—and we can accept that—then we have to realize that the substance of our lives is made up of time and time-synonymous energy.

So it isn't just what we do in the class here that counts, but it's what we do away from the class that counts. What we do here, of course, counts. But what we do here will become more transcendent and perfected in love if we are functioning when away from here as we are intended to function. And the perfect love of God will enable us to cast aside sophistry and wit and bring into manifestation the real Spirit of the Lord, the real Holy Ghost, the real breath of God in our lives.

I think one of the problems that I faced myself in accepting this idea was the fact that I was of the opinion that perhaps the Holy Ghost was so holy that it would annihilate me. I thought that I would become full of holes, that God would shoot me full of holes, there wouldn't be anything left. And I was afraid I would lose my life by becoming too holy. And I'll just bet you, if some of you would admit it, you've had some of the same ideas.

So you try to hold onto your life and you wind up losing it

because what you're holding onto isn't anything that really is the same, has no constancy whatsoever. First, you find yourself drooling oatmeal all over your chin as a child. The next thing you know, they take the bib off and they say, "No more bottle for you." Then you're walking around. Then they send you to school, and then you get into the schoolyard, and the next thing you know you're in high school. And the first thing you know, you're out on your own working at a job. And then you have a whole bunch of concepts, and when you get a little older, you change all those for some more concepts.

So who are you, anyway, that you're trying to hang onto? You've let go of yourself many times already. What are you trying to hang onto, some kind of a status quo? I think that's what most people do, though. They hang onto the status quo of the old man. He's old from the day he was born and he's tired. And he dies tired. And the eternally new man is the man of the Spirit, who recognizes that he has to be renewed in God every day and changed.

We simply do have to change. We can't remain the same. And the proof of that is in the fact that George Lancaster back there in the corner, he was a bartender once. He doesn't mind me telling this on him at all. And I'm just as proud of him as punch. He's one of our real devotees. But, you see, the fact that he was a bartender made him to know a lot of people and he loved people and he understood people, and he always knew that the whole thing was phony. You can't even pour a drop of wine down him now.

One time I was out for some kind of a lunch with him, and I asked him, "Shall we have a little tiny sip, a thimbleful of wine?"

And he said, "No, nothing doing." He said, "I gave it up."

So I had to turn around and say, "Well, I'm going to follow your example, George."

Which is a bit interesting, because this perfect love is practical and down to earth. You can use it in your daily life to improve your business, your understanding, and your friendships. I think many of us get too serious at times about our families and ourselves. We get too overly concerned. I'm not against anything that will help us. If worry will help us, fine. Let's all worry together.

Continuing on with this perfect love, I want to admit that all of us will do things and say things at times that may not always be agreeable to others. I mean, I've been a bull in a china closet in my life many times, but it has never been through intent. I have never tried to sit on anybody or hurt anybody. I've sometimes opened my mouth and put my foot in it. You know what I mean.

But the thing is, you either have to be a man of action or a man of inaction. You can be so scared to live that you don't do anything. And I believe that perfect love casts out that fear. And I believe you have to run the risk of trying to serve God, of doing your best. And if you're going to head an organization like this, you're going to have to be unafraid to make statements. If you make a wrong statement, well, you just have to trust that people will understand that. The lives of all of us have had many shames, if not in this life, then we've had them in the past. And there isn't any one of us that hasn't made a mistake. We haven't been on this planet this long without making some mistakes.

But regardless of that, I think the apostles and the prophets and the great men, spiritually speaking, down through the ages, have been full of mistakes. I think they've made a lot of mistakes. But what would we have done without them, mistakes and all? What would we have done without them? I'll say it'd be dark ages.

So we have to face the realistic view that we are moving onward to a perfection that we seek from whatever plateau we are presently on. I intend—God granting me the long life to do it, and God granting me the wisdom to be able to understand how to do it, and God granting me the friends like you to help me do it—to see that that university develops a series of practical courses in many subjects that we hope will be written in a manner that most people can understand, that will enable people to put some of these practical, philosophical, religious, and even political and social ideas into the test tube of daily living, where you and I can learn to live, you see, a little better than we did the day before.

I think that all schools and all classes and all instruction and the whole business here on this planet that we call life is all intended to improve the strain. I think there are retrogressive forces in the world. I think there are forces and things that we can do that will regress us as well as progress us. And I can cite several of them.

I agree that LSD and all dangerous drugs can regress man. I do not believe they will progress man. I believe they are retrogressive agents. I believe that beer, wine, and whiskey, taken to excess certainly, can regress man. Used moderately—very moderately—they may have a medicinal place. I know in Europe, the Europeans have a glass of beer and they feed their children wine like water. And the way they handle it, I can't say that I can find as much fault with them as the way we handle it here. They understand it. However, when you get to really know the truth about it all, you find that the creation of fermented beverages was originally brought down here by the Luciferians. It was not an activity of God. That's why the proverb says that strong drink mocks.⁵

However, I also believe that cigarettes and tobacco should be discarded if possible by the students, but as most of you know, I never condemn any of you who do smoke. I don't condemn anybody for anything. It's their business. But I still am going to take a stand and say that I think we'd all be better off without it. I think it is a retrogressive agent also in a minor way. Physically, I think it is a deteriorating agent, in many cases responsible for lymphatic diseases, emphysema, lung cancer, throat cancer and also tuberculosis and heart trouble. So I think we'd be better off without it.

I think sex is another act which, while it is very vital to the procreative world we live in—we have to keep creating, we have to keep having children or we'd all die out, we have to give lifestreams a chance to come in—I think excess sex used entirely for pleasure can raise people up to great heights of ecstasy in one minute and drop them down the next to such a terrible state of confusion that they don't know whether they're coming or going. And I think that can be a retrogressive agent when it's abused.

I think the love of a man and a woman, if they're disposed to be in love, can be a very beautiful experience, and they can be helpmeets to one another and do a lot of good for one another. And I think the celibate who wants to choose the celibate course can make his peace with God in the divine romance. And he or she can even, in many cases, become attached to a spiritual being. And it will not be a sex activity. It will be a raising up of the sex energy to the head, where it becomes a sacred activity because the word *sex* really is *sax*. And it comes from *sacerdotal* and *sacred,* the sacroiliac.

And I think all things are wrong only in their abuses. And so the perfect love that drains us of fear must take dominion over all of our acts and make them spiritually creative acts. We have to begin to do as God did.

Perfect love will teach us how to create a perfect body. Great saints have had sicknesses. Don't think they haven't. Look at Ramakrishna. He died with cancer of the throat. There have been many crucifixions. Saint Bernadette had cancer on the knee. Great afflictions have come to great saints.

But on the other hand, what I am citing for you this afternoon is the spiritual power of the creative divine mind in man that is able to create by perfect love the perfect body. And forgetting the karmic patterns that anybody may have or the projected patterns of human hate that they may have projected against them, man left alone, who will perform a creative act on his body, can completely rejuvenate and regenerate his body by the Christ mind.

One of the most beneficial things to do is to regenerate the mind before you try to regenerate the body. Otherwise you're almost doing like Jesus said, before you start putting wine into a bottle, you first get a new bottle.[6] And the chalice of the consciousness or the chalice of the mind should be renewed so that the renewing content will come in, and then the content can be imbibed by the soul and one can start about the business of building a perfect body by the perfect mind.

But you know who the bugaboo is? You know who the serpent in the trees is? The winding, sinuous emotions, the puny little ego that with the puny intellect, that always opposes the Christ mind, combines together—the puny intellect and the puny ego—and gets his feelings hurt because someone doesn't notice him.

Right when somebody's trying to lead a spiritual life, right when somebody is trying to do their best to renew their mind, right when they're doing the best they can to renew their body, along comes the human ego and gets its feelings hurt. And then the ego, with its hurt feelings, starts to generate the emotional whirl in the solar plexus. And that's like a spinning top, and it just pulls the mind and the whole being, the body and all, into a drain—only it's a reverse spiral. You're going right down the drain. You understand what I mean. It just seems as though the world is literally going to fall apart if you get your feelings hurt.

And what is the cure? I think the cure is Christ-understanding, providing you can vigilantly see that Christ-understanding is given voice at the time you need Christ-understanding: to stand up here and say, when the boat starts to rock and the storm of the emotions comes up, "Peace, be still, and know that I am God."[7]

If we would only do that, we wouldn't be disturbed by other people. When the boat starts to rock, right away seize it. Don't wait. Don't wait until you're all stirred up and then try to control it, because then you've got a demon on your hands and it'll be stronger than you are.

April 6, 1969
Colorado Springs, Colorado

CHAPTER 15

The Threefold Flame and Identity

We want to get into this lecture on the threefold flame and your identity. And I want to point out to you first of all a very gross concept that most people have of themselves. They somehow or other think of themselves as a physical being. And because we live in the physical body, we are constantly oppressed or depressed or, in some cases, inspired by the way that body functions.

If it functions poorly, we feel that we're not too happy about it all. But if the body functions very well and we're vibrant with good health and feel good most of the time, we don't mind identifying with this body. In fact, people will say they rather like it. They paint it up, they powder it up, they pamper it, they trim its hair and fingernails, and do a lot of things to it to make it look better. And mainly they dress it in very good apparel.

I think this is a fine idea. It makes life interesting. But in actuality this body is so very little a part of the total man. It's really, as Krishnamurti said in *At the Feet of the Master*, "The body is the horse on which you ride." You don't care to identify with your horse, do you? But at the same time, people do.

So we're going to talk about the threefold flame and identity, and we want to point out that man's life is in actuality a flame.

You probably have not thought of yourself as a flame. And therefore I want you to think of yourself as a flame, because when you in this audience start to think of yourself as a flame, you will be involved in a bit of temple magic. And this temple magic is white magic, not black magic. It is essentially a valuable experience in defining reality.

The electronic nature of the universe is quite apparent to us, that is, if we are discerning. Science has given us great insight in recent years as to the power electricity plays in many of the functions of life. But now we have to realize that we ourselves are a bit electronic and that we are a vibratory creation—not a creation that is static and stands still without movement, but a creation that pulsates with life.

And life is God. And the scriptures say that God is a spirit. Now, if God is a spirit and we are made in the image of God, then we, too, are a spirit rather than a body. The body is our overcoat. We put it on. We wear it. It carries us about. It functions, but it is not ourselves. We are a flame and we are a tripartite flame, that is, a three-part flame.

In modern video transmission, you will probably, if you study it a little, notice that in colored video transmission we make use of three primary colors. This happens to be a part of the color spectrum. And by using it properly, we are able to bring in almost all of the tones of life on this television screen that we can bring into manifestation in the world of art and the world around us in our environment.

Now we are going to find out that the flame that we are is three parts, that the parts have colors and qualities with the colors, that the color of pink and blue and yellow is involved here. And that is the threefold flame of our identity. On this Chart of the Presence and the causal body and the Holy Christ Self, the descending dove from the Father to the son through the heart of the great Christ Self, we see the Paraclete here or the Holy Spirit descending on the head of finite man.

We see finite man here with a circle drawn in the chest cavity.

The Chart of Your Divine Self

And there we see three plumes. One is pink, one is yellow, and one is blue. These three plumes are the plumes of identity. And qualitatively—not quantitatively but qualitatively—they manifest through the pink the quality of divine love, through the yellow they manifest the quality of divine wisdom, and through the blue they manifest the quality of the will of God.

I do not care how scientific you are or how intellectual you are or how many masters or teachers you may have studied under, you can never change these unalterable basic truths of the universe and the color relationships that we are describing to you.

The blue is correlated to the will of God. And Mary the Mother of Jesus, who is so often depicted with a blue veil over her, is actually manifesting her service as the handmaid of God. "I submit. I obey thee. I do thy will, O God." Overhead we have the blue sky. It covers the earth. And unless it is obscured by clouds, we always see it in the daytime, a blue sky. Some parts of the world where we have a lot of smog and aerial refuse, this sky is washed out. It doesn't look very good.

Here in Colorado, where we have a relatively pure air similar to the air at Darjeeling, India, we have this beautiful blue sky. And actually it is to remind us of the will of God, because we always think of the blue sky as good. If a sky is blue, we are pleased. People remark again and again about the blue sky here in Colorado, and they like it, but they do not know why they like it. They like it because it relates to the will of God. And people inherently, because of the affinity of the flame that they are, really desire to relate to the will of God.

We will find out, if we are very careful to watch through this class, that deliberately intentional mechanisms of destruction have tried to tear man away from his natural self, his Real Self, his cosmic identity, his cosmic affinity, to pull him down just like you'd put dirty water down a drain. But that's not God's plan for us.

There are what we will call "spirits of darkness" that depend on stealing light from us. They want to vampirize us. They want to take our energy because they have none of their own. They cannot get it from God because they have rebelled against him. The only way they can get it is from people. And the more discord people throw out, the more jangle in the world, the longer these spirits of darkness can survive in the astral world, the longer life that they have. And their tenure will run out when human beings become perfect.

The moment man starts loving his neighbor as himself, at that very moment there will be no possibility of their stealing any more light from people and they will fade away into the nothingness that they are, because they have no real reality. But as we give them power through accepting their negative feelings about other people or our destiny, about our nation or other nations, about anyone, the moment we accept these ideas, they become real to us, and we act accordingly.

So we must be aware of the wisdom flame, because it is not just enough to have intelligence although intelligence carries within its own word structure the true meaning of intelligence, the *in-telling* of God, which should make *gents* out of us, shouldn't it? We should be a little bit more diplomatic if we have the intelling of God coming into us. You know, *intelli-gence* [*intelli-gents*]. Oh, you didn't get that one.

Anyway, this is the way it is at Punkin Center* as well as Colorado Springs—everywhere in the world. That intelligence as man measures it by his diplomas and his fraternal associations, by his class distinctions, this does not guarantee to him that he is going to have wisdom along with his intelligence.

How many men and women have you seen who were, so to speak, loaded to the gills with worldly wisdom who could not function in an executive capacity at all and failed the first time they were put on trial and ever thereafter? And how many people like Henry Ford have you seen who with very little education were

---

*Punkin Center is at the junction of state highways 94 and 71 in eastern Colorado. At one time it had a gas station, a general store, and a coffee shop (all painted orange) and a population of four.

able to take command of a vast empire and develop it?

You see, while intelligence must not be spoken of disparagingly, for certainly under God's guidance the intellect was intended to be cultivated, it must not become a substitute for genuine wisdom, which is developed by experience and by compassion.

So the Christ mind is the yellow plume. And we find these flames interpenetrate our being. We have the Christ mind with its vast cosmic intelligence storehouse. We have the love of God that never reflects upon a man's bank account or any of his possessions in determining to render him a service.

God is the great giver and the flame is the great giver of life to us all as we will find out. The flame imparts life to us. It does not take from us. And we, made in his image, if we are to remain in his image or to function in God's image, we cannot be vampires. We cannot be predatory creatures preying on one another with base motivations. We must, if we are to emulate the Christ, emulate him in the thought of service, completely unmotivated.

The old story has been told, I have often smiled over it myself, about the bank president. A man said that he could always tell who were the prominent people in town by sitting in the bank and watching the people come in and listening to the bank president greet them: "Morning, Miss Jones." "Hello there, Bill! How are you?" "Mr. Smith." And a few nods here and a few nods there. He knew the size of the bank account of these people just by the way the bank president greeted them.

There is no motivation in God. He doesn't look at the size of your bank account. He doesn't even look at the size of your causal body. In fact, from what I know of God, he sometimes looks at the most anemic, weak, and sickly creatures in his kingdom because he thinks they need his love more. And this is true, and we should be a little bit that way.

But we have got to learn—and I'm not saying that God should learn this, but I'm saying that we should learn this—that there is a time to let certain segments of life learn to stand on their own two feet.

There is one problem involved in this, as we'll perhaps cover in "The Social Gospel,"[1] where people become overly sympathetic to elements of life that are not willing to assume the responsibility for their own God-given opportunities. And we pour out our love and our service to them, as we do sometimes to foreign countries, and we receive back a slap in the face and a curse for our efforts. And this is true.

Therefore, as people who value divine judgment, we must learn also to understand when to give and when to withhold of ourselves. And sometimes, à la the Divine, we must learn to chasten other people in order that we might demonstrate our love by chastening, as well as at other times by lavishing our affection upon them.

But God give us the wisdom to know when to do this. Otherwise we could create a tremendous karma, you see, by reversing this process, just turning it upside down. And when in doubt, give a little—but don't give everything, because you could be wrong on that, you see.

So we are covering love that is not involved in the vampire activity of human sympathy, where it is pulled upon because people want you to feel sorry for them. I do not say that we should not pray for such as these. I think they need a great deal of prayer. But they must reach up. They must make an effort to find reality themselves.

"Man, know thyself" is a fiat of the Great White Brotherhood. Man has got to come to the point where he makes self-intelligent effort to find his Divine Presence. I am convinced that from the beginning God was literally dumping himself on humanity, that he was drenching people with his love, but that they did not respond.

And I am convinced that out of his own wisdom he gradually withdrew, because he realized that this was not the answer. It was not the answer, of just giving and giving and giving of himself and his gifts. But there was an element of true stewardship involved here, where the steward had to learn the value of his talents and prove unto the Deity before the Deity would open the windows of heaven to him.

There are schools today that teach of the abundance of God and how he would lavish it upon them. But we must look practically not to one life or to just a few segments of lives, but we must look to the total world picture. We must also look with the wisdom eyes of the Great White Brotherhood, and we must realize that God has only withdrawn from man as a tactical maneuver calculated to arouse in him a hunger for this great reality that God is. Because when God was close to man, and when he has drawn the closest to man, sometimes people have failed to appreciate him.

Now, I want to point out something about the flow of the flame. I want to point out that the flame of reality that is in the heart is very, very small in most of humanity. And this flame is not visible under normal circumstances to the physical eyes of man. It is probably no higher than an eighth or a quarter of an inch in the heart chambers.

In case of transplants, I assure you that the flame remains with the individual, because it is a part of the etheric rather than of the physical. Therefore, these silly questions—which I shouldn't call silly, but nevertheless they seem a bit silly at times—they come in, they want to know, "What happens now if I have a heart transplant?" The number of letters we've been getting, you'd think that half the people in the organization were wondering about whether they were going to have a heart transplant.[2]

In the case of a heart transplant, the threefold flame, of course, remains with the individual, as I've said before, because it's a part of the etheric. In fact, all of the organs of the body are only a manifestation in the physical. And if you do a transplant of any organ, you still have your same etheric record. This is something that medical science is going to find out about one of these days.

If you do a kidney transplant, the record of your other kidney will remain in your etheric body. There will be an overtone of the donor kidney, of course. It will show a vibration. But unless the conditions that created the diseased organ in the first place are corrected, eventually we would see a manifestation of the same disease, in most cases, coming back into the physical in due course of time, because the electronic pattern is actually that which holds the karmic record, you see. It has to be. You can't change it.

So this flame flows and it flows very minutely. And one of the activities and functions of the Keepers of the Flame Fraternity and of The Summit Lighthouse itself as an organization and agency of the Great White Brotherhood is the teaching of the methods of increasing the flow of this flame so that it becomes larger and larger.

In fact, we have seen people whose plume of love was so large that it stood outside of their physical form and spilled over on the side, where the wisdom ray came way up above them like this, and then the blue plume came out like that on the other side. So, seeing the reason for the activity is to increase this threefold flame, this means that we are seeking the expansion of the reality of the individual, because you are not your body but you are this flame.

At first, of course, this may seem a bit uncomfortable to some people who have always thought of themselves as a body. And they can't imagine looking in the mirror and seeing this flame in the mirror. In fact, they'd probably be frightened and run out the door if they saw the flame.

But actually it's just like this: Whatever environment you are in, there is an adaptability in your consciousness. It is just like in the matter of the spherical body as described in one of our advanced lessons. It's the same with the child in the womb. The child is curled up in the womb, and it's perfectly comfortable in this natural environment, warm and cozy in a fluid, like a fish, very happy there, so happy they kick and bounce and can hardly wait to come forth. And they have even been heard to cry—did you know that? They've been heard to cry inside the womb, make noise with their mouth.

So this is a rather interesting thing, because the fetus itself is really, of course, the embryonic adult male or female body. And once again we see that it is not this little miniature creation that is actually the child, but it is the threefold flame. And it conveys and carries identity.

You go and talk to some of the nurses sometime up in the maternity wards, and they can tell you some real stories like this. They'll say, "Every baby has a distinct and different personality." Well, is this hereditary? I mean, was it mama and papa through their genes and chromosomes that put this personality in? Is this just the manifestation of chemical elements and so forth?

Of course not. It's a manifestation of the soul. And the soul is different. The soul personality is different. It's naturally different, because people are different. Let's face it. Yet they all have the same potential.

Getting back to the pattern of the threefold flame again, it has a flow and the flow must be increased. And I want to point out something strange to you about this threefold flame. When we look at it frontally, it looks almost like a Boy Scout emblem, similar to the fleur-de-lis. But if we look at it from on top, if we come right down on top of it, it looks like three balls in a pawn shop. We are dealing here with three spheres, and attached to the spheres is sort of a gradually receding root structure. It isn't really a root, it's part of the flame, but it comes down, you see. So this gives us a little different vision of it.

Well, if you stand on one side of the flame, it may look a little different than the other. Do you see that? From the standpoint of the three balls, you're looking down on top of it. It depends on what relationship your body is and your eyes are to the position of the flame. If the flame is not moving, it's just stationary, you can get all kinds of different angles to it, you see, which will reverse the process, won't it?

But you should be aware of the right and left in relationship, then, only to your own physical body because you will find that the left hemisphere of the brain, when it is affected, as in strokes and paralysis and so forth, it will affect the right side of the body. It's always reversed. And this is an interesting concept, but it's true. It's just like the optical images that we see. In reality, all of the people in this room in my eye are upside down. You're all hanging by your heads, but my brain reverses it in my consciousness.

Now, I want to try to explain to you, in connection with this flame, something about the personal id. The personal id, the identity, the self, basically has no connection with this flame because the flame is the identity of the Father within you. Do you understand me? This is the Christ identity of man, and that is what we must cultivate.

We have to cultivate the flame identity, because the human personality is constantly changing. People will absolutely change from the time they're babies until the time they're five years old. And they change when they're ten years old. They change when they're fifteen, and they change when they are twenty. And then when they become twenty-one and they grow up, then they change again. And they change all the way through life and they're constantly changing.

People are in a constant state of flux, mental flux. And it's really something. But people get rooted and wedded to this changing personality, and they think that's themselves, and they cherish it because they don't understand it. And we'll try to give you some insight into it as quickly as possible here.

The personal id actually equals the akashic records of all embodiments you have ever had. In other words, the personal identity of you is involved with every one of your embodiments back to the time you first set foot upon this planet. Therefore naturally, seeing you've probably been kings, queens, serfs and bartenders as well as everything else, blackguards and pirates, heaven only knows what, you do have within you the demons of many of these negative creations.

And these, of course, must be transmuted by the student, because they are the shadow and the smoke that was referenced by God to Abraham when he said to him, "The burning and smoking lamp will pass before you."[3] The burning is necessary because this shows transmutation. The smoke comes up because we are having combustion, and we are having combustion because we had something to burn.

And whether you realize what I'm saying or not, this is actually the constructive aspect of what men have called "hellfire" and "brimstone." It's the burning out by the divine process, without harm to the personality at all, of the elements that need transmuting.

Why, I can go to anybody in this room and say to them, "Have you ever done anything wrong?" And any honest person here will admit to having done wrong. And when they admit it, they will say, "Well, I don't want that in my world." Well, you've got it in your world. It's in your world if you did it, and you've got to clean it up. Everybody does. If it were not so, all of the messiahs we have seen down through the ages would have saved the world a long time ago and we'd now be living in a golden age of peace and harmony between everyone. The very fact that we are not shows that failure has occurred.

But it is not total failure. It's only partial failure. It's the kind of failure that shows we're trying. And it means that we should sweep aside and say "Skiddoo" to a lot of the erroneous thoughts and philosophies that have tried to deceive us with a childish religion that actually thinks that the heavenly Father sits up here somewhere in an antiseptic corner of the universe with a big white beard as in the Sistine Chapel. They think he's sitting up there looking down on the earth and saying, "Well, you're going down. And you're going up. And I'm arbitrarily going to decide..." It's like a game of daisies, "She loves me, she loves me not. He loves me, he loves me not" and so on—that God is just whimsically deciding that he's going to choose this one or that one.

That is not the case. We have to choose God, as the masters have taught, and we have to compound Deity within ourselves alchemically. We have to transfer Deity and we have to transmute and we have to refine. And this is the wonderful Christ process whereby with the will tethered to the divine will, we are able to manifest reality for ourselves. Otherwise, you see, it would never work.

The flame is will, wisdom, power of perfection. All of that is inherent within the flame. The carnal mind and its acts untransmuted or unchanged enters life and leaves its record on the lower being of man in the liver. This is correct. The liver is a sewer, and the life records of human beings are actually recorded in the liver. That's what the word means: liv-er, life record, in the old Senzar tongue— *live r*ecord. The Christ mind is different from this lower life record. And the Christ mind always carries people up.

What is the real id, the real identity of man? This is where we've got to walk the razor's edge, and this is the most important point I'm trying to make to you. A lot of people want to abolish this lower identity. They are wrong. They cannot abolish it. It is a carte blanche to heaven if they use it right and don't abuse it.

God could have made us angels, beings subjected to his will like puppets. We would be programmed like computers. We'd fly through heaven, we'd carry out the divine mandates, and eventually we might even come to the point we'd created in ourselves a certain degree of his love. But in the meantime, we would carry his love. We'd be angels.

Human beings, made a little lower than the angels, are going to be crowned with more glory[4] because they will come through the crucible of suffering, and God will be born in them. They will have their own Bethlehem, their own nativity. The straw in the manger of their heart will repose there. And on that straw the little, miniature Christ Self, as an extension of the higher Christ Self, the macrocosmic Christ, as a flame is blazing there within the heart.

And the real identity of man is a fusion of the lower personality and a merge, where the lower personality gradually lays off that which is corruptible and puts on that which is incorruptible. And eventually the lower self—as above, so below—the lower self becomes God-identified. This is what a master does. This is what a master is. This is what you're all aspiring to be, ascended masters. And this is your God-plan.

God did not create you to turn you into pirates, thieves, black-guards, and every other kind of ill-begotten personality manifestation. God created you to be his only begotten Son, to be in the image of that Son. Do you see the point? And the whole human race was created that way, gloriously created.

And so, in closing, I'd like to say that the real id is a composite of the Christ mind and the emerging human personality as it is glorified by light. And to wind it up, this is a daily process. And we will touch upon many of these things and reintegrate them and rephrase them and clarify them as the class proceeds. But we did want to touch a bit on the threefold flame and your identity, because while you may not even understand what I have said, there are some of you that won't understand it only because you haven't thought of yourself this way.

Yet, on the other hand, biological science is now coming out with possibilities of even transplanting human heads and putting them into a machine and then wondering whether the soul will enter in. And they could keep people alive just inside their brain. And eventually this brain would just sit there in space and be aware of all things through some scientific apparatus that could be constructed. We don't want that. Others are freezing corpses in the hopes that a thousand years from now they'll be able to take care of the cancer they have or the heart condition, all these things.

We are not looking to science or the earth for our immortality. We are satisfied with the disintegration process, because we know that we have an integration process while we are here that, if we follow it out to the fullest degree, we will achieve our immortality—and that without any question.

There aren't any two ways about it. The masters have gone before. And any person that doubts the masters' authenticity or reality can very easily in the course of time prove to themselves again and again the reality of the masters.

I'm not going to do it this minute. You're not going to receive it this minute. But it is a provable process. And when we see that process, we realize our divine identity as our immortality, and we realize that in this changing, ephemeral manifestation, we do not have immortality but mortality.

There is a fraternity in this country that as part of their ceremonies has people sit before a mirror and look at their own embodiments. I'm not criticizing this process, but I'm sure that all of us could go back and back and back and see ourselves as Sufis, see ourselves in Ur, see ourselves in Babylon, or as Risë Stevens did,[5] see ourselves in the Colosseum or elsewhere in the world.

We might proceed to examine the fabric of all these embodiments. But as far as I am concerned, I'm looking to the future, because these are all root structures feeding the present. And what we are concerned with is what we shall be. "For when he shall appear, we shall be like him; for we shall see him as he is."[6]

Thank you.

December 28, 1968
Colorado Springs, Colorado

CHAPTER 16

Man's Identity and His Real Plan

The mystery of identity is not as complicated as it seems at the point of its inception, at the point of its origin, at the point of its beginning. The mystery of identity is like a clean, white slate. Nothing is upon it except the purity of God.

This concept has been promulgated before. It goes something like this: "Mine eyes are too pure to behold iniquity."[1] And therefore, we cannot relate ourselves with iniquity, but only with the purity of God.

So our real identity originated in God and is Godlike, is qualified with the qualities of God. But along with it, with the precious gift of identity, God gave something else. What was that? It was free will. And so, we all share in free will as one of the facets of our identity, and this is what has gotten us into trouble—not individually alone, but as a whole human race, from time immemorial.

Some people think that perhaps God had a bad idea. They say, "Well, why didn't he just create us perfect?" Well, he did, which brings us to a strange duality: the duality of the level of our God Presence and the little manifestation of selfhood that we call ourselves but which, in reality, is only our freewill motivation. It's sort of a doorway, and it really leads two ways: we can go through the doorway to the left or we can go through the doorway to the right. It's an arch. It can be an arch of triumph or an arch of defeat. And that, of course, is basically our identity.

But that is not God's identity, you see. God's identity is the image that he gave to us. It's a part of us, a part of the dual self, half of it. The other half is linked entirely to will and motivation. We do what we want to do and we create ourselves.

A lot of people don't understand that. They always thought that God created them. Well, he did. But what he made was pure and perfect. What they have made is not pure and perfect. So we have two creators, the first creator and the secondary creator. And what we have to do is cause the secondary creator to eventually become one with the first creator, which is God.

We have to identify by our will motivation with the wisdom of God and the will of God. Then, you see, we become that oneness ourselves. But people don't understand that; they get confused on this whole issue. It's so easy to do it, because now you see it and now you don't.

First you see that all things come from God. You can understand that. There's a source and everything comes out of that sun, out of that source. And then you look at the sort of a chimera of human consciousness, a variegated manifestation.

I hope that you understand what I mean, because I am trying to put into finite words man's vision of the infinite. You see, the purpose of this realm is actually an expansion of the spectrum of life. And what has happened here is that the light has shined down in this dimension here, and it has expanded its own spectrum, and then we are allowed in this time span to get involved in that.

We get involved in all kinds of choices because we have a lot of synthetic appetites. I am sure that God didn't create beef stew. That's what I am trying to say, you know. So we created it, we created these hungers. We created many of these dishes that we more or less become accustomed to.

We identify with these things as though they were actually a part of our life. In reality, they are no part of our life at all when we come to the other side of the road. When we reach the point where we're living in the heaven world, we don't have any need for human meat. You remember how Jesus said, "I have meat to eat that ye know not of."[2]

So we begin to develop, then, a hunger for the spiritual meat even while we're here involved with many material things. But too many of us get confused, and we think that these material things are everything to us, and really they are not. They are only a series of appetites that have been handed down from our grandmothers and our great-grandmothers and our forefathers. We've inherited them as a race. But it doesn't mean all of that. It doesn't mean anything in reality as far as the immortality of the soul is concerned, and I'll show you why.

First of all, supposing you made your ascension tomorrow. They'd just be excess baggage, wouldn't they? What use would you have for a big house?

The whole idea can be illustrated by the analogy of death itself. When a rich man or a poor man, either one, dies, what do they leave behind? Naked they came into the world, naked they go out.[3] They can take nothing with them.

So the only things that we can take with us are the things that we give away. Isn't that interesting? Had you ever stopped to think about that? One of the masters one time told us that. The master said, "I give you my love. All else I have already given away." I thought that was very beautiful, and it illustrates to us the nature of identity.

Identity is ephemeral. Let's go back and take Mary Magdalene. Let's put her in the position momentarily of being a prostitute. All right, all of her friends knew that, didn't they? They all knew this is what she was. People that knew her intimately, they knew this is what she was. So if someone asked you, "What about her? What does she do for a living?" "Oh, she's a prostitute." You understand?

It was a very natural thing. They just talked about it as a common occasion. But when she became a Christian, she changed, didn't she?

Well, I allow that we have to recognize the potential for human change in all people, not just in ourselves. And we ought not to deny it to ourselves, either. We ought to recognize the potential to change.

I find one of the greatest of human cruelties in relation to the identity of man is that people like to put you in a hole, a round peg in a round hole. They stick you right in there and stereotype you. They like to say, "This is the identity of so and so. This is the kind of person they are. This is what they believe. This is what they think. This is what they do." You understand?

Well, that, of course, to me is only the passing stream of identity. It keeps on flowing. Don't people change? I believe they do. I believe they change physically and they change spiritually and they change mentally. We should allow people to have change and to experience it for themselves.

Unfortunately, some people have negative change. Many times when they fall low enough, they know the only way they can go is back toward God. They just simply can't see it's a dead end street. They go down and they're not satisfied.

Why is this? Because in reality, man is a dual being, as I said before. What do we mean when we say a dual being? When I say a dual being, I mean that he is made up of a divine image and a human image; and the purpose of life is to allow the human image to use its own free will to become Godlike.

Somehow or other, God doesn't enjoy very much having a group of puppets that he's made surrender to his own will. You can see that, can't you? Isn't that perfectly natural? I don't think even you as an individual would be very happy in making the right choice of living for God and for Christ and for the masters and by the right teachings unless you could make that choice yourself, unless you made it of your own free will. If someone else made it for you, you wouldn't like it. I don't think I would like it, either.

You might know that you were eating good food, you might know that you were properly housed, you might know that everything was very nice and everything was being done for you, but somehow or other that wouldn't be satisfactory. You'd say to yourself, "Well, I am not exactly contented, because I didn't elect to come here. I came because God forced me to. He made me do it." And somehow or other you just don't like that idea. And somehow or other I don't feel that God would like it, either.

I have a feeling that God would be very displeased with a bunch of puppets and robots, little puppy dogs that he had fenced into a corral or into a kennel or something and said, "Now you stay there, Fido. You do exactly as I tell you to do." And it doesn't go for the making of a god.

So why do we have this initiation in duality? Why do we have initiatic experiences? We have initiation given to us because the real purpose of life is to make man into a god. God started out by putting the stamp of the divine image on man. That is his identity. And the master plan for the ages is to create a godlike man, free from all of the dregs.

In order to give you some idea from a modern text by a man who has some understanding of this, but not a complete understanding of man's identity and his real plan, I am going to read you from an introduction by György Kepes.

> Thus, vision, our creative response to the world, is basic, regardless of the area of our involvement with the world. It is central in shaping our physical, spatial environment, in grasping the new aspects of nature revealed by modern science, and, above all, in the experience of artists, who heighten our perception of the qualities of life and its joys and sorrows.
>
> Vision is a key to man's creative power, even on the most rudimentary level. Our eye receives only the random flow of light stimulation; the light rays that impinge on the retina have no intrinsic order. But our dynamic tendency to create order

transforms the basic sense impressions of light signals into meaningful forms. From the welter of sensation bombarding the retinas of our eyes, we articulate structures, images, and from the intermingled, interconnecting, shifting stream of optical images, we separate persistent patterns, things, events.

Thus, to perceive an image is to participate in a forming process; it is a creative act. In the simplest form of visual orientation and in the most embracing unity of a work of art, there is a significant common basis: the sorting and organization of sensory impressions from the visual field.

But vision, though the key orderer, nevertheless receives its scope and scale from what it orders. Our visual experiences are drawn from the features of the visible world around us. The strength, the richness, and the order of the visual forms that we create depend, to a certain extent, upon the nature of our visual surroundings. If, in the world, man sees around him the rhythm of nature's processes revealed, and if the colors, forms, and movements he sees are expressions of organic events, then his vision is nourished by the "primal sanities of nature"—to use Walt Whitman's words. If the primal sanities of nature can be absorbed through his vision, if man is led to see them, he can reproduce them in the world he shapes for himself.

Today, we have lost the benefit of these natural guides because we are surrounded by the "second nature" of our man-made environment, an environment that has not grown according to nature but has been shaped by one-sided and shortsighted interests. The appearances of things in our man-made world no longer reveal their character: images imitate forms; forms cheat functions; functions are robbed of their natural sources emanating from human needs. Our cities, our buildings (counterfeit inside and out), objects for use, the packaging of goods, posters, the advertising in our newspapers—even our clothes, our gestures, our physiognomies—are often without visual integrity. The world that modern man has constructed by and large lacks sincerity and scale. It is twisted in space, without light, and cowardly in color. It combines mechanically consistent patterns of details within formless wholes. It is oppressive in its fake monumentality; degrading in its petty, fawning manner of face-lifting. Men living in this environment, injured emotionally and intellectually by the terrific odds of their compassless society, cannot avoid injury to their sensibilities, the basis of their creative faculties.

To give direction and order to this formlessness, we have to go back to our roots. We need to regain the health of our creative faculties, especially of our visual sensibilities. There is a reciprocal relationship between our distorted environment and our impoverished ability to see with freshness, clarity, and joy. Fed on our deformed and dishonest environment, our under-nourished visual sensibilities can only lead us to perpetuate the malfunctions of the environment that we create. To counteract this spiral of self-destruction, we have to re-educate our vision and reclaim our lost sensibilities.[4]

I think this will illustrate, perhaps, one of the intents of our forthcoming Ascended Master University, which will be to reeducate the vision of humanity taken in any stage of their evolution and in any age in their chronological development—in other words, a child or a child-man or a man or an old man; it makes no difference. We can take people at any age and attempt to reeducate their vision according to ascended master concepts, and thus eventually this will permeate the world order and induce the kingdom of heaven as an automatic function of the higher mind in man.

Unless we are able to recognize this relationship between our identity and our own creative acts and impulses, we probably are more or less drifting people, drifting in a sea of mind, which almost becomes mindless in its manifestation. This is because we become automated creatures of habit. We have an idea in our consciousness that a certain thing is valid. We say, "Well, I'd like to do that." And we function a great deal on the basis of whimsy and also sentimentality.

Sentimentality becomes one of the forces that seems to drive mankind to bargain his life away and impoverish his environment. He wants to do a certain thing because that old tree has always stood there. It's always stood there, and he doesn't stop to realize that the overhanging branch makes it difficult for him to get his car in the garage. So he doesn't want to cut it down because grandmother planted it, and he leaves it there. And this sentimentality is actually destructive in a way, because as soon as his son finds that he has lain to rest his father, he cuts off the branch and maybe the whole tree.

So we see that people should be capable of moving with the flow of the universe, or the divine Tao, the divine endowment. There is a flow in the universe. Perhaps we may imagine it as coming from the yin and yang, the negative and positive forces of the universe. And this flow cannot and will not be stopped by any of us. We may stop progress in our own time, if we want to, by insisting upon the sentimentality of whatever we wish to keep or preserve of our human nature. But if we are determined to actually pursue an *avant-garde* realization of God, we have to be willing to let go and make progress, keep alive, be eternally young because you can accept the fruits of the Spirit of the coming age.

The young people here today can little imagine themselves as old men with beards. But I assure you that the time will pass swiftly and they will stand right where the older people now stand. So in view of this tremendous flow and the continuation of the flow, the identity of man which we have termed ephemeral has to be considered because ephemeral means the passing scene. And we have to consider that the scene is passing whether we want to acknowledge it or not, and we are very, very foolish people if we want to let life pass us by, as far as opportunity goes.

So we've got to look at this identity of ourselves and be willing to make changes. Because we're not only making them for ourselves, we're making them for our God. This is what Saint Paul said, "We . . . are changed . . . from glory unto glory, even as by the Spirit of the Lord,"[5] which denotes to us that there are glories terrestrial and glories celestial. And in and among those glories, both terrestrial and celestial, we find planes of glory, like the steps on a stairway or like a ladder. We go up that ladder, the ladder of terrestrial glory. We go through all the human experiences that we think we find happiness in.

Jesus himself said, "Search the scriptures; for in them ye think ye find eternal life: and they are they which testify of me."[6] He dwelt among mankind, yet said, "I have meat to eat that ye know not of."[7] "I must be about my Father's business."[8] He denoted in his consciousness that he had a higher walk than the average man and woman.

The average man and woman today on the streets of America and the whole world are completely brainwashed, fake as this man said, in their monumental stupidity, or something to that effect. They themselves are stereotyped images. They wear certain clothes. They wear certain ornamentation. They do certain things. It's the fashion of the times.

The current vogue, wherein many of our high school people are wearing long hair—and I am not speaking to condemn them; I am simply making a statement of fact—was originally started— without their knowledge, of course; they didn't ask the permission of anybody to start it—by certain Marxist Communists who were using it to divide and create a generation gap where none existed between the various ages.

The reason I have pointed this out to you is because it is a synthetic agency which is intended to create a division among people when there is no division between their hearts if their heart is in the right place. I have been in Haight-Ashbury.* I have been all over the country and made personal investigations and motion pictures of many of these functions. And I have found out in my own experiences that many of these young people are highly idealistic and

---

*In the 1960s, the Haight-Ashbury section of San Francisco was known as a center for hippies, alternative beliefs and lifestyles, psychedelic drugs and marijuana, and non-traditional mores.

very fine and highly intelligent people, capable of absorption into our social order.

They, however, are not all completely satisfied with our social order, and I think there is perhaps one constructive change that we have to recognize that will come forth from this—because you cannot do anything, whether it's good or bad, without having some fruit from it, and I assume that there are some good fruits that come from bad causes, albeit Saint Paul says, "They who say, Let us do evil, that good may come, their damnation is just."[9] So he pointed out that the law of karma is that which functions, and I think a man would be very, very foolish today if he wanted to do evil just so good would come of it.

Nevertheless, I think that while innocent evil occurred in the case of many of these people throughout the nation, at the same time some constructive good of change will come from it that will probably bring about a greater introspection on the part of humanity as they begin to examine the phoniness of their ideals.

I had a conversation not long ago with one of America's formerly great evangelists. This evangelist told me of a great meeting that they had. And at the close of that meeting they took up bushel baskets of money. And I said, "Well, that's fine. You really did a good job, then."

He said, "Yes, everything was fine—until I went out with the minister of the church after the service was over."

And I said, "Will you describe to me what took place in the church?"

He told how the Spirit of God had moved in the people and there was a tremendous outpouring of love and all of that that went on.

And I said, "Well, what happened after this evangelistic meeting that disillusioned you?"

He said, "Well, I got out on the street with the pastor and he said, 'Come on. Let's get in my car. Let's go somewhere and pick up a couple of women.'"

And he said to the minister, "Aren't you married?"

The minister said, "Yes, but what difference does that make?" So my friend looked at him, and he said, "Well, it makes a lot of difference to me."

He said, "I heard you were a square. But I didn't know you were that bad. Just get out of the car and I'll go out and find one myself." Bang. And out, down the street he drove. And this was down in the southern part of the United States in what's known as the Bible Belt, which was a more shocking manifestation.

But I recall the words of Jesus Christ where he said to Saint Peter, "Satan has desired to have you, that he may sift you as wheat."[10] Those who would follow the tenets of the Brotherhood, then, should understand that Satan never will bother anybody he's sure of. If he thinks he's got you, he's going to leave you alone. But the closer you get to the light, the more he's going to do to give you some trouble or cause you a fit, as somebody might say. And I think that no greater fit in this world can occur than for a man to lower his ideals or engage in the business of hypocrisy.

But I must tell you this, because we pull no punches here at the Summit. In order to examine the actual nature of evil and good under the microscope and lens of our consciousness, we know that in human conduct, honesty and sincerity ought to go at a premium. If we were having an auction, in other words, they ought to bring the top dollar, because they're worthy of the recognition of people and I think appreciated by most people. I think the hypocrite is one of the most damaging creatures on the face of this earth today, because he doesn't have to be a hypocrite.

You know, it's quite popular today for a man to be like Hugh Hefner, the owner and manager of *Playboy* magazine. It's quite popular to be that way. You could openly live that life and follow almost any other profession. But to be a preacher and then turn around and do the nasty and vulgar things that some of these fellows are doing is the most anti-Christ action in this world. Only someone who was satanically oriented would do this.

And I want to tell you that, furthermore, you don't even have to do it yourself in some cases in order to be accused of it. In my own life, I have lived as close as I can to the cross, that is, to the way of God. But I once in a while find people who will turn around and use their evil tactics to try to defame me. And I am amazed at it, but I can understand it because Jesus himself was accused long ago of being a glutton and a winebibber and a friend of publicans and sinners.[11]

Well, I would find myself perhaps justly accused of being a friend of publicans and sinners, because I am willing to associate with all people, just as Jesus did. And I feel this is the role and mark of a spiritual man. You can't be a spiritual man and live always on the mountaintop. You have to be willing to come down to the multitudes and allow the hem of your garment to be touched by the woman.[12] Do you understand what I mean? (I am not running women down, by the way.)

What I am getting at is, you have to make yourself available to people. And if you're living on the mountaintop, in what is known as a cloistered situation, you may be able to do a great deal of good there for a specific function. But for soul development, I recommend the initiation of the world. And I recommend that if you can preserve yourself in that hostile environment as an honest man, you will make it not only in this life, but should any lives come after, you will also make it. And ultimately, by pursuing that course, you will have the correct vision of yourself and God. And you're going to turn out to be the kind of a person that's a candidate for the ascension, believe me.

You will never turn out to be a candidate for the ascension by shutting yourself up into a closet somewhere and having nothing to do with people because they're not good enough for you or for God. God himself comes down to this earth through people, and he contacts people, and that's how he's able to deliver people.

A lot of people have told me personally that this work of The Summit Lighthouse has given them tremendous insight and spiritual experiences. They've had wonderful experiences. Why? Because, basically, it is guided by the masters.

But the question has come up, I must admit, where some people have said to me, "Well, I am a positive thinker and I don't like to think of anything evil. Why do you sometimes talk about the other side?" And I have tried to explain this, time and time again, that if we were all saints and we were talking only to saints, we would be able, then, to talk only about the spiritual side of life.

But when you stop and think that there are negative forces in the world that keep people from attainment—just think of that, keep people from attainment—you have to talk to them about it sometimes in order to make them realize the subtlety of it. A lot of times it's very subtle. It rides just underneath the surface of consciousness, and there it will defraud us of our spiritual inheritance if we do not wake up and live.

So I felt in the giving of this talk on the identity of man and the real plan of man, we should understand that there also is a fraudulent plan, which probably is a willy-nilly plan, I must admit, that is largely pleasure-based, where man says, "Well, I like good food. I like coffee. I like chicken and turkey and steaks. And I like wine, women, and song."

They've always had these things on this earth, and that's one of the things that defrauds people of their spiritual inheritance. We don't have to have that kind of a life. But we've got to be prepared to understand those to whom this kind of life appeals. And we should not condemn these people. We should try to help them, by the power of our inner nature, to find their own reality and contact with God.

So let's forget all about that now. We are through with it. We're through with that aspect of vision. But I've touched upon it.

Now, when we come to deal with the process of involving ourselves in our own identity, we have to first of all possess the quality of enlightened vision. If we do not have enlightened vision, we are more or less lost. We're lost in the maze of human conduct and consciousness, our own or someone else's. But if we recognize that our Presence can give it to us, we can then understand the mystical significance even of a meditative period.

What is a meditative period? It's a period when you cut your connections to the world thought and you establish your connections with the divine thought.

What are the dangers in meditation? One of the dangers in meditation is that you will fall asleep and go into the astral realm, that you will become purely psychically oriented. You have to be able to direct the meditation with your conscious mind until such a time as your higher spiritual mind is able to take over. And you will know it when this happens. You must be able to remain in control of your own environment and yourself, directing yourself as a boatman along the shore so that he doesn't get hooked up or snagged up on something. You have to be able to use that long pole and push yourself off if you see a rock.

And if you're not conscious and you're functioning in a trance state, beware of this state of consciousness, because it can often be as dangerous as automatic writing, which is also one of the very great dangers that people encounter in the psychic realm.[13] It has to do with the identity of man, too, because it's one of the dead ends that people sometimes get in.

You should understand, one and all, that the identity of man should be fashioned after the identity of God. "Well," you say, "how do I know this God? And what does God do for me?"

First of all, he does not have to come forth in human utterances in order to actually do things for you. You've probably noticed in some of the dictations, especially some of you who have actually come here many, many times, that once in a while you have a dictation that is mystical, that is not always clear to the conscious mind as to just what it means, but somehow or other you get a tremendous feeling. You begin to wonder just why is it that so much is being done for you, and you know it's being done, but you can't put your finger on the pulse of it, and you don't know what's happening.

That is because there is a soundless Word. In other words, God's vibrations do not have to extend to the mere utterance of human words and language and speech, which, after all, is just intelligent sound. What is language and speech? It's intelligent sound.

For example, today we say "chair." We could say *Stuhl*,* and it'd still be a chair, wouldn't it? It wouldn't make any difference what you said. In some other language, you could call it a "dodo." Well, if you called it a "dodo," it would still be a chair if it meant that to you. It's all a matter of image substitution, do you see? It's a matter of image substitution and familiarity.

That's why the Tower of Babel functioned the way it did. When the angels came down, all they did is confuse the speech centers in people. And so different words had different meanings. And the ones that believed one thing or heard one thing, they went off with all the rest that talked their language and they parted company with those who didn't. It was quite an experience.

Now, however, what we are interested in primarily is man's identity and his real plan. I've tried to touch on this. Man's identity is from the Divine Source all the way. Remember that. God is the Creator of that inner spark in man. But you, supposed to function as a god, are the creator of your own darkness. You create hatred. You create feelings of lust and destruction. You create all kinds of ideas.

A lot of times these are fanciful dream ideas, ideas that Sigmund Freud would probably have written about if he were alive today. He probably would have defined it a little bit more. Why? Because he lived more or less in a sort of a dream world, which is actually fringing on the astral, on the border of the astral world. None of this has anything to do or any relevancy with the true spiritual man.

Meditation will give you, for example, often a tremendous feeling. I can do it right here and now—by God's grace, I have the power to go into instantaneous meditation. I might do it just for an

---

*German, "chair"

experiment, just to show you what I am talking about. And then you can judge for yourself. Some of you will pick this up and some won't. But we'll try it and just show you what I mean.

[Mark meditates for fifteen seconds.]

Did you feel that, any of you? Who felt it?

One, two, three, four, five, six, seven, eight, nine, ten, eleven, twelve, thirteen, fourteen, fifteen, sixteen, about seventeen people here felt it. Everyone might not feel it. Your senses might not be momentarily opened as quickly. But I went into that state of meditation to show you what I was experiencing. I will tell you what it was.

I was experiencing a tremendous trembling of electrical energies, a very high vibratory rate. These energies were basically the universal power of God that crisscrosses across all time and space. It's the warp and woof of creation. Those energies are vibrating just like electricity all the time through space. They have no time to behold evil. They have no identification with evil whatsoever. They are purely good. But they're not goody-goody good. Do you see what I mean? It's not the Pollyanna sort of goodness, but it's the goodness that is creative. It's creative energy. And if you lost your body, that would still be there and you'd still be there. But you might not know how to plug into it, how to tune in on it, you see.

So you have to realize that this creative energy, this creative feeling, to many people becomes a point where they get enmeshed in that spirituality and they say, "Well, I've contacted God in meditation. You should feel that power I felt. Oh boy, I really had an experience."

But you know something? You can fall in love with that feeling. And you can become a person who just wants that feeling like a person wants drugs or sex or whiskey or a cheap movie. You can fall in love with that feeling. And in order to really be spiritual, you have to go beyond that to the nature of God and love him for just being himself. Love the power of the creative vision itself—not for the sake of that power, but because there is an intelligence beyond that power.

And here is the strange thing. That's your real identity. It's the ocean of God's Spirit. That ocean is everywhere. I can go to India and contact God. I can be here in America and contact God. Wherever I am, I can contact God and so can you.

Why doesn't everybody develop an awareness of that? Now, about seventeen to eighteen people in here could feel that. Why couldn't everyone feel it? Some may get it even later today. They have a latent structuring in their glandular system and the opening of their spiritual eye.

The point I am trying to make is that this can be felt by some. And if it can be felt by some, then it can be felt by everybody. But that in itself is not God; it is the nature of God. There are so many people that get confused by this nature of God that they do not actually come to know him. The real God, then, is the creative essence and the creative plan that is locked as a cosmic engram within your very bones and within the structuring of your whole spirit.

You have an inner plan and that plan is a victorious life plan. That doesn't mean that you have to work as a telegraph operator or a moving picture star or as a Florence Nightingale. It doesn't mean any of these things. You may do any of these things and still be godly. That's not what I am talking about. I am talking about developing the creative power of being able to tap the power in the universe and then become the acquaintance of the Godhead as the divine mind (rather than the carnal mind) functioning as the creative mind in you.

The carnal mind in most people becomes the functioning structuring of their being. Do you see what I mean? And everybody finds it very compatible when they're with people of a carnal mind, because it doesn't rub them the wrong way. But the moment they come in contact with the Christ or with Jesus or a Buddha or someone that talks about something else, this may bother them. It may bother the carnal mind.

So don't be surprised if sometimes people shun you or your

vibratory action simply because they are not affinitized with you. Don't think this is unusual. This is natural law. It's natural law always. And you have to understand that law.

So when you're dealing with the identity of yourself, realize that identity is a changeable identity. And realize, above all, that you can develop the creative aspects of your life until you can completely identify with God, the God that is behind the manifestation of power, the God that is behind the manifestation of wisdom, the God that is behind the manifestation of love.

Many people make the terrible mistake in their whole lifetime of suspecting that the all-important aspect of their life is their twin ray. Well, I think there's no question but their own twin ray has some import to everyone. But a person can get hung up on that and find that their twin ray has been ascended for two thousand years. Then they go all around hunting for every gal on the whole planet to find out if she's their twin ray. This is a hang-up. And it's a dangerous one at that.

What you really want to do is find the creative aspects that God has put within you, your life plan, and put your energy into that plan and leave it to the Creator to draw you to your twin ray. What can possibly happen if you become a highly developed person is this: your twin ray will come to you if they're ascended. If they're not, they may be drawn to you on the earth plane of matter, providing you're not already hooked up. But if you're already spoken for and you have a wife or a husband, it's kind of ridiculous to expect that your twin ray is suddenly going to come floating around the corner and say, "Here I am."

It's just a bit ridiculous. And an awful lot of people sacrifice everything for that. And the love that they have becomes only sex love instead of God love. You don't want it. You can get this all over the world. It's not what you want. What you really want is divine love. And a lot of people mistake the human love for the divine love.

I didn't say that you should be unkind to one another. I think people can be kind and understanding and loving to one another and courteous. But they don't have to turn around and get involved in all this touchy-touchy business like sensitivity training, where you see some guy feeling a guy's bald head and then another guy has got his hand on some lady's knee, and all this type of stuff in the name of sensitivity. And as my friend Al Schein out there would say, "Fiddledeedee."

That's exactly what it is. It's a bunch of human foolishness that doesn't take anybody to God. And when you try to mix religion with that, then it becomes all the worse. And I think in the state of California, I've found quite a few religions where they are basically oriented that way instead of being oriented to God's way.

I will agree there may be some human contentment in it all. But after all, people don't really like to be deceived. I think a very interesting thing has to do with the "pigeon drop" cases that most of the police departments are familiar with, where someone comes along, and they say to some woman on the street, "Oh, my friend over here just found $10,000 in hundred-dollar bills. Maybe you'd like to participate in this. I'll be willing to give you half of it if you'll put up some good faith money."

So the woman goes to the bank and draws out $5,000 and she hands it to this guy for safekeeping and he wraps it in a newspaper. And then he turns around and he pulls a switcheroo on her, sleight of hand, and the little package which he has of her $5,000 becomes another package in which there's worthless newspaper. And he hands that to her for safekeeping, but she doesn't even look at it because she trusts him. Later on she gets suspicious and looks at it and then calls the police, and you have another victim of the famous "pigeon drop" scheme.

Things like this go on all the time in the world. People become victims of human love and human delusions of grandeur and human ideas of riches and all that. If people put their heart with God and trusted in God, they wouldn't be looking for human schemes all the time, and then being deceived.

But this illustrates that people do not like to be deceived, because I want you to know that for every ten "pigeon drop" cases that go to the police departments of this nation, there are probably ninety to a hundred cases that never say a word. They just take their licking and the losses and they say, "Well, I learned a lesson. I was a fool." And they go off and forget about it, too ashamed to tell even the police department that they were so badly duped.

You should understand, then, that in this organization we are going to tell you the truth about these things, because it is important to you to learn who you really are. And please understand for all time that the human ego is nothing but the human ego.

You just saw Constantine on the screen. Constantine's been dead a long time, and I happen to know a great deal more about him than I am saying—and he isn't anybody that's here, so don't get that idea. But the point I want to make is that this changing identity we have is this way. You take one of our ladies here and you bring her back to her girlhood, like Bridey Murphy. I don't believe in hypnotism, but you go ahead and just do it without hypnotism. You just make her think about when she was a little girl. She starts telling you some anecdotes from her girlhood.

Over the years, the trauma and pressures of human experience have molded her until she's not the same little girl she was when she was nine or ten years old. She's changed. We can always accept the element of change in ourselves as long as it occurs in ourselves, because it's so gradual. It's like some man that goes off somewhere to India, and he's gone for five or ten years. A lot of changes take place in him and we haven't seen him all these years, and when we see him, all these changes are all at once before us. We can recognize this. But somebody that's with him over in India all that time, they don't even notice he's changed, it's so gradual.

And the gradual changes of life often come to us, although traumatic experiences come, too, where terrible things will suddenly turn the hair gray overnight just like that, boom. Or you might lose your eyesight overnight. I am talking about the world. I am not talking about you people. While it could happen to you, you're a cross section of the world, that's not the idea. I just want you to understand that changes come to people.

I met a woman at Mount Shasta one time in spiritual work whose hair had turned completely red, as red as you could ever imagine. And I said to her, "Well, you're using henna, aren't you?"

She said, "No."

I said, "What do you mean, you're not using anything?"

She said, "I am not using anything. That's the way the Lord did it for me."

So I looked at her hair and it was absolutely a glorious red. And I said, "What color was your hair when you were a girl?"

And she said, "Red."

So you see, it went back to the same stage it was in before, by the grace of God. And I thought that was a tremendous thing.

Now, when you get back to this identity, you have to understand that you, yourself, one and all, are not going to be any different. And that's one of the problems of humankind. People think, "I am going to be different than someone else. I have an ego, and I am a great artist. I am a great painter. I am a great musician." Well, all of the talents in the universe are available to everybody. If you want to put the time into it, go ahead.

I can remember very well in one of my past lives where I rode a horse and I was considered quite a horseman, in fact, rather notorious, and quite a swordsman. When I came back into this life, I was in the service in World War II, and I came home and I went out in the country to one of my friends who lived there who had a riding horse. And I said, "Let me ride that horse."

And he said, "Fine. I'll help you mount."

"OK."

So I got up on the horse, you know, and I was very proud. My mother was there. I thought, "Gee, that's wonderful. I'll be able to ride this horse." But I didn't know anything about reembodiment at the time. But I got on the horse and down the road I galloped past a graveyard like Ichabod Crane. And as I passed this graveyard, suddenly the horse got frightened by a passing car and he reared up, and I slid off and landed into a mud puddle with my army khakis on, and I got soaking wet, and the horse went on down the road and left me there in this freezing wind and rain.

So I had an experience that I could very easily be unhorsed. Then somebody found out afterward that I was this other character who had ridden a horse, and they said to me, "Well, how could this have happened to you if you yourself were a horseman?"

And I said, "Well, you may have been a horseman in one life and not be the next time."

In order to really keep a momentum of being a horseman or a swordsman or anything else, you have to actually engage in that business from the time you're a child in any lifetime to pick up the momentum you had where you left off. If you don't do it, you may not even be experienced in it at all. It's very natural.

So I feel that I have explained to you something about your identity, that your identity is not the passing scene. Your identity is not the circumstances or experiences that happen to you. These happen to you so that your real identity can shine forth, and your real identity is your Holy Christ Self and your God Presence, individualized.

I don't think you'd like to pick up the threads of history such as you saw today. Supposing you were one of those people that were throwing the people to the lions. My goodness. You wouldn't like that idea now. You wouldn't throw people to the lions now, would you? Well, that's the point. Maybe you were thrown to the lions. You wouldn't like that, either, would you?

So the whole idea is that a person has to recognize that there's an ongoingness about life. And I want all the people in this activity to try to get as much out of it as they can. You can't possibly get any more out of it than you can actually understand—although I suppose you don't have to actually fully understand it in order to get something out of it. I think, however, you do get more out of it if you understand it. So this is why you should study to show yourself approved unto God.[14]

I am only giving you guidelines. I'm not trying to live your life for you. You have to do that.

So I hope that you have gotten something out of this lecture, and you understand that your real plan is the plan of the Spirit.

There's one point I might like to end with. Where does the Great White Brotherhood fit in? And how is it that there's a difference in people at the spiritual level of the ascension?

Take Saint Germain and Jesus, for example, or Lord Buddha. I do not know the actual micrometer measurements of their aura and neither do you, and I am not too concerned about it. But it has been said of Lord Buddha that his aura today is bigger than the whole earth.

This is possible when you view Saint Paul's statement where he says that the resurrection of the dead is sown in dishonor and is raised in honor,[15] and where he says that one star differs from another star in glory,[16] and compares that to the resurrection of the dead, meaning that a person in their spiritual experience can gain a bigger and bigger and bigger expanding causal body. Anybody can gain this. It isn't some prerogative that I have that you don't have. You all have the right to do this.

So Gautama Buddha, apparently, through his meditations and through his spirituality in all ways and through his ability to enter in to the higher communion with the deity, gradually expanded his causal body until it became bigger than the earth.

Then you have other masters where maybe all they can get out is maybe a couple of miles, but they're still ascended masters. How in the world is that, you say? That's that one star differs from another star in glory. They're both stars, but one is bigger than the other. And we all have the right to expand our star. This equates also with the statement in Kahlil Gibran's book, *The Prophet*, where he says, "It is a flame spirit in you ever gathering more of itself."[17] In other words, you can gather more of God even though you are God. "Greater things shall you do because I go to my Father."[18]

The individuality of man, then, and his plan individually, is based on freewill choice of spiritual experience and spiritual advancement. Nobody on this planet in their right mind is going to push any of you into that spiritual experience. But you may push yourself into it. And when you do, let's make it a safe experience, a sane experience, and keep both feet on the ground while your heads are in the clouds.

Don't think that God is impractical in these dimensions. He is not. And I equate his mind as functional with the Great White Brotherhood and the great masters of the Great White Brotherhood. They function with God. Do you understand me? They function with God to help solve all kinds of human problems.

We have known many cases where the intelligence gathering agency, such as K-17, the great master, has gathered intelligence for the Brotherhood. This has been correlated, laid on the council table, and afterward it has been used by the Brotherhood to prevent war. Did you know that? They've turned around and used the information to prevent war. Sometimes they do it by leveling karma on individuals.

In the cases of Janis Joplin and a few of those others who were in the rock 'n' roll set who were taking strong drugs, they actually had the karmic hammer lowered on them as an example to some of the young people in America today.[19] The Brotherhood made that request. They said, "Can we do anything to help the young people to see the dangers?" I am trying to show you that.

So the Brotherhood functions very practically and pragmatically in the world. They're not just some kind of a strange, mystical organization floating around in some strange body with a little tail of light or something, like a paramecium. They're not part of Walt Disney's *Fantasia*. They are very practical men. And, believe me, they can do the miracles they say they can—and so can you.

Thank you.

January 1, 1971
Colorado Springs, Colorado

CHAPTER 17

"Why Callest Thou Me Good?"

Surely no tongue can tell, surely no thought can explain the programming of the cosmos, the beautiful magnificence of the eternal Father, which so little appears to our vision. Then we come to a point of cosmic law which speaks to us of the mystical, the inward sense, the sense of our heart, of the eye behind the eye, and we understand inwardly, not necessarily outwardly, that the blessing of our perceptions by the grace of God creates an expanding inward sense.

The Master Jesus said, most correctly, "Why callest thou me good?" Yet Christendom has not understood—because of tradition, both tradition of error and tradition of truth. For truth is traditional, yet error is also perpetuated, and men know it not.

And so we realize the statement he made, "Why callest thou me good?" was followed by this concept: "There is none good but one, and that is God."[1] We have, then, a common denominator of worldly goodness and badness, and also a mystical reality, the fruit of Christ, the beauty of soul, the luster of the divinity within, which, if we identify with it, removes us from the arena of the world sense, the concept as to whether or not we are good or bad.

In examining the happenings of countless lives throughout the world from inner levels, utilizing vast banks of cosmic computers and the computers of soul consciousness, we have found, without question, that one of the greatest tragedies in human lives is the fact that individuals ponder as to their own goodness or badness.

And by an amplification of this sense of goodness or badness, people are made to feel either good or bad because of some action that they have taken at some time of their life. They've done something bad or they've done something good. If they put a dollar in the little kettle of the Salvation Army, I think that's a good thing to do, but they do it and right away they say to themselves, "Well, I'm doing something for God." And often we find that the things that are done are token actions that are actually carried out in order to improve our own sense of personal worth, and this is a great tragedy because the inner luster of the soul already possesses great abilities.

There is, however, a point I would like so much to clear up tonight for some of you who need it, and some who don't might enjoy it anyway, and it is this: that individuals upon this planetary body often confuse what we might call soul abilities—perceptions, facilities, and the nature of soul, the ability to extend itself out from the body, to move physical objects in some cases in a phenomenal manifestation, to engage in contact with the departed (a questionable act in the eyes of the masters unless the one we're contacting is not deceased but the one we're contacting is translated or raised), psychic abilities, the ability to perform mystical acts—with spirituality.

Spirituality is based upon a cosmic code of honor that pays homage to the God within not only oneself but in one's fellowman. It does not equivocate. You cannot argue with this fact, because God has made of one blood all people to dwell together upon the face of the earth.[2] And there is one spiritual life fount. It is to be found in the soul sense and in the soul itself, and that life fount is magnificent in everyone.

In the Keepers of the Flame Fraternity, which some of you belong to and some do not at this moment, we have in one early-degree lesson the admonishment that we should take the simple statement,

"O God, you are so magnificent!" and this should be repeated many times a day in moments of reverie. This automatically produces an inner contact with God.

Many people's contact with God consists of the same type of action that a parent may expect to receive from his children, and that is the running up to the parent and saying, "I would like to go here. I would like to go there. I need some money. I want permission to do this. I want permission to do that." And so the dependence upon God is not one of identifying with the nature of God.

Imitation is the highest form, not only of flattery, but also of honor. To imitate the divine nature, to be godlike within, is not a question of human self-righteousness. This does not exalt us above our fellowmen in an ordinary sense or in any sense. What it does do is it brings to us the cosmic afflatus, the actual radiance and luster of the Spirit so that we who are spirits rather than bodies may understand how to become like unto God—when we already *are* like unto God.

What is it, if it is not a matter of "now we see through a glass darkly"?[3] This frosted glass through which we see has behind it the divine luster, and we have placed the glass over it, the lens of our consciousness, our ability to perceive; and we do not see God because we have not put ourselves in that position—as though it would be a desecration to do so.

What did Paul say? "Let this mind be in you, which was also in Christ Jesus: who, being found in fashion as a man, humbled himself, and became obedient unto death, even the death of the cross. And he did not think it robbery to be equal with God, but made himself of no reputation, and took upon him the form of a servant and was made in the likeness of men."[4]

We fit the latter injunction, don't we? "And was made in the likeness of men." This is our gravest error, and the only difference between a grave and a rut is one of depth. Isn't it true? That's our great error.

"Why callest thou me good? There is only one good and that is God." If we would stop our unnecessary self-concerns about our personal righteousness and make a crystal clear, which means a Christ-clear, determination of what we are in character—not what we are in demonstrating the psychic ability to move objects at a distance or even to heal the sick just to be seen as a spiritual teacher or a person of great spiritual power—if instead of that we would see ourselves as a part of the Universal, if we would recognize that the glory of God in the face of the universal Christ can spring into action in any one of us at any moment, we would find that it is that inner action of the law fulfilling itself through the open door of our open consciousness that fabricates the divine Christ intent for us individually.

And as we do this through rote or ritual, which some have said means right-you-all, the moment that we begin to do this over and over again, to repeat it as an action, as we repeat our carnal actions that pass away as a vapor upon the window, we will find ourselves growing in grace and the knowledge of God and the inner attunement of the Universal Christ Jesus whereby we may assimilate ourselves and be assimilated into the Body of God, the immortal birthright for which we came first into embodiment. And then the statement, "Why callest thou me good?" will not apply to us, for "there is only one good," which means that there is a universal storehouse in cosmos, and all of the good of all of us, because it is derived from God, returns to this storehouse.

It is this magnetic identification with God that Jesus Christ reached up to and thereby put down the bolt of his energy through his aura, through the billowing garments that surrounded him. And through the energy shaft that came from that storehouse and penetrated his aura and the great cosmic buildup of this magnetism of God in his aura that he called virtue, which means goodness, this energy went out into the woman who had the issue of blood, and the issue was dried up and the woman was healed.[5] Why? Because the magnetism of God from the universal storehouse like a bolt of lightning flashed through the consciousness of the Christ, and he was a great lodestone, a magnificent electrode. And any one of you can be that electrode in action, if you desire.

"Why callest thou me good? There is none good but one, and that one is God." We do not live, then, in the palliative sense of "Father, forgive me. I have sinned," in the sense of condemnation. We read in the writings and we read in the akashic records the statements of the Master, "The Son of man came not into the world to condemn the world."[6] Tonight we would imbue your consciousness, not with a sense of condemnation. This belongs to those who desire to create the images of the fall of man in your consciousness and keep them alive as a guilt sense which prevents you from reaching forth unto the Tree of Life and handling the fruit of the Tree of Life and being a servant of the Most High God.

Having the guilt sense, man then feels the separation sense along with it. And born out of the separation sense is this yo-yo consciousness—"Now I am up and now I am down." "Swing low, sweet chariot, coming for to carry me home." But as one vicariously saved, we postulate, we bring forth, we approve of the concept of universal love. "Swing low, sweet chariot, coming for to carry me home."

Listen. Listen well. If the vicarious atonement were correctly understood, take note, correctly understood by man, why, the whole world would be saved in the sense that the whole world would be a part of the goodness of God in consciousness and in attainment. There would be no guilt sense existing in the consciousness.

And it is the guilt sense and the sense of world guilt and world pain, *Weltschmerz,* and all of the guilt that people have all over the planetary body—guilt between the races, national guilt between the nations, individualized guilt because people think that secretly they might have done something that they don't think God would approve of, they may have developed tastes through their traditional responses to the world aura—many, many things may take place in consciousness, and all of these many things suffocate us and bring us to a situation where we are literally smothered by condemnation and we cannot rise. And man is so easily led to a point, almost to the brink of self-destruction, where he feels unworthy of God and God's love.

Yet what did Jesus say? "The Son of man came to save that which is lost."[7] The Good Shepherd leaves the ninety and nine of the flock to go and seek and find that which is lost,[8] and in the parable of the lost coin, the woman proclaims, "I have found this which is lost!"[9] Everywhere we see divine concern for that which is lost.

Is it any wonder, then, that mankind in his dogma, in his self-conceits, in his failures to apprehend the teachings of the Brotherhood and the proximity of God to the human soul, has misunderstood all of this? I tell you that people all over the world in the theaters of orthodoxy, they significantly believe that they are doing the will of God. And Jesus told us, "The time will come when he that killeth you will think that he doeth God service."[10] Do you see? Because the real truth proclaims the emancipation of every person who really wants to be emancipated. And there is only one source of freedom, and that is God-freedom.

Dogma today in the world order, from an ecclesiastical standpoint, has done greater harm to the cause of the Universal Christ and the presence of the living God than anything else in society. It creates a false premise that topples the whole pyramid of life and brings to mankind a false sense of security as well as a false sense of judgment. And these false senses developed in the human ego and human person become barriers that separate people from the presence of the masters.

Beloved El Morya, beloved Saint Germain, all of the great masters of wisdom, together with Christ Jesus, who is indeed an elder brother of our race, would, if they could, lift the whole panoply of human consciousness almost in the manner of this handkerchief.

[Mark lays down a handkerchief and lifts it up the center.]

Representing, then, the human race we have the summit consciousness—I'm not talking about The Summit Lighthouse, I'm talking about the highest divine consciousness on the planet—here at the apex of our handkerchief. All of the human race are positioned somewhere from the lowest points to the highest on the ladder of life, and you cannot lower the consciousness of anyone in this great panoply of consciousness without lowering the whole, and you cannot raise it in anyone without raising it in the all.

In Jesus we find that through his consciousness he was able to ascend unto the Father. As he put it, "I ascend unto your God and unto my God."[11] We find him going through walls. This isn't difficult, if you want to do it, but you see, it won't save your soul. It is a *product* of the activity of overcoming the world. It is a *product* of a man's attainment. It is not his attainment.

Those who can go through walls, who can float in the air, who can make iron rise upon the water, who can heal the sick, who can project their consciousness all over the world—these are not necessarily even the children of God. These are individuals who are involved in what we may term psychic abilities. Did you know that recently in Moscow they had a convention of psychics behind the Iron Curtain? Did you know that they are very advanced in psychic phenomena? Did you know that the power of extrasensory perception in the world is gaining recognition every day? Oh, yes.

An ascended master can do this. An unascended master can do this. Any one of you can become an unascended master, a candidate for the ascension. But here's something awfully strange. Just because you can do these things does not assure anyone that you will actually complete your ascension. Your ascension, at the present stage of human life, is based on fifty-one percent of the balancing of an individual's karma.

Emerson wrote of the law of the circle.[12] We hear about the boomerang that was developed in Australia. Ella Wheeler Wilcox says that a man can send out his thoughts from the track of his mind, and whatever he sends out on this track will come back.[13] Emerson's statement "come full circle" is the same thing. And whether we call God, "God" or "Brahma" or "Vishnu" or "Siva," or whether we recognize the divinity of Jesus Christ or the divinity of ourselves, all are a product of the mind of God from the very foundation of the earth.

Obviously, individuals have a set span of existence in their mortal sense, and the purpose of that existence is clear. It is to *meld* oneself in consciousness into the God consciousness of the planet, which is like the magnetic flux of our earth, or the solar patterns that appear around the planetary body. And through this melding process, we are actually coming into the universal consciousness. In other words, we individually per se are plugging into that consciousness.

But what do most people do? Most people leave themselves outside that consciousness. As Edwin Markham said, "I drew a circle and shut Him out; He drew a circle and took me in."[14] I won't quote it all but just the points of it, you see.

We draw circles and we shut God out because we proscribe our individual personality according to standards that we have learned from the cradle to the present hour. And we fail utterly to apprehend the principles of the Great White Brotherhood because the traditions and principles of the Great White Brotherhood, which we proclaim here and which are a part and forte of our inner understanding, are not a part of the educational systems of the world because they have been crowded out of those educational systems. We have developed our reasoning into a syllogism whereby our logic becomes a door that flutters in and out, and we determine whether something is right or wrong by whether it conforms to our understanding.

This is ridiculous in itself, because no syllogism can always possess in its inherent factors all of the *necessary* factors. Do you see what I mean? There are factors that are x factors and y and z

that are left out. There are factors of the Spirit that we know not of. And therefore all of us should come to that beautiful understanding of divine potential—our potential.

Tragically enough, there was a time in my own life (and I hope you'll forgive me for even speaking of my own experiences, I'm not trying to accentuate the personal) when I was absolutely crushed, as a child, by a sense of guilt. I recognized my worldly imperfections. Actually, I wasn't all that imperfect. Probably by the standards of the world someone might have said I was a terrible square, but I thought I was really very far from the divinity of God.

I have not now reached a point where I am satisfied with my rate of progress, and I really have never talked to any of the masters who are satisfied with theirs, even beyond the ascended state. Most of the ascended masters feel this with a great sense of expectancy and a certain joy, an awareness of anticipation, that behind the veils and curtains of cosmos that extend themselves beyond the ascended state, wonderful things are going to happen to them. And in a sense this is really magnificent, because people think in eschatological terms. They think entirely in the doctrines of final ends. Some day the world will end. Some day they will die or they will end. Some day everything's going to end. And of course, it goes to cycles and a cycle comes to an end.

But cycles are endless. And therefore, the lives of people are endless. We cannot actually believe that a baby child today that is born in an incubator or out of an incubator, in a nursery or even out of a nursery, in a hospital or out of a hospital, does not show and reflect thousands and thousands of years of culture in less than one year. Sometimes in even five months a baby can develop fantastic skills. I remember our own little boy developing the skill of reading at the age of one, and by the time he was two he was reading many, many books, could actually sit down and read.

Well, if you go to these nurseries and talk to the observant nurses that are there, they will tell you that there is a vast difference between children. You have children who are very advanced, and you have children who are not advanced, and they see it within three and four days and sometimes within twenty-four hours in the nursery.

What is it that is affecting the child? Is it a matter of environment? Is it a matter of heredity? Well, if so, whose heredity is manifesting? Obviously, the individual child, because there is a difference between people, and we cannot believe that in the genes and chromosomes, we cannot believe that in the inherent factors of physical existence, that all of this is communicated. We feel that this is a manifestation of soul consciousness in the young child. How wonderful. How beautiful.

But are we substandard, ourselves today as adults? Do we come to a point of stultification? Do we stop our action, the growing process that commenced with nativity and then moves forward while we're in the hospital and even in the first year so that in the first year we can learn to walk and in many cases talk and begin to adjust ourselves to the mechanisms of this our world? We see this all around us.

But we see also these great abilities I spoke of, called "psychic perceptions," and by reason of the very fact of their existence, they indicate to us that many wonderful things can happen to us in the manifestation of certain developments. But then there is the moral sense that Jakob Böhme indicated. He was the shoemaker over in Germany who became a saint, and he is referred to in the writings of Dr. Richard Maurice Bucke of the London, Ontario, asylum for the insane. His vast studies, which were incorporated into a large volume called *Cosmic Consciousness,* showed that the sense of survival, the sense of immortality, is one of the key factors governing the manifestation of cosmic consciousness.

Dr. Bucke spoke about Jakob Böhme. He told about this great mystical sense, the sense of an uneducated man who knew not letters suddenly finding himself filled with all of this vast cosmic storehouse of knowledge, so that the world literally beat a pathway to his door in order to be blessed by him, to receive the fount of knowledge which he indicated, which was a very real part of himself.

This is you I'm speaking about, not just Jakob Böhme. It can be you. It can be me. It can be all of us, any of us, and all of the people of the world, because we have one fountain source. And our ministers today do not understand this—not because they are vicious people or little worms peering out of an apple, the apple that Adam and Eve are supposed to have eaten, out of the sense of good and evil, out of the fruit of the tree of good and evil.

This story tells us, of course, if we are at all perceptive, that out of the sense of good and evil comes the serpentine sense of the deviousness of the human mind whereby God becomes denied, in fact, and we find ourselves groveling between a crushing sense of sin and of guilt and perhaps a sense of self-righteousness because our deeds seem to take on the cast of greater nobility, greater decency.

The moral sense is within, and the moral sense that is within is a part of cosmic consciousness. It is a natural attribute of divinity. It comes to us because it was implanted in us from the beginning. It is the Christ. "All things were made by him; and without him was not anything made that was made."[15] The Logos, the first fruit of the Creator's Word, the only begotten Son of the Father was before Abraham. He said, "Before Abraham was, I AM,"[16] which clearly shows us that the consciousness of God always was and did not begin to be.

We do not understand this great master of cycles, because we find ourselves a little missing link chopped out of the whole vast cycle of chains, the manifestation of all chains of events that start from the very foundation of the earth and move to the present hour and then move onward into the future, which, as fast as we are able to perceive it, clearly is the falling sand in the glass of consciousness. This sand comes down to us, and most people are buried beneath the dunes of it. They do not understand the future. But what did Kahlil Gibran, the great poet, say about man and about words and about thought? He said, "For thought is a bird of space, that in a cage of words may indeed unfold its wings but cannot fly."[17]

In order to fly, in order to be a free bird that inhabits space, we have to possess the abilities of God, the mystical sense, the sense of union, the sense of oneness with all that lives, the sense of immortality, the ability to let go of the weights of sin that so easily beset us and to put on ourselves the whole armour of God.[18] We need faith. This is a requisite. Without faith, the Master Jesus could demonstrate no good works wherever he went.

I'm going to tell you something. If, as I suspect, in the years ahead the miracle of the flowers that has taken place here and has demonstrated itself conclusively to us,[19] and the healings that have accompanied it, are to enlarge themselves, it will be because people just like you, in whom the flame of God is, will begin to recognize it and have the faith in yourself.

You believe in yourself. This is one of the great attributes of divinity. If you don't believe in yourself, how can you expect God to believe in you? And you have to believe that God put his spirit, he lit the taper within you with the first advent of life, and that lighting of that taper is, as the Elohim of Peace said today in his magnificent address to us, the lighting of the votive light upon the altar of being.

We should think for a moment of what we are in the eyes of God. We think mostly of what we are in the eyes of our fellowmen. The stinging, biting concerns that involve themselves with the human psyche, the opinions of men seem to be far more important to us than the opinions of God. And I think we should reverse the process and we should be a little concerned with what the Father thinks of our noble efforts. Are we truly identifying with the things that pertain to life, or are we willingly allowing the graces of life to slip through our fingers? And slip they will if we do not lay hold upon eternal life. We are here in this world solely to know God and the powers of God, because they are worthy to know.

I have not said that everyone who knows God has to more or

less dump every other knowledge to one side. I fully believe that the knowledge of maneuverability, the knowledge of how to deal politely with our fellowmen, of how to govern our affairs and order our minds and our spirits according to divine grace are natural functions of the Holy Spirit. While they may have been a part of our life primarily by rote throughout the years, I feel that this rote is an approved one, that we may not condemn ourselves simply because we have developed some reasonable sense of sophistication.

But I challenge any man, any woman anywhere in life to recognize that the portion of the cosmic knowledge that they are using or the amount of cosmic knowledge that they have is usually so infinitesimally small that it is almost vain for people to say, "Well, I have used the fountain of God's knowledge in my life." Primarily, people have used a little bit of it, and when they are in the dearth or depth of trouble, they turn around and turn to Almighty God and they say, "Father, help me." They appeal.

And what does he do? Many times he answers right then and there. Johnny-on-the-spot, the living God. God is not proud. Pride is the questionable prerogative of man. I question it because while I acknowledge that it is a related part of free will, I do not believe that it is a true part of the Godhead, and therefore I don't think it should be our part, either. I think we lose a great deal by it, do you see?

I will be willing to stop whenever you want to raise your hand. I am only trying, under the direction of the Great White Brotherhood, to bring these blessed people who have come here from all parts of the world, of our nation, as much of Christ truth on this, the last day of our conference, which like the steps of a stair, has been built from a certain point of origin to this night, which is a climax in our entire arrangement for this conference.

I ask, then, your indulgence while I, under God's direction, bring forth those ideas and thoughts, those ideals of consciousness which the masters have felt would be in some small measure a feeding of the sheep of God, those who have a more than ordinary devotion simply because they recognize what has happened here in the past, in years gone by, and in the long journey of the soul across the sands of life.

Some of you have come a terribly long way. You have attained an almost frightening and dizzying height of spiritual experience. There are times when you actually feel somewhat lost because of the summit of your own consciousness. It has reached up to such heights that you almost feel as if it is broken off and disconnected from the world itself at large. Take heart. There are many waiting in higher octaves.

And there is the obscure or dark night of the soul referred to by Saint John of the Cross. The obscure night comes to people at the very point when they are left to rest, not upon the spiritual power and the steps of wisdom that are built beneath them as foundation, but rather on that measure of attainment which is the fruit of the soul, and then disconnected from contact with both God and man. In the experience of the dark night of the soul,* individuals are asked to render, out of the antahkarana of the inner experiences and balance that lies and lives within them, a mystical accounting. This occurred in the life of Jesus Christ at the exact and precise moment when he cried, "My God, my God, why hast thou forsaken me?"[20]

There are no people upon this planetary body who ever passed through the experience of the dark night of the soul who will not feel exactly in that manner that the Master felt at that moment— completely forsaken of God—because it is a necessary experience that must come to all to prove whether or not they have actually attained those inward experiences which are the strengths of God, built by free will into the consciousness of the individual, in such a manner as is calculated to make that individual capable of being the god of his own universe and capable of going by divine direction

*In teachings in later years, a distinction is drawn between two different dark nights. The dark night that Mark speaks of here, part of the initiation of the crucifixion, is usually referred to as the dark night of the Spirit. "Dark night of the soul" usually refers to an earlier experience on the path, when the initiate is facing an accelerated return of personal karma.

after his ascension to any new solar planet anywhere in cosmos to which God wants to appoint him, taking over the job of being a planetary Logos for that planet.

People say, "Why, that's *ridiculous*! With all of the billions of people upon the earth, there are not enough planets that I could be a Logos of a planet." Well, beloved ones, I think that people have a very vague sense of what is really behind this great basket of creation, this egg of the universe. Why, look down with a microscope into the microscopic kingdom that is beneath your eye, and even in the little paramecium and the various creatures that are manifesting in the submicroscopic realm, you will see a tremendous world that is there in just the head of a pin. How many angels can dance on the head of a pin? Why, an infinite number, for angels do not displace time or space. We have to develop, then, this sense of the expansiveness of the nature of God.

Of course, the purpose of creation is to fit man to become an overseer in the house of God. We are being tested. We are being developed. We are passing through these experiences in order that we will be able to guide men. It may be the prerogative of God that he could, if he wanted to, maintain a sort of a tight-knit control over all of cosmos whereby he would remain as the Lord of lords and King of kings, seated on the throne of the universe and absolutely dominating it.

Or he could turn around and say to his sheep, "I am grooming you to sit with me upon my throne, the throne of my authority. I am anxious to give you the same ability that I have, because this is a part of your solar initiation. This is a part of your cosmic initiation. This is a part of my joy. It's going to be a part of your joy someday, because you're going to go ahead and go back in that great computer-like complex of the infinite storehouse of wisdom within your own being, and you're going to be able to draw from that computer of consciousness the specific and helpful information that you can even give to those various individuals who have also come up through the initiatic process to a certain place in cosmos where they are able to work with you in the developing of this planet."

They will be overseers, the governments of the planets. Analyze the word *government*: g for God, God's overmen. Do you see? This is the will of God, to appoint overseers, people who have demonstrated these abilities and have mastered their worlds.

People have the very corruptible idea that somehow or other we are more or less here in this physical world facing the awful tragedy of death, when the arterial systems of our body will slow down, our blood will not circulate, and our thoughts will become senile. And then, because it is no longer valuable that we have the heart of life beating within us, we are laid away, like a piece of old marble or discarded inner tube, into a grave where our physical form rots away. And that is the end of it all. Some people believe that.

Others think, well, perhaps we're going to be laid away until the day of judgment, when suddenly Jesus is going to burst forth. This idea doesn't ever take into account, mind you, the fact that we have had so many millions of people already existing on this earth that have lived in the past. And now Christ is going to come forth, and all the graves are going to open up all over the world—even including that poor man who stood on top of a girder in a factory and put his coat over his head and jumped into a pot of red-hot iron. All they saw was the soles of his shoes that rose to the surface. And then God's going to suddenly summon all these people and these old moth-eaten bodies are all going to come together. They're not concerned with the soul, but they're all going to rise from the dead.

And in this great—well, I really wouldn't know what to call it; it would be a hodgepodge of confusion with all of these people coming up. Christ is going to come down, floating on a fleecy white cloud, and he's going to sit there with a big gold scepter, and everybody's going to take a telescope and look at him from all over the world. They're going to be able to see him from all around the world, and they're going to sit there and then he's going to say to all people,

"You are the goats, and I'm going to send you to Hades. You are the angels, and you're going to come up to heaven."

Why, my dear ones, this entire facility is a dramatic presentation of how we are actually being separated from the goats and from the sheep every day. The judgment of Christ is a matter of each hour, every minute. It's going on all the time, and we become participants in this drama as we emancipate ourselves from the quicksands of life that are here to swallow us up, as we suddenly rise as a full-blown Son of God and a joint heir with Christ, able to take dominion over the earth and master ourselves and the whole range of authorities which are given to us to demonstrate that God never made a mistake in the first place, because we're proving to the Father that we can accept the Christ consciousness.

And it is the Christ consciousness that gives us the great fruit of Eden. We can eat of the Tree of Life. "The leaves of the tree were for the healing of the nations."[21] Isn't that wonderful?

When we understand it, Grandma is not in some never-never world, just in limbo, waiting to be born after Christ comes—you see, she only has one life, they tell us. And we're not in a situation where people are just being born and born and born again, and the same old round goes on, you know, "round and round she goes, and where she stops, nobody knows."

The world has not made a great deal of progress simply because religion has been the bane of mankind's existence. Isn't it strange, the very thing that was intended to free man becomes the cross that he carries? He doesn't understand life. He doesn't understand God.

It doesn't mean that God couldn't come on this fleecy white cloud. He can do anything. It's just that the way it's set up. It doesn't quite work that way. Instead of that, right now today we can tune in with these higher powers and build into our consciousness each day greater fruit of the spirit.

The Brotherhood does not want me tonight to try to take you through all of the golden threads of cosmic law. They don't want me to suddenly reach out for each one of you and grab the golden ball thrown before Atalanta.* No. We all "run in a race, . . . but one receiveth the prize."[22] Well, in God's kingdom we can all receive the prize—it just may not happen all at once.

So we gather knowledge as the little nub that is the beginning of antahkarana, and we begin the unraveling of the cosmic process within ourselves and we gather these tapestries and these threads that we can weave into the tapestry, point by point of knowledge.

For God is not going to abandon us. He clearly states that he will not leave us without a Comforter,[23] and so it is to the Comforter that we dedicate our lives, the Holy Spirit that is within us all and within the race. They are all God's children, whether they know it or know it not. Out of the fount of that knowledge, and out of the fount of the wonderful feeling of cosmic joy, can be spun the ideals of God that we can build into action in the world community and in ourselves. For the kingdom of heaven is within us now.

God bless you.

January 2, 1972
Colorado Springs, Colorado

---

*In Greek mythology, Atalanta, daughter of King Oeneus, agreed to marry only a suitor who could outrun her in a footrace. (Those who lost would be put to death.) Hippomenes, a grandson of Poseidon, asked the goddess Aphrodite for help, and she gave him three golden apples. Every time Atalanta took the lead, Hippomenes threw a golden apple ahead of her and she would run after it. Hippomenes thus won the race and married Atalanta.

CHAPTER 18

The Drama of the Ascension versus Attainment through the Bodhisattva Ideal

This evening our subject is the ascension as one magnificent pathway to the heart of God and the bodhisattva ideal of the Buddhists and members of the Far Eastern branches of the Brotherhood. I believe that clarification of these two pathways is sometimes important to those sincere students who want to know those little details that can have an impact upon goal-fitting. Hence we have chosen at inner levels to reveal some of these facets to you tonight for your edification and so that your choice of pathways may be made clear.

Let us make clear then, also, that we prefer the path of the ascension as the choicest goal for the student of the light. But remember, if we skim off all the cream from society, we will have a very thin skimmed milk left. I want to define for you first in miniature both pathways and then explain the matter of choices and why some of the great masters have chosen to take the bodhisattva pathway even though they were able to qualify for the ascension.

The first pathway leading to the ascension is one of degrees spiritually attained and mastery of the self by the individual. This includes complete emotional and mental control. In order to attain and manifest mastery, we do not need to manifest mastery according to human terms and definitions. Mastery is a divine achievement. And the accreditation of cosmic mastery comes before the Brotherhood and according to their tenets. It has nothing to do with human opinions of what a person is, and this is why many of you have met masters on the street, unascended beings, of course, but adepts and masters nonetheless, and have not known them—because they may even drink a bottle of 7UP and occasionally some of them have been known to smoke cigarettes.

Yes, I said it. They don't approve of it, however, for anyone else. And they don't even approve of it for themselves. They just occasionally do these things in order to conceal themselves in the mass consciousness.

However, in the main you don't have to worry about that. Most of the adepts don't do these things at all. The reason why I mentioned it at all is because I want you to understand that human opinions of people do not necessarily prove anything.

Manly Palmer Hall from Los Angeles tells an interesting anecdote concerning Saint Germain. I don't claim this, but he claims in this book more or less that Saint Germain sired a child after he was ascended. And he says that Saint Germain at that particular time, as was the fashion of the times, carried a silver snuff box, and that the son that he sired was slain in a duel and lay there covered with a cape. Saint Germain pulled back the cape and saw that it was his son, and then he took a pinch of snuff up his nose and turned his head, and he said, "He was my son." His grief lasted long enough to take the pinch of snuff. This story is told in one of the books by Manly Palmer Hall.

Whether or not it's true, and I have neither endorsed it nor disendorsed it, the fact does remain that adepts and ascended beings of the Brotherhood, as well as unascended masters, do occasionally do a few things that are common to man, I think primarily because they do not want to attract the full attention to themselves that they would otherwise attract. It's an interesting thing, and just a point in passing. This is not my theme.

So don't be too quick to judge others. Don't decide that because somebody uses a word of slang or somebody does something that you wouldn't do that they are immediately cast down in your mind from that pedestal that you have placed them on, in ruins on the marble floor, because we really cannot judge outwardly. And we ourselves ought not to judge ourselves outwardly.

Instead of that, we ought to have a mounting aspiration toward the ascension. We ought to be lost in the clouds of glory surrounding goal-fittedness and not be trapped by the dying flowers along the pathway, the flowers of illusion that hold us more or less enamored with their jewel-like quality and then their fading. These are meaningless. What really counts is the process of overcoming, true adeptship, true mastership, true overcoming, true victory.

So the ascension is our goal. And what is the ascension? The ascension as we now understand it is conferred upon an individual who has balanced fifty-one percent of his karma. That has been the decree now for quite some time. Human beings are not required to balance one hundred percent of their karma from the human level. This has extended vast hope to large numbers of people. They don't have to be wholly perfect, just fifty-one percent perfect. But there's a catch in it, and I'm going to tell you the catch.

After you ascend, you have to balance the other forty-nine percent from inner levels. And then you find yourself trying to beckon to the poor man to get out of bed because he's got work to do. You're a master and you're standing over the poor corpse lying there, and you say to him, "Come on! Come on! We've got work to do. It's a certain hour in the day. Get up. Get up." He doesn't hear you at all, he's completely oblivious of you. And you send other directions to him from your level and you say, "*Please,* don't go that way, no. Now, that's psychic over there and that's spiritual over there. Come on over this way." And the guy keeps right on going that way.

And the more you talk to him, the more he seems to ignore you. It's as though he decided that you were a mentor that was not actually truly spiritual. And he prefers to listen to the foolishness of his own mind. But you're ascended and you have karma with this man. You've got to bring him into greater light. You're an ascended being. It's really fun from that level, too, especially with human beings. You know how the masters say that they never can depend on human beings.

These are the ascended masters, you see. They've been right down here with us. They've had all the temptations that we've faced, and they've overcome them. But they still have forty-nine percent of their karma to balance.

Now, the question has been raised, "Does everybody ascend at fifty-one percent of their karma?" No, they don't. Some people, by choice, when they reach that fifty-one percent level, don't stop there. They stay on earth and serve humanity until they may have balanced eighty percent of their karma or ninety, and then they pay the other ten percent when they get upstairs. This is a matter of choice. The election of the ascension is often actually given to the individual. They can choose to accept it and go up there and sort of escape from the world of form into their glorious eternal victory—but still they have to pay their debts. So they do. And they elect to pay it that way.

There's something in the Bible about this. It says, "Some men's sins are open beforehand, going before to judgment; and some men they follow after."[1] Isn't that an interesting point? But it happens to be true.

I want to tell you, then, that the ascension is a glorious attainment. And it is just like the description that you will find in the book by Dr. Ingraham called *The Prince of the House of David*, where Adina writes a description of Jesus' ascension in a letter to her father.[2] The ascension also is to be found in the New Testament,* and from the New Testament we can gather some insight into it.

The late Bishop Pike was very confused by the ascension. He, of course, adopted the intellectual examination of the process. And he said—and what a silly trap this is—"When we ascend, where do we go? Which way is up?" And he said, he couldn't see it.

We have to understand that the earth is round. Christopher Columbus proved that. And we know it, of course, from other scientific factors today—spatial explorations, trips around the moon, etc. But when you stand over in China, your head is pointing one way on the terrestrial globe, and when you're standing over here, it's pointing another way. So somehow or other Bishop Pike got his geometry mixed up. He didn't quite understand the process of the ascension.

It is not a process of just dissolution of the elements of the body. In other words, it is not like a cremation. What actually takes place is that the Spirit of the Father accepts the total being of the Son in this cloud that receives him out of human sight. And in effect, man is then found everywhere at the same time, just like God is.

Heaven is a place within ourselves in consciousness. It is not a physical place in space somewhere. It can be anywhere and probably is everywhere. So in effect, when Jesus went up on Bethany's hill and disappeared from physical view, he assumed the posture of Spirit. And if you can compare the universe to a sponge, he became like the water that is absorbed by the sponge. He was absorbed into the Godhead. He returned to the Father.

This is no desecration, by the way, in any sense—microcosmic or macrocosmic. Right now you're a little sponge, maybe five or six feet high. You have absorbed a spark of God's life in yourself. And when you came out of your mother's womb, you were a little bit of a shaver, and you grew. But that's all relative. And in effect, what

---

* "And when he had spoken these things, while they beheld, he was taken up; and a cloud received him out of their sight" (Acts 1:9). See also Mark 16:19; Luke 24:50–51.

happens is that in the process of the ascension, the being of man and his consciousness is absorbed by the Godhead and he gets into a bigger sponge. So the body of all cosmos, in effect, becomes his.

Master of cosmos, he is then possessed with the ability at will to transfer himself to any point in space or time, where he can appear at will to anyone he wishes to, as the Master ably demonstrated after his ascension. He came into closed rooms through locked doors. He walked on the water. He prepared fish on the fire for them to eat.[3] Even though he probably was somewhat of a vegetarian himself, he prepared fish for them—low in sodium content!

The general idea here is that an ascended being is not some sort of a God-king, in the sense of the world's Caesarean concepts, like Julius Caesar. He doesn't just sit on a throne somewhere and order people around. Here we're dealing with a cosmic being, but now remember that this cosmic being in reality is a member of a great Brotherhood. And please understand the Fatherhood of God. God is the Spirit. The Brotherhood is made up of other consciousnesses, but they're all one.

Have you ever read with some degree of questioning and doubt in your mind this statement, "Let us make man in our image, after our likeness?"[4] Don't you understand that the universe is very, very ancient? Don't you understand that in this ancient universe there have been outbreathings or manvantaras of God a long, long time ago and that one of these days the present age will end?[5]

In other words, we have the outbreathing of God from the Central Sun, for symbolic purposes we will say. This is where the mouth of God perhaps takes ahold of the balloon of cosmos and begins to blow. And the breath of God going out expands and expands and expands through space, and eventually God fills everything with this creation, which is actually the *Grund* and the *Ungrund*, if you want to say it in the German—"the created" and "the uncreated."

And so we find space is expanding and can be proven scientifically to be expanding. This is, of course, the natural course of divine events or cosmic episodes. So, space gets so big. We have the expansion and maturity of Cosmos. And the idea is transcendence. Each age of God-ideation is intended to be more transcendent than the last, because in effect, God is maturing in his universe. I don't know whether you'll all understand this or not, but it is drawing upon the magnetic law of transcendence.

People of course get hung up on this sometimes. They say, "If God is already perfect, how can he expand anymore?" They don't understand what perfection really is. You can have the qualities of perfection in a nutshell, but you can still fill the earth with them. And you can improve the qualities of the nut meat. You can improve the qualities of life from a spiritual standpoint.

For heaven's sake, qualitatively speaking, there's nothing wrong in God himself expanding his own nature. Why? Because God is all of us and all of cosmos and then some put together. But we have some part in it because we've got a little bit of God imprisoned within us. That's the imprisoned lightning, the imprisoned splendor of the ages in ourselves.

And God himself fashioned this way of life. The only way that the divine lightning can strike in human affairs is by the permission of the human will. Therefore, every son of heaven who receives this fire that leads him to the goal of his ascension receives it the same way and is traveling the same road, and ultimately he will become as masterful as God himself. But he's going to find, when he gets a little higher in the divine peerage, that there are those who have been there before.

How many of you have ever heard of Sri Magra? I doubt you have. Yet I'll bet you your souls will leap just at the sound of the voice of his name—Sri Magra—a former Lord of the World from other ages.

You ought to understand, then, that in this vast universe there are undiscovered ascended beings that are not necessarily made known to man. Why? Because spiritual and cosmic work is so diversified. We hope to be able to show you during this conference some slides of the Pleiades and various parts of the solar system taken through some of the giant telescopes of our land. And I want you to particularly examine those slides. You see globules of light in the most amazing and harmonious manifestation that you ever could imagine. And you ask yourself, "Why, how little this world is in comparison! All these vast distances, all this tremendous sea of light—is all of this without purpose? Is all of this without life?"

Of course not. Let us not be so ridiculous. If one drop of water can contain a sea for parameciums, and they can all be swimming in there with their little tails, do you think that this creative cosmos is just limited to this earth? Of course not. We have intelligent life throughout all of cosmos. And just because we come to one dead world or the remnants of dead worlds like the planet Maldek, which now forms the asteroid belt in our own solar system, this is no reason for us to discount the existence of life somewhere else in the universe.

But it really wouldn't make any difference, do you understand, whether life were on other planets or other parts of the universe or just here. From the standpoint of us as people, our life is more or less important to us and should be. Why do I say this? Because there is a statement that goes like this: "Man, know thyself." This inscription written over the old temples is a manifestation from elder worlds of spiritual art. And the priesthood of Melchizedek is a very ancient priesthood. I doubt if most of the people in our world today would like to live according to those tenets, which brings up a point.

The priests of Melchizedek are never involved in any form of sexuality. And this is a very strange point perhaps to many people. Naturally, because they do not involve themselves in this, they can truly be called those who have no father and no mother. Because they are not involved in cycles of generation but only in cycles of regeneration, that which never begins can never end. Then how can living people suddenly become priests of Melchizedek? It's possible because there are many mysteries that are not known to the general public. And we have no intention of discussing some of these mysteries other than just touching on them. But we are going to discuss with you the bodhisattva ideal in contrast to the ascension as goal. The bodhisattva ideal, of course, proclaims no penury of spirit, but proclaims attainment. In other words, it is necessary for a bodhisattva to have something.

So many times I meet people here who will say to me, "If I had a million dollars, Mark, I tell you, the Summit Lighthouse would really be rolling in the money. But I only have but my old-age pension, so I can just help a little bit."

Well, it's easy to give away what you don't have. Things might change if people had that million dollars. And I'm comparing this to spiritual attainment just for a reason. In other words, a bodhisattva is one who has overcome, who has attained mastership.

I will make contact with a bodhisattva here tonight, and those of you who are sensitive will be able to at least realize that there is such thing as a bodhisattva on the planet. In fact, there are many. I would just want to demonstrate this for a moment if you will permit me. Please relax. Separate your hands and feet wherever you are. [28-second pause]

We don't need a lot of time. How many here felt that contact? Around twenty-one people. Well, obviously something was happening. Just because you might have been one who didn't feel it doesn't mean it didn't happen, and I didn't create it as an illusion. Nor was it a figment of these twenty-one people's imagination. If we had sustained it for a longer period time, more people would have felt this particular contact. If only one person beside myself had felt it, this would have proven something. I was making contact with a very famous Himalayan adept who is a bodhisattva. I will not identify him for reasons of my own choosing.

The point I want to make is that a bodhisattva does not choose to ascend. As a rule, they remain here. And by their vibrations, the force of their divine thought, they affect millions of the evolution of this planet benignly. They do work for the Brotherhood at inner levels, and they identify themselves with the planet.

A story told by an Indian yogi many years ago familiar to some of you concerning the bushy-tailed squirrel will give you the concept which I will make clear to you. He said, a little squirrel with a bunch of baby squirrels came to the edge of an ocean. And there the little squirrel parked with her brood, when along came a big wave and swept all her baby squirrels into the sea and drowned them. The little squirrel got to shore someway or other, and she looked back at the ocean and she said, "Oh, naughty ocean, I will dip my tail in you and I'm going to take all of the water out of you and I'm going to dry you up until you give me back my babies." And she started doing this and she just kept right on a going, swishing her tail in the ocean and then swishing the water on the dry land. "I'm going to dry up that great big ocean."

Well, in effect, the bodhisattvas have been compared to this story, because regardless of what human beings do on this world, the bodhisattvas continue to maintain a high state of cosmic immutability in their physical bodies. Their physical bodies do not deteriorate but are charged with living light to such an extent that many of these beings—and there are several in the Himalayas—dwell there in caves.

And don't think, by the way, that you're going to go over there and discover them, because they are not that readily available, as we very well know. [At one point on our pilgrimage to India] we were not far from Kullu, [in the western Himalayas], and the Chogyal of Sikkim invited both my wife and our party to come over to Sikkim, to Gangtok [in the Eastern Himalayas]. But the Indian border guards would not allow us to cross, because of the danger of war and preying Chinese from China—we were near the border of China, you see. And before we could actually negotiate with the Chogyal by telephone, our schedule prevented us from further staying in Darjeeling. That is a part of the area where many of the great masters live. It is not far from Kanchenjunga. The great masters live there in caves, and I'm not referring to yogic masters in the ordinary sense of human yoga achievement. I'm referring to the masters who have attained the bodhisattva ideal.

I do not recommend the bodhisattva ideal for people. I feel that if there is such a compulsion in human beings, placed there by God, then that compulsion will act in their own world and these may refuse the ascension even when they have the privilege of accepting it, because they have some desire like the bushy-tailed squirrel. They want to remain on this planet until every living human being on this planet has finally attained his ascension, and then they'll go.

They're willing to go at that time, but they don't like the idea of taking heaven by storm, or taking heaven, period, and allowing this earth to become the abode of vampires or vultures and everything else. In other words, they don't like human vultures and they don't like all the things that are going on in the world today with people preying on each other and causing all these problems.

So they insist that if they can't have control over the earth, they're going to have control of themselves. And these bodhisattvas are a great assistance to the hierarchy as far as maintaining a vibrational contact upon the planetary body that is very stabilizing to the planet. I think sometimes that the earth would probably split in two if it were not for the pure and holy Christlike vibrations of the bodhisattvas.

Let us not, then, discount all of these beings and say that all we are interested in are the ascended masters. And by the way, I received this from the ascended masters. So it is with their sanction and authority because they consider these brothers equally important to the evolution of the planet.

However, I think that the bodhisattva ideal should not become the goal of the average person in the Western world, and I think that few in the Eastern world should follow it, either. I think we should try to obtain our ascension. I think this is the real goal of humanity and the one we should prefer. I simply like to have you, as the hierarchy likes to have you, cognizant of this segment of world society. These ascended beings are great but these bodhisattvas are also very great beings.

Please don't confuse the bodhisattva with some guy that wears a turban over in India and tells you he's a great yogic master. One of them came to New York and he was found with a blonde in a bathtub, practicing "tantra yoga." This happens to be true. And he was arrested by the New York police for that very reason. And if some of you don't believe it, you can see the records of various police departments and investigate this for yourself, and you'll find that I'm telling you the absolute God's honest truth.

There is no room for hanky-panky in the Great White Brotherhood. If a person even starts in their earliest novitiate in the Brotherhood and then begins to get engaged in all of this tantric yoga, this sort of sex yoga and all of that junk, they can anticipate speedy and swift expulsion from the Brotherhood and the sign of excommunication will be given to them quickly. Please understand this. The Brotherhood is pure and the Brotherhood is divine. And the Brotherhood is concerned with the Christlike virtues that ought to exist in the mind and spirit of everyone upon the planetary body.

It would be nice if we could chase all the blackguards of the world off the planet. But of course you can't do that. There are fakirs in every line of endeavor. You have men today that are not printers, and they go out and they tell people that they're printers and that they're union printers and everything else. I know of one man that forged his papers in the union and was kicked out of one plant after another all over Ohio and West Virginia until finally he decided to quit working as a printer.

We have people who have forged their doctor's credentials and worked in hospitals and performed major operations upon people for as long as five and ten years and never saw one single day of medical school. Did you know that? This is a matter of record.

As I said, we have fakirs in almost every human endeavor, and there are spiritual fakers, in the Orient and in the Occident. Your heart must become a scale of balance. These people invariably trap themselves. You should realize this. I want you people to know this. They will trap themselves, but it isn't always readily apparent to the uninitiated. Sometimes a lot of people are fooled. Some pretty fine people are fooled. And I think there is probably nothing worse than being fooled.

You should understand that the public today is very gullible and very ignorant, and there is a great deal of ignorance among the general masses of the people about true spiritual manifestations and about the Great White Brotherhood. We have a lot of misunderstanding about everything I'm talking about—the Great White Brotherhood, the bodhisattva ideal, the ascension.

All of this becomes very confusing to the average person. They're brought up on Darjeeling tea and coffee from South America and pancakes made from white flour and lots of honey and sugar on top of them, and moving-picture shows and now television, and reading, writing and arithmatic the school teaches. They're going to get married someday and probably have children, and then eventually they'll die and have to pick out a tombstone. And this is just sort of an a, b, c, d, e, f, g, and finally you come to the end.

It's a matter of eschatology. You finally reach the point where the whole thing ends. In reality, it doesn't end at all. If it does, it never began. It's the old riddle of the serpent swallowing his own tail.

So we have to understand these differences in our own mind and get a fixation on what we're talking about. We are not products of just our environment. We also have a heredity, and the heredity factors are very strong and this is what makes the great distinction in people's abilities. A mind that is never used to thinking cannot possibly be the same as a mind that is trained to think.

I'll bet you in this room and in the next room here we have some people who don't even know what a syllogism is. Are you afraid to admit it? Put your hand up if you don't know what a syllogism is. Let's see how many people. Oh, all right, there you are, right there. So you see that the very reasoning processes that are taught in ordinary courses in philosophy are not readily apparent to you, because you're a segment of the masses.

Do you know what deductive reasoning is? That's a syllogism—syllogistic reasoning. Human reasoning is not even understood by the masses of people, and so there's an awful lot that we have to learn about our own sciences.

Is it not, then, natural, seeing that the schools do not teach the ascended master laws and that most of the people who get up to teach them don't even know which way is up, that you wouldn't really get the truth in a lot a cases? You get a lot of garbage. And you know, I consider that Sanskrit garbage is one of the worst of all.

Have you ever noticed in some of these books that come out of India, they talk about, for example, the *Atman* to some guy down in Arpic, Arkansas. Actually there's a lot of wonderful people down there—I happen to like those people pretty well. But there are a lot of people in other parts of the country who don't know about the *Atman*.

So if they read about the *Atman* down there in Arkansas in the Baptist Church, they'll say, "What in the world is an *Atman*?" And then these writers go a little further and they talk about karma and they get into all these words that are in these books. And these poor people, they just don't understand that theology, because most of the writers don't even have a glossary. And if the glossary is there, you need a couple of dictionaries to figure out the glossary. So when you get all done, it's sort of an algebra or a calculus to the average person. They don't know what it is. And so they never really learn these laws.

And yet these laws are just as simple as pie. They are not really complicated. The bodhisattva is someone who decides that he wants to stay here. He's already had attainment. He's won his ascension.

He doesn't take it. He stays here and he tries to help the earth out by anchoring his vibrations into the earth pattern. An ascended being is one who has accepted the gift of the ascension and has probably paid off from fifty-one to a hundred percent of his karma. Now do you understand?

The choice is yours. I want to make that clear.

April 9, 1971
Colorado Springs, Colorado

Notes

CHAPTER 1 • *The Avatar*

1. Matt. 7:14.
2. Hilarion, "Understanding the Kingdom of Self," *Pearls of Wisdom,* vol. 15, no. 9, February 27, 1972.
3. Heb. 12:6.
4. Hab. 1:13.
5. Exod. 20:5–6.
6. 1 Chron. 16:34, 41; 2 Chron. 5:13; 7:3, 6; 20:21; Ps. 106:1; 107:1; 118:1–4, 29; 136; Ezra 3:11; Jer. 33:11.
7. Rev. 2:17.
8. Mark 15:39.
9. John 10:10.
10. Rom. 1:21.
11. Rom. 8:28.
12. *Leaves of Morya's Garden,* Book Two (New York: Agni Yoga Society, 1954), p. 13.
13. Matt. 7:7.
14. John 14:6; 10:1.
15. Matt. 26:40.

CHAPTER 2 • *Antahkarana, the Web of Life*

1. John 11:35.
2. John 14:12.
3. Ezek. 1:16–22.
4. Matt. 23:13–28.
5. 1 Cor. 6:19, 20.

6. See Rev. 17.
7. 1 Peter 4:8.
8. Gen. 3:24.
9. Luke 21:33.
10. Gen. 3:4.
11. Matt. 7:13.
12. 1 Cor. 15:32
13. Ps. 16:10
14. From "Love Divine, All Loves Excelling," a hymn by Charles Wesley.
15. Gen. 3:24.
16. 1 Cor. 15:41

CHAPTER 3 • *The Artisan in the Temple*

1. Prov. 23:7.
2. 1 Cor. 3:16–17.
3. The Center for the Study of Democratic Institutions was a think tank established in 1959 by Robert Maynard Hutchins, former chancellor of the University of Chicago, with the aim of influencing public policy in many different areas. It was criticized for its advocacy of left-wing causes and in particular for providing a platform for individuals who praised Communist regimes and called for the overthrow of the United States government. The center was influential in the 1960s and early 1970s, but closed in 1987.
4. John 5:17.
5. 1 John 5:8.
6. 1 John 3:2.
7. "Little Things," a poem written in 1845 by Julia Abigail Fletcher Carney.
8. John 20:29.
9. Heb. 11:1.
10. Heb. 11:6.
11. Alcyone (J. Krishnamurti), *At the Feet of the Master* (Chicago: Rajput Press, 1911), p. 12.

CHAPTER 4 • *Exhalation and Inhalation of the Breath of God*

1. Gen. 2:7.
2. 1 Cor. 15:41.
3. 1 Cor. 2:9.
4. Rom. 8:28.
5. Rev. 4:8.
6. Acts 11:7.
7. Matt. 18:10.

8. Giuseppe Mazzini (1805–1872) was a key figure in the struggle for an independent and unified Italy. His political ideals had their foundation in a deep spirituality, leading him to vigorously oppose Marxism and its materialism. In *An Essay on the Duties of Man* (New York: Funk & Wagnalls, 1898), he wrote, "Workingmen, brothers! ... Yours is the solemn mission to prove that we are all the sons of God, and brethren in Him. You can only prove this by improving yourselves, and fulfilling your duty."

9. John 3:16–17.

10. Matt. 28:18.

11. Rom. 8:17.

12. See Matt. 22:44; Mark 12:36; Luke 20:42.

13. 1 Cor. 2:9.

14. Gen. 1:26.

15. The creation of the spiritual man is described in Genesis 1:27, "God created man in his own image, ... male and female created he them." After Adam and Eve ate of the fruit of the tree of the knowledge of good and evil, "The eyes of them both were opened, and they knew that they were naked; ... And [Adam] said, I heard thy voice in the garden, and I was afraid, because I was naked; and I hid myself" (Gen. 3:7, 10). The four lower bodies of man (including the physical vehicle) are described allegaorically as "coats of skins" in Genesis 3:21: "Unto Adam also and to his wife did the LORD God make coats of skins, and clothed them."

16. Gen. 3:1–6.

17. From "God Moves in a Mysterious Way," a hymn by William Cowper (1773).

18. Acts 20:24.

CHAPTER 5 • *Creation*

1. Constantine the Great, emperor of Rome A.D. 306 to 337, was the first emperor to convert to Christianity.

2. Theodora was the wife of Justinian I, ruler of the Eastern Roman Empire from A.D. 527 to 565.

3. Gen. 1:1.

4. Gen. 1:27.

5. Gen. 1:31.

6. Gen. 1:28.

7. Col. 3:9; Gal. 3:27; 1 Cor. 15:31.

8. Mark 2:22.

9. Matt. 5:5.

10. Matt. 6:10.

11. From *A Psalm of Life,* by Henry Wadsworth Longfellow.
12. Eric Hoffer (1898–1983) was an American moral philosopher. According to his own account, he was born in New York, the son of German immigrants, losing both parents at an early age. He lost his eyesight at the age of seven, and when it inexplicably returned at the age of fifteen, he developed an insatiable appetite for reading. He spent the years of the Great Depression as an itinerant worker, ending up on Skid Row, Los Angeles. He tried to enlist in the Army during World War II, but was rejected for medical reasons. He signed up as a longshoreman on the docks of San Francisco, where he worked for the next twenty years. In 1951 he published *The True Believer: Thoughts on the Nature of Mass Movements,* a study of the psychological appeal of revolutionary, nationalistic, and religious movements. This was followed by a series of books praised for their original thought on social and historical issues. He was hailed by the *New York Times* as "a genius against insuperable odds, capable of amazing insights into history." Hoffer was awarded the Presidential Medal of Freedom in 1983.
13. Luke 17:21.
14. Ps. 23.
15. Prov. 29:18.
16. Matt. 28:18.
17. Heb. 11:37.
18. Matt. 22:12–13.

CHAPTER 6 • *Penetration, Focalization, and Control of Consciousness*

1. Prov. 4:7.
2. Hab. 1:13.
3. Gen. 3:22–24.
4. Dictation by Kuan Yin, April 12, 1963.
5. Thalidomide was introduced in 1957 as a treatment for anxiety, insomnia, and morning sickness. Use of the drug in the first trimester of pregnancy resulted in severe birth defects, including deformed or vestigial limbs.
6. Matt. 6:7.
7. In a dictation delivered earlier this day, the Great Divine Director spoke of "the banner of freedom which we wish to wave over the face of the earth."

CHAPTER 7 • *Thoughts Are...*

1. Luke 24:39.
2. 2 Cor. 5:16.

3. Acts 17:23–28.
4. Matt. 5:39.
5. James 4:7.
6. 1 John 3:2.
7. Matt. 28:18.
8. John 1:3–4.
9. John 8:58.
10. Matt. 19:30.
11. Luke 9:44.
12. John 5:17.
13. Mark 9:29.
14. *The Tempest,* act 4, scene 1.
15. John 11:41.

CHAPTER 8 • *The Use of Thoughtforms
in the Expansion of Consciousness*

1. Dictation by El Morya, November 29, 1970.
2. Matt. 10:42.
3. Gen. 1:26.
4. Gen. 1:28.
5. 2 Pet. 3:5.
6. John 5:30, 17.
7. Ps. 82:6.

CHAPTER 9 • *Instruction on Evoking the Illumination Flame*

1. Phil. 4:7.
2. 1 Cor. 14:8.

CHAPTER 10 • *Developing Ascended Master Love*

1. Gen. 1:27.
2. Ps. 139:14.
3. Rom. 13:8.
4. Matt. 10:34.
5. John 13:34.
6. Mark 12:30–31.
7. Rev. 21:16–17.
8. Matt. 3:10
9. 1 Cor. 3:13
10. 1 Cor. 15:31.
11. Heb. 12:6.
12. Prov. 4:7.

13. Charles M. Sheldon, *In His Steps: What Would Jesus Do?* (1896) has sold more than fifty million copies, making it one of the best-selling books of all time.
14. Prov. 29:18.
15. John 2:17.
16. John 2:16.
17. 1 Cor. 13:12.
18. Mark 11:14.
19. Luke 11:35.
20. Mark 16:15.

CHAPTER 11 • *Purity of Heart*

1. Matt. 5:8.
2. Matt. 5:48.
3. James 2:23.
4. Matt. 19:17; Mark 10:18; Luke 18:19.

CHAPTER 12 • *Waves Upon the Sea*

1. Ezek. 33:11.
2. Luke 17:21.
3. John 8:58.
4. James 4:8.
5. John 14:12.
6. Gen. 1:27.
7. Matt. 5:18; 16:27.

CHAPTER 13 • *The Accent Is Love*

1. Gen. 1:27.
2. John 4:24.
3. Col. 2:9.
4. Rom. 8:17.
5. Mark 5:34.
6. John 5:39
7. John 8:32.

CHAPTER 14 • *Perfect Love*

1. 1 John 4:18.
2. Isa. 53:3.
3. Robert Louis Stevenson, *A Child's Garden of Verses.*
4. Gen. 11:1–9.
5. Prov. 20:1.

6. Matt. 9:17; Mark 2:22; Luke 5:37–38.
7. Mark 4:39; Ps. 46:10.

CHAPTER 15 • *The Threefold Flame and Identity*

1. Mark delivered a lecture titled "The Social Gospel and Dissent" later that day.
2. Heart transplants were very much in the news at the time of Mark's lecture. The first human heart transplant was performed in South Africa by Dr. Christiaan Barnard on December 3, 1967. The first heart transplant in America was performed on January 6, 1968. More than one hundred heart transplants were performed worldwide in 1968.
3. Gen. 15:17.
4. Heb. 2:7, 9.
5. While Risë Stevens, mezzo-soprano, was singing Orpheo's aria of lamentation at the foot of the Acropolis, she "lost all touch with reality" and felt herself in ancient Greece, "mentally and physically" living a former life in which she had acted on that very stage. Later she wrote about the incident, saying she finished the aria as if she were in a trance and "fell prostrate on the body of Euridice." It took five minutes of thunderous applause to bring her back to the present. See Kyle Crichton, *Subway to the Met: Risë Stevens' Story* (Garden City, N.Y.: Doubleday & Company, 1959), pp. 237–38.
6. 1 John 3:2.

CHAPTER 16 • *Man's Identity and His Real Plan*

1. Hab. 1:13.
2. John 4:32.
3. Job. 1:21.
4. György Kepes, ed., *The Education of Vision* (New York: G. Braziller, 1965), Introduction, pp. i–ii.
5. 2 Cor. 3:18.
6. John 5:39.
7. John 4:32.
8. Luke 2:49.
9. Rom. 3:8.
10. Luke 22:31.
11. Matt. 11:19; Luke 7:34.
12. Matt. 9:20–22; Luke 8:43–48.
13. From the ascended masters' perspective, automatic writing is one of the most dangerous types of mediumistic activity. In this process, an individual allows the physical body to be controlled by a spirit that writes or

types messages. Most people who engage in this are caught up in their ego; the spirits engage them with personal messages and flattery. (In fact, this is the point of vulnerability of many people who engage in psychic activities.) By repeatedly ceding control of the mind and body to astral entities in this way, individuals may eventually lose the ability to control their own consciousness, and thus they become subject to all manner of "voices" and projections from the astral plane that they can no longer control or distinguish from the real world.

14. 2 Tim. 2:15.
15. 1 Cor. 15:43.
16. 1 Cor. 15:41.
17. Kahlil Gibran, *The Prophet* (Alfred A. Knopf, 1950), p. 95.
18. John 14:12.
19. Four of the most prominent rock stars of the 1960s died at very early ages. Brian Jones (of the Rolling Stones) died of drowning in July 1969. Jimi Hendrix died of an overdose of barbiturates in September 1970. Janis Joplin died of an accidental heroin overdose in October 1970. Jim Morrison died six months after Mark's lecture, possibly of a heroin overdose. All were age 27 at the time of their deaths.

CHAPTER 17 • *"Why Callest Thou Me Good?"*

1. Matt. 19:17; Mark 10:18; Luke 18:19.
2. Acts 17:26.
3. 1 Cor. 13:12.
4. Phil. 2:5–8.
5. Matt. 9:20–22; Luke 8:43–48.
6. John 3:17.
7. Matt. 18:11; Mark 5:25–34; Luke 19:10.
8. Matt. 18:12–13; Luke 15:4–7.
9. Luke 15:8–9.
10. John 16:2.
11. John 20:17.
12. Ralph Waldo Emerson, *Essays,* first series, "Circles."
13. Ella Wheeler Wilcox, *Poems of Power* (1903), "You Never Can Tell."
14. Edwin Markham, "Outwitted," paraphrased by Lord Maitreya, in Mark L. Prophet and Elizabeth Clare Prophet, *The Science of the Spoken Word* (Gardiner, Mont.: Summit University Press, 1991), p. 17.
15. John 1:3.
16. John 8:58.
17. Gibran, *The Prophet,* p. 66.
18. Heb. 12:1; Eph. 6:11.

19. Annice Booth describes this miracle in *Memories of Mark* (Summit University Press, 1999): "On April 14, 1971, by a fiat of Alpha and Omega, the Retreat of the Resurrection Spiral was established as the place prepared where devotees of the sacred fire might come and learn from the messengers the disciplines of hierarchy and prepare for their ascension.... Prior to the dictation each of us was asked to bring a flower to the sanctuary, wearing it upon our person as a corsage or in the men's lapels. During the dictation Omega called our attention to the fact that all our flowers had wilted and died. And then, at the close of the dictation, our flowers were fully restored as immortelles, appearing as dried flowers, yet having within them the flame of the resurrection. We noted that for months thereafter all our flowers that were used in the sanctuary became immortelles."

20. Matt. 27:46; Mark 15:34.
21. Rev. 22:2.
22. 1 Cor. 9:24.
23. John 14:16.

CHAPTER 18 • *The Drama of the Ascension versus Attainment through the Bodhisattva Ideal*

1. 1 Tim. 5:24.
2. J. H. Ingraham, *The Prince of the House of David* (New York: Pudney and Russell, 1857), pp. 450–51.
3. John 20:19; Matt. 14:24–33; John 21:9. In the Introduction to 1984 *Pearls of Wisdom* hardbound volume, Elizabeth Clare Prophet presents a new revelation from El Morya that Jesus made his ascension from Shamballa at inner levels, after his passing in Kashmir in A.D. 77. At the conclusion of his Palestinian mission, it is recorded that Jesus rose from Bethany's Hill in the presence of five hundred witnesses. In doing this, he left a record for all time that the ascension is the goal of life for every son and daughter of God. He also demonstrated certain spiritual aspects of the ascension process, as explained in this chapter.

   Jesus entered his final incarnation with only that minimum portion of karma unbalanced (about seven percent) that was necessary for him to retain the tie to the earth plane and the evolutions evolving there. (See Sanat Kumara, *The Opening of the Seventh Seal,* p. 245.) He received the initiations of Maitreya and the masters of the Himalayas during his years of study in the East. (See Elizabeth Clare Prophet, *The Lost Years of Jesus.*) He demonstrated the full mastery of time and space in the many miracles he performed during his three-year mission, and after the resurrection he proclaimed, "All power is given unto me in heaven and in earth" (Matt. 28:18). He thus walked the earth as an "unascended ascended master," demonstrating aspects of the nature of an ascended being, as Mark explains here, even while retaining a physical body.

Jesus challenges all of us to follow in his footsteps: "Right on earth you can walk as ascended unascended beings. Would you not like to be an unascended ascended master? An unascended ascended lady master? This means that you have the power and authority of an ascended being while you yet walk the earth in robes of flesh. This is possible in this age.

"Hasten, then, the balancing of your karma. Let not one opportunity pass to be Sons and Daughters of Dominion. And then watch. Watch the great opportunities that the Cosmic Lords and hierarchies shall present to you to be victors over hell and death, to have the all-power of heaven and earth, and to extend it unto the children of mankind" (Mark L. Prophet and Elizabeth Clare Prophet, *The Masters and the Spiritual Path*, pp. 153–54).

4. Gen. 1:26.

5. For additional teaching on these cycles of the universe, see Chapter 4, "Exhalation and Inhalation of the Breath of God."

MARK L. PROPHET AND ELIZABETH CLARE PROPHET are world-renowned authors, spiritual teachers, and pioneers in practical spirituality. Their groundbreaking books have been published in more than thirty languages and over three million copies have been sold worldwide.

For more information about the work of Mark and Elizabeth Prophet, including their Pocket Guides to Practical Spirituality and their series on the Lost Teachings of Jesus and the Mystical Paths of the World's Religions, visit SummitUniversityPress.com.